P9-DIW-738

CURRENT ISSUES
IN VICTIMOLOGY RESEARCH

CURRENT ISSUES
IN VICTIMOLOGY RESEARCH

THIRD EDITION

Laura J. Moriarty
MONMOUTH UNIVERSITY

Robert A. Jerin
ENDICOTT COLLEGE

CAROLINA ACADEMIC PRESS
Durham, North Carolina

Copyright © 2017
Carolina Academic Press, LLC
All Rights Reserved

Library of Congress Cataloging-in-Publication Data

Names: Moriarty, Laura J., editor. | Jerin, Robert A., editor.
Title: Current issues in victimology research / [edited by] Laura J. Moriarty
   and Robert A. Jerin.
Description: 3rd edition. | Durham, North Carolina : Carolina Academic Press,
   [2016] | Includes bibliographical references and index.
Identifiers: LCCN 2016044624 | ISBN 9781611638660 (alk. paper)
Subjects: LCSH: Victims of crimes--United States. | Victims of
   crimes--Research--United States. | Victims of crimes--Legal status, laws,
   etc.--United States. | Victims of crimes--Services for--United States.
Classification: LCC HV6250.3.U5 C87 2016 | DDC 362.880973--dc23
LC record available at https://lccn.loc.gov/2016044624

Carolina Academic Press, LLC
700 Kent Street
Durham, North Carolina 27701
Telephone (919) 489-7486
Fax (919) 493-5668
www.cap-press.com

Printed in the United States of America
2018 Printing

*In memory of all my loved ones who left this world way
too early for me. May you rest in peace until we meet again.
With loving memory of Mom, Aunt Mary, and Aunt Helen. — LJM*

*To my family and special friends — your support makes
everything possible. — RAJ*

CONTENTS

PREFACE

Current Issues in Victimology Research focuses on topics of concern for those who study victims of crime, or what we refer to as victimology. There is a myriad of topics that we could have included in this third edition, and thus it was tough narrowing the scope of the book. Ultimately, we focused on manuscripts that either summarized existing literature on the topic, giving the reader an update on where we are on the issue, or on manuscripts that contributed because of the uniqueness of the topic. An interesting coincidence with this edition is the synergy of the work presented with authors citing each other's work independent of them knowing who the other contributors were to this edition.

We are pleased to have seven chapters updated for this edition. Likewise, we are pleased to have seven new chapters written for the book. One chapter is a reprint of an excellent article on campus rape adjudication. The compilation of these fifteen chapters provides the reader with an understanding of some of the most current issues in victimology research.

The reader begins with an overview of victim services, where Kurst-Swanger reminds us that "Since the early 1970s the crime victims' movement has truly come of age, emerging as an influential political and social agent of change." She presents the past, present and future of victim services in the United States, providing a cursory review of some of the historical perspectives guiding the evolution of victim assistance programs, illustrating the types of issues that have confronted crime victims and explaining how such services help to minimize the impact of crime, and exploring some of the challenges and opportunities that victims will face in the future. In her update of the chapter, Kurst-Swanger incorporates future challenges and promising approaches of crime victim services. As she states, "[a]lthough tremendous gains have been made in the development of victim services and policies which support victims' rights, challenges do lie ahead for the future. Those challenges, however, can pave the way to innovation and promising new approaches to the delivery of victim services." She then continues explaining these trends with an emphasis on trauma-informed care and technology.

The next chapter examines batterer intervention programs — what some refer to as BIPs — to determine how well these programs are succeeding in reducing domestic violence recidivism. As Gordon and her colleagues point out, after reviewing the literature and reporting what others have found when conducting meta-analyses, it may very well be that researchers are not asking the right questions when they evaluate BIPs. In the original chapter, the authors noted that methodological issues had severely limited the strength of the evaluations, and they suggested that the focus should shift to other program variables when conducting program evaluations. They specifically mentioned that all the goals of a program should be evaluated and that treatment fidelity should be one major component of any evaluation. In their update, a decade later, they note that "research has improved . . . [with the] focus on more than just the cessation of violent behavior via the examination of official reports." They pose this question: "Has the literature shifted to identify the impact of violence as seen through the lens of the victim, define domestic violence differently or examine or assess offender responsibility?" and conclude overall that the current literature still finds mixed results.

Chapter 3 is a new contribution examining whether electronic monitoring of domestic violence offenders is working. Moriarty and McDermott provide an overview of electronic monitoring highlighting the pros and cons of these devices in relationship to cost, effectiveness, and victim satisfaction with the devices. They find general support for using the devices, especially GPS, when used in concert with a larger coordinate response to domestic violence, especially at the pretrial phase.

Likewise, Chapter 4 is a new contribution focusing on domestic violence with emphasis on improving police records of repeat domestic violence. As Marie Mele states, "[T]he chapter reports on a collaborative effort between researchers and police officials, generated by a common interest in assessing the nature and extent of repeat domestic violence in one U.S. city. This collaboration was informed by the understanding that because domestic violence is repetitive by nature, greater understanding and prevention of this crime can be achieved by studying the pattern of repeat victimization. Research on repeat victimization has fostered better understanding and prevention of crimes such as burglary, robbery, and vehicle theft. Research on repeat domestic violence similarly suggests that the analysis of repeat victimization may enhance our efforts to prevent domestic violence."

In Chapter 5, Elizabeth Quinn updates her chapter on repeat victimization and problem-oriented policing. It is positioned in the book after Mele's work to facilitate understanding regarding repeat victimization — a topic not well understood. Quinn specifically looks at repeat victimization and problem-orientated policing. Using the same approach that is used with putting resources where needed based on "problem-oriented" policing, Quinn argues that repeat victimization should be viewed as analogous to "problem-oriented" policing, meaning that resources and services should be more focused or directed at victims who are more likely to be victimized again.

The next chapter addresses the issue of black women victimized by the police, a very important, and timely, topic given the public awareness generated by "Black Lives Matter." Breea Willingham forces us to critically examine gender in this regard as the purpose of her chapter is to "critically examine Black women's experiences with state-sanctioned violence and to find out why they are often neglected." She explicitly asks: "Why do the cases of Black women and state-sanctioned violence go unnoticed? . . . And . . . argues that what is happening with Black women and police violence is significantly more than simply ignoring these women's stories." Her powerful chapter reports on oppression of black women and commonplace victimization by the police. She concludes with this finding: "The details of Black women's encounters with police that I have provided further illustrate the ways in which Black women are marginalized, thus contributing to their invisibility, and address how impossible it is for them to survive in a criminal justice system that not only victimizes them, but was not designed to protect them."

In Chapter 7, Manzi and Dunn update their chapter on the legal aspects of hate crime victimization. As they point out, even though we have statues to augment the penalties when an offender is convicted of a hate crime, there are tremendous obstacles to implementing such penalties, the least of which may be getting prosecutors to actually employ the statues. In this update, the authors discuss emerging issues in hate crime legislation including sexual orientation and gender identity and anti-Muslim hate crime. They conclude with the observation that "much work remains to be done to combat hate crime in this country. Legislation must expand to encompass still unprotected groups; and an environment must be created that encourages victims to report instances of hate crime, police to investigate those reports, states to prosecute those charged with hate crimes, and courts to punish those convicted of hate crimes."

Chapter 8 is an update to an original chapter focusing on child fatality with a focus on determining whether the deaths are intentional or unintentional. As McDougle (formerly Diehl Lacks) and Zeppa maintain, child fatality is a major social problem nation-wide. With causes of death including sudden death syndrome, sudden unexpected death in infancy, abuse, neglect, and homicides, it is evident that the topic of child fatality cannot be ignored. However, the authors also point out that discerning whether a fatality is intentional or unintentional is difficult. Law enforcement needs to be trained and educated in such discernment in order for reporting of such incidents to increase resulting in more accurate statistics.

Chapter 9 is new to the reader, and focuses on child maltreatment investigations and the development of Children's Advocacy Centers (CAC). Bracewell begins with a discussion regarding what is meant by child maltreatment, followed by how it is investigated and how these investigations have changed over the years. She concludes with a lengthy discussion about children's advocacy centers. As described within, "A CAC provides a child-friendly, nonpartisan location for children to be interviewed in reference to alleged child maltreatment, specifically child sexual abuse, severe child physical abuse and neglect, and child witnesses to violent crime." Through the use of CACs, we have been able to better understand and detect child maltreatment, and thus have a greater likelihood of preventing such victimization.

Chapter 10 and Chapter 11 are new chapters to the reader focusing on elderly maltreatment and neglect. As the authors all point out, the growth in our aging population will present unique challenges to identifying and responding to elder maltreatment. In Chapter 10, Bellas and his colleagues set the premise that elderly maltreatment is still very much a private matter and as such we have difficulty in defining, measuring and treating it. They argue that we must protect those who cannot protect themselves: in this case, the elderly.

In Chapter 11, Policastro and her colleagues start out by observing that "criminologists neglect elder neglect." In other words, it's a topic that as they say is "glaringly missing from the literature." Moreover, the lack of research on this topic is problematic, as they point out, especially when you consider that the studies on elder mistreatment find elder neglect to be the most common type of elder mistreatment. The authors report on research they conducted comparing elder neglect cases with elder non-neglect cases. A number of significant findings were uncovered with the most important ones having to do with stress and caregiver burden being good predictors of neglect.

The next three chapters shift the focus from elderly maltreatment and neglect to college campus victimization. In Chapter 12, Bromley and Perez update the chapter on college crime victimization and the various approaches used to deal with the challenge. The authors provide a detailed overview of campus crime with the update focusing on administrative responses to campus victimization. Examples of programs and practices to deal with campus crime and subsequent victimization are detailed from a variety of different universities.

Chapter 13 is a new addition providing an overview of college sexual assault. While Bromley and Perez touch on this topic in Chapter 12, Dolinsky and Gurska provide an extensive overview of it. Their chapter contains rich information on sexual assault legislation directed at institutions of higher education and responses to sexual assault legislation.

Chapter 14 is a reprint of a published article by Kirven where she writes specifically on the campus rape adjudication process. Very timely with the Title IX public discourse, all three chapters add to our understanding about aspects of Title IX with this chapter focusing specifically on the campus rape adjudication process.

Chapter 15 is an updated chapter on youth internet victimization. Since last published, the internet and devices used to access the internet have exploded. Bryce provides an overview of the technologies involved in internet victimization, the statistics related to these types of crime, and strategies for preventing and dealing with such victimization. The chapter concludes with insightful information about internet victimization with specific crime precaution strategies presented.

This reader is a compilation of many varied topics that normally are not found in one collection. Since the field of victimology is emerging and topics of interest within it are wide and diverse, we find the reader to add to the expanding body of literature, and to serve well as a companion to any traditional victimology text book. We hope you enjoy reading the book as much as we have enjoyed collaborating with the authors and compiling it.

Laura J. Moriarty
Robert A. Jerin

ACKNOWLEDGMENTS

We are indebted to many individuals who have supported us through the completion of this third edition of our reader. First, we thank the authors; truly there would be no third edition without your willingness to work with us and to revise your work to fit our expectations of the book. We are pleased that once again we have been able to publish the work of some of the best known scholars in the field of victimology. Second, we recognize the support of our institutions — Monmouth University and Endicott College. Having recently moved from Virginia Commonwealth University to start a new administrative post as Provost, I am particularly appreciative of the support of my new colleagues in contributing to the book and serving as reviewers, and in providing me with time to get it done. Further, Bob and I would like to acknowledge our past and present colleagues, students, administrators who have been instrumental in providing advice and counsel on how to reach the goal of completing this third edition. Third, we thank the staff at Carolina Academic Press, especially Keith Sipe and Beth Hall. CAP is an excellent publishing company to work with, allowing us the freedom to compile the third edition with very little interference. We appreciate the support. Fourth, we thank our families and friends. Like Bob said above, "your support makes everything possible." Lastly, but most importantly, we would like to recognize the tremendous courage of the survivors of criminal violence. We hope this book provides greater insight into their fight for understanding and justice. If nothing else, we hope a great awareness results.

CURRENT ISSUES
IN VICTIMOLOGY RESEARCH

CHAPTER 1

VICTIM SERVICES: PAST, PRESENT AND FUTURE

Karel Kurst-Swanger
STATE UNIVERSITY OF NEW YORK AT OSWEGO

INTRODUCTION

Since the early 1970s the crime victims' movement has truly come of age, emerging as an influential political and social agent of change. Today, crime victims have a greater voice in the criminal justice system, have rights which have been recognized by state governments, and have access to a wide range of services intended to meet their specific needs. In fact, it is fair to say that much has been accomplished in the past forty years to aid the plight of crime victims in the U.S. Such social and political change has come about as the direct result of the tireless efforts of victim activists, both volunteer and professional, who have been dedicated to ensuring crime victims receive proper treatment and that the law is responsive to their needs.

Perhaps one of the most notable accomplishments has been the evolution of victim assistance programs to assist victims in recovering from the aftermath of crime victimization. While arguably we are all affected by crime, the experience of being a crime victim can be very traumatic, and in some instances, it can be quite devastating. Physical injury, emotional trauma, and economic loss often leave enduring marks on victims. Although it is difficult to predict the exact effects certain crimes will have on victims, we do know that victims across a broad spectrum of crime types can experience temporary or permanent injury, short-term or long-term psychological distress, and economic losses that are often difficult to recoup. Some even experience what is referred to as "secondary victimization," which is harm toward the victim created by the system, rather than a criminal defendant. Clearly, the establishment of services to assist victims through the recovery process and the

3

arduous criminal justice system has been a welcome change to many communities.

This chapter will explore the past, present, and future of victim services in the United States. First, a cursory review of some of the historical perspectives guiding the evolution of victim assistance programs is discussed. Appreciating the broad spectrum of services and services providers available today is best understood within the context of the political and social environment within which victim assistance services first emerged. Second, an overview of the core services available nation-wide to assist victims is provided to illustrate the types of issues confronting crime victims and how such services help to minimize the impact of crime. Lastly, this chapter will explore some of the challenges and opportunities facing victim services in the future.

HISTORICAL PERSPECTIVES

The evolution of crime victim services is best described as a social movement. The movement began in the mid 1960s amid a period of radical change in the U.S. and reform in the criminal justice system. It is difficult to mark an exact date from which the movement began; however, Young and Stein (2004) note that several factors influenced its initiation. One factor was the outgrowth of the field of Victimology itself, which emerged as a subfield of criminology after Edwin Sutherland's well-known textbook entitled *Criminology* was published (Jerin and Moriarty, 1998).

Second, the establishment of crime victim compensation programs in several states spurred the dialogue in state governments regarding the needs of crime victims. California led the way in 1965 when it established the first compensation program, followed by New York, Hawaii, Massachusetts, Maryland and the Virgin Islands (OVC, 2015c).

Third, the rise of the second wave of the women's movement during the 1960s and 70s, helped to sharply define the types of crime that targets women specifically, namely domestic violence and sexual assault. The women's movement was instrumental in advocating for specialized services for women, such as domestic violence shelters and rape crisis centers. In turn, the burgeoning crime victims' movement helped to fuel the success of domestic violence and sexual assault activists (Kurst-Swanger and Petcosky, 2003). Walker (2000) also notes that the civil rights movement and the anti-war movement of the 1960s and 70s, in addition to the women's movement, helped to set the stage for the emergence of the victims' movement.

Young and Stein (2004) also note that another factor influencing the rise of the crime victims' movement was the escalating crime problem troubling many communities across the U.S., accompanied by a growing dissatisfaction with the criminal justice system. Parallel to this was the plethora of cases reaching the U.S. Supreme Court which involved offenders' and prisoner's rights. Crime victims issues were noticeably absent from such due process decisions. Victim activism was thus born out of the inequities and frustration brought to victims by the criminal justice system. Their courage and resolve coalesced into grassroots organizations which demanded legislative change and helped to establish victim services.

Two examples are worthy of mention here. Mothers Against Drunk Driving (MADD) was founded in 1980 by Candy Lightner after her 13-year-old daughter was tragically killed by a drunk driver who had three prior drunk driving convictions and had been out on bail from a hit-and-run arrest. Today, MADD is one of the most influential non-profit organizations in the country (www.madd.org). The Stephanie Roper Committee and Foundation, now known as the Maryland Crime Victims' Resource Center, Inc. (www .mdcrimevictims.org) was founded by Roberta and Vince Roper after the brutal murder of their daughter Stephanie in 1982. Their efforts have created real reform in the State of Maryland and they continue to provide critical services for victims. Grass roots organizations such as these have made a significant impact on legislative reform and the growth and development of services for victims by serving as a strong political voice for victims.

Other coalitions such as the National Coalition Against Sexual Assault and the National Coalition Against Domestic Violence were formed in the late 1970s to address the specific needs of victims of sexual assault and domestic violence. In 1975, the National Organization for Victim Assistance (NOVA) was established to promote victims' rights and to expand services for victims. Activist groups such as these were assisted by the National District Attorneys Association and the American Bar Association, each creating special committees to consider the needs of crime victims (Young and Stein, 2004).

Coalitions and activists' groups worked diligently during the 1970s and 1980s, which initiated a movement that influenced government policies and programs. For example, their efforts lead to the inclusion of victim services in the Federal Law Enforcement Assistance Administration (LEAA) funding in 1974. Through LEAA, several victim assistance pilot projects were created. These first victim assistance programs were intended not only to provide necessary services for victims, but to encourage victims to cooperate with authorities to improve prosecution rates. LEAA funding expanded, and by the end of the decade, many states had at least a few victim service programs, and 10 states had networks of programming. The early programs provided a core of services, including crisis intervention, counseling, assistance through the criminal justice system, compensation and restitution (Young and Stein, 2004). In 1979, however, the U.S. Congress did not renew LEAA and thus all federal funding for victim assistance ended (Derene, Walker and Stein, 2007). It appeared that the movement had suffered a blow that would be difficult to recover. Yet, victim's activists groups and the criminal justice professionals who had become their allies, joined forces to create enough political momentum to progress the movement forward, despite the funding setbacks.

In 1981 the Attorney General's Task Force on Violent Crime recommended that a separate Task Force be convened to study victims' issues, and in 1982, President Ronald Reagan initiated the Task Force on Victims of Crime. The Task Force held public hearings in cities across the nation resulting in a final report which offered 68 critical recommendations to the President. The findings of these Task Forces were influential in the advancement of the victims' movement and victim assistance programming. Shortly after the recommendations were issued, the Office for Victims of Crime (OVC) is established by the U.S. Department of Justice within the Office of Justice Programs to implement the recommendations. The Victims of Crime Act (VOCA) is passed in 1984, creating a venue in which victims could receive compensation and programs could receive stable funding. Additionally, other public funding streams became available to accommodate specialized services for specific victims. For example, the Family Violence Prevention and Services Act, Title XX Social Services Block Grant, and Emergency Assistance for Families providing funding for services for victims of family violence (Davis, Hagen, and Early, 1994). Also, the Violence Against Women Act, passed by Congress in 1993, authorized funding for prevention and intervention programs for crimes that address the needs of women.

Over the course of the next two decades, the crime victims' movement is firmly established, resulting in policy change and program expansion. One special project has evolved to capture the rich history of the movement. An oral history of the movement was documented with those who live it and is available at http://vroh.uakron.edu/.

Crime victim services became institutionalized in many communities across the U.S., although funding issues continue to plague their operations. Programs have come to rely on a mix of federal and state dollars, as well as the support of private foundations, community fundraising, and local government support. Programs and services for crime victims expanded from their initial home in voluntary organizations, to become embedded in the daily functions of police departments, prosecutors' offices, courts, probation and parole departments, etc., providing evidence that the crime victims' movement has been hugely successful in changing the mindset and operations of the criminal justice system.

CRIME VICTIM SERVICES

Today, crime victim services are offered from a variety of different professional public or private venues, such as police departments, hospitals, prosecutors' offices, probation or parole departments, or non-profit community agencies. Services are rendered at the federal, state and local level. Most programs offer assistance to lessen the impact of crime on victims and their families, as well as witnesses. Such assistance can also help reduce the secondary victimization that often accompanies victims' interaction with the criminal justice system. Although a wide range of services may be available to victims, the core services available include crime victim compensation, crisis intervention, counseling, advocacy, information and referral, each of which is described below. Also, a brief overview of specialized victim services is noted, including innovative services which involve interaction with offenders.

Financial Assistance: Crime Victim Compensation

Crime victim compensation programs assist victims in recouping some of the financial losses incurred as a result of being victimized by crime. Each state administers its own program to directly reimburse victims of federal or state crimes. In addition to state revenue, the states receive funding from the federal government through the Crime Victims Fund. The Fund, established in 1984 through VOCA, is the major source of financial support for compensation programs nationwide. The Crime Victims Fund is unique in that it relies on dollars from offenders convicted of federal crimes rather than taxpayers. The fund draws its support from money collected by the U.S. Attorneys' Offices, federal courts, and the Federal Bureau of Prisons through criminal fines, forfeited bail bonds, penalties and assessments. In addition, as a result of provisions made to VOCA through Title VI of the USA PATRIOT Act of 2001, the fund can also receive donations, gifts, and bequests from private donors.

Each year, dollars are deposited into the fund and then dispersed to the states. Congress, from time to time, has issued a cap on how much money can be placed in the fund, thus limiting the total amount that could ultimately be devoted to crime victim service programming. Even with the funding caps in place, the fund has grown substantially since its inception in 1985 when approximately $68 million dollars was collected. According to the Office of Victims of Crime (2015a), the fund balance was approximately $9 billion in 2013.

The fund supports a number of different initiatives including; the investigation and prosecution of child abuse cases in American Indian and Alaska Native communities, assistance programs for those victims in the federal criminal justice system, state compensation and victim assistance programs, and remaining funds can be deposited into the Antiterrorism Emergency Reserve, which supports emergency expenses and other services for victims of terrorism or mass violence within the U.S. and abroad. The fund is administered by the U.S. Department of Justice, Office for Victims of Crime (OVC, 2015a).

Of course, a direct benefit of the Fund to individual crime victims is through crime victim compensation programs. Compensation provides reimbursement to or on behalf of a crime victim for a variety of crime-related expenses such as: out-of-pocket medical or dental expenses, funeral and burial costs, mental health or financial counseling, lost wages, loss of financial support, court transportation cost, crime scene clean-up, temporary shelter, replacement or repair of windows or locks, and dependent care expenses to allow victims to attend court. Also, some victims may be eligible to receive reimbursement for the replacement of essential personal property such as eyeglasses, medication, dental or prosthetic devices. Compensation benefits and allowable awards vary from state to state, as do the eligibility requirements. Most compensation programs however, require that victims be innocent victims of violent crime. Also, most state laws require that victims report a criminal incident and cooperate with the proper law enforcement authorities.

Research conducted shortly after compensation programs were developed found that victims are generally unaware of such compensation programs and are discouraged by the cumbersome application process (Elias, 1983; Roberts, 1990). Thus, victim assistance programs have played a critical role in notifying eligible victims of compensation availability and assisting in the application process. The Office of Victims of Crime (2015b) reports that a total of 275,470 crime victims were compensated a total of $751,015,672 during fiscal years 2013–14.

Crisis Intervention

Crisis intervention is the immediate, time-limited support of victims and their families during times of crisis. Crisis intervention is such an important service for victims of crime because of the immediacy of need. The goal of crisis intervention is to assist victims in resolving the most urgent issues facing them while helping them to enhance their coping strategies (Roberts, 2000). Depending on the role of the agency providing the service, crisis intervention personnel can provide much needed psychological support, validate emotional experiences, assist in establishing safety, ensure the delivery of appropriate medical intervention, arrange for other necessary services such as, housing or psychiatric assistance, and facilitate the involvement of family or friends to assist the victim further (Kurst-Swanger and Petcosky, 2003).

Services are rendered in a number of different venues, such as police departments, hospital emergency rooms, court rooms, protective agencies, in the home, or on the telephone. Usually, crisis intervention is provided as a service shortly after victimization. Some victim service agencies even have the capability to arrive on the scene of a crime to assist victims immediately after a crime has occurred. In cases where a place of business has been victimized, crisis intervention may be offered in group sessions with employees. For example, bank or store robberies, bombings and other acts of terrorism, or employee shootings, etc.

Crisis hotlines are utilized extensively since they typically operate 24 hours a day, 7 days a week. Hotlines generally provide crisis counseling, emotional support, information and referral to other important services or programs, and critical information about the criminal justice system. National, state, and local hotlines are available, although some are focused on specific types of victimization, such as domestic violence or sexual assault.

In addition, crisis intervention services can also be offered via a crisis response team or through what is sometimes referred to as critical incident debriefing. Crisis response teams are generally mobile teams which are assembled after a critical crime incident has occurred. Team members, whether they are volunteers or paid staff, have specialized training in working with groups and/ or communities in crisis. Some communities have crisis response teams in place which are specially trained in critical incident debriefing, and thus, they are readily available to respond to local needs. Teams may exist within particular institutional settings as in school districts, universities, or large companies or they may be more multidisciplinary in structure and available to serve the community at large, such as the American Red Cross, victim service agencies, and mental health programs, etc.

The National Organization of Victim Assistance (NOVA) has been a leader in assisting communities in coping with collective trauma. NOVA can assemble a specially trained team within 24 hours of a community request. The team works to assist local leaders in identifying groups at risk of experiencing trauma, including first responder professionals such as police officers, emergency medical personnel, fire fighters, crisis response and assisting communities in coping with collective trauma. The team can also lead crisis intervention sessions with groups of individuals who have suffered trauma. Such groups are helpful to professionals, victims, witnesses, or secondary victims to "debrief" their experiences and begin the coping process. Additional, NOVA team members can provide training and information for local caregivers to continue the healing process (see website at www.trynova.com).

Counseling

Mental health counseling or therapy is another critical service for victims and their families. Counseling is usually short-term in duration; however, some therapy services for victims may be offered by skilled clinicians for longer periods of time. Counseling can be offered to victims and their families through individual counseling sessions or in group sessions and is generally provided by a professional with an advanced level of training. The support group model of counseling has been found to be especially helpful to victims of violence (Tutty and Rothery, 2002). Support groups may involve victims of specific types of crimes such as intimate partner violence, sexual assault, DWI, homicide, or robbery, or they may involve a mixture of crime types. Counseling differs from crisis intervention in that victims and/or their families have longer periods of time to explore their feelings, fears, and anxieties, to work toward developing coping strategies, and to make functional decisions about their future.

The psychological consequences of victimization can be quite devastating, resulting in more long-term problems, such as post-traumatic stress disorder, adjustment disorder, depression, eating disorders, substance abuse, self-injury, or suicide. These emotional difficulties can be mitigated by effective counseling models. However, it is also important to note that not all victims of crime require therapeutic intervention. Many are able to recover with the support of friends and family, while drawing on their own coping strategies.

Advocacy

Advocacy is another critical element of victim assistance. Victim advocates can ensure that crime victims and their families are treated fairly by the police, district attorneys, defense attorneys, compensation board, the courts and correctional personnel. Also, advocates can work to assist victims in navigating a variety of other institutions, services or programs such as, insurance companies, funeral homes, schools, the media, employers, and medical care providers, etc.

Crime victims each have unique circumstances, thus victim advocates tend to be flexible in order to accommodate the individual needs of the victims they work with. The advocate's strength is in their knowledge of the systems and the individuals with whom victims have to interact with after a crime has occurred. Since crime victimization tends to leave many people emotionally vulnerable, advocates can help victims get the services or information that is important to them. For example, they may, depending on the sponsoring agency, aid victims in the following types of actions: prompt return of their property, securing an order of protection, filing of crime victim compensation, explaining the processes of the criminal justice system, prepare the victim or witness for court testimony, accessing other financial or mental health services, securing transportation to attend court, navigating issues with employers, notifying family and friends of the crime, assisting victims in completing a victim impact statement for the court, etc. Victim advocates often also accompany victims to court or are present to support victims during interviews with the police.

Victim advocates also work to ensure victims' rights are protected within their communities by engaging in advocacy on a broader scale. Advocates often represent victim's needs on local or state coalitions, task forces, or special projects. Advocates can work with local institutions, such as police departments, court system, hospitals, schools, etc. to improve the systems response to victims within their community. They may also work toward the development of or reform of public policy to improve the plight of victims. In an effort to advocate for their clients, they may also provide education and training to a wide range of professionals, such as police officers, judges, attorneys, hospital staff, etc.

Information and Referral

Victim assistance also involves a service referred to as information and referral or I. & R. Victim service workers provide information to victims regarding a wide range of issues such as: information about the procedures of the criminal or civil court system, the status of their case in the court process, including the apprehension and detention of suspects, trial proceedings, and sentencing outcomes, or information about eligibility and procedures involved in filing crime victim compensation. Also, staff may educate victims about the dynamics of victimization and provide information regarding the recovery process and what to expect from themselves and others for the short and long term. Victim assistance staff may also provide referrals for victims for further financial, mental health, housing, transportation, or medical services.

Crime victims may also be provided valuable information through Victim Information and Notification Everyday (VINE) programs or Statewide Automated Victim Information Notification Programs (SAVIN). SAVIN or VINE programs, or what has been commonly referred to as Automated Victim Notification (AVN) programs were first established in Louisville, Kentucky, in 1994 to provide continual access to critical information regarding an inmate's custody and case status. The automated telephone notification system was originally designed in Kentucky after the brutal murder of Mary Byron by an ex-boyfriend whom had been released from jail. In recognition that a notification call could have potentially saved her life, the automated system was developed to ensure that registered victims would automatically be notified of changes in the status of offenders. The Office of Justice Programs, Bureau of Justice Assistance, with the authorization from the Consolidated Appropriations Act of 2005 (PL 108–447) provides funding to states to build, implement, or improve their SAVIN system to create the capability to share such information on a nationwide basis.

Today, 47 states, the District of Columbia and Puerto Rico operate an AVN program, many of which are available to the general public. Although there is variation on how AVN programs are operated, they generally notify their registrants via email, text message, telephone, and postal mail regarding the status of an offender's release, death, transfer, court dates or escape (Irazola et al, 2013).

Specialized Services

In addition to the services noted above, some victim assistance work involves meeting the unique needs of victims of specific types of crimes. For example, shelters operate to provide emergency housing for women and children victims of intimate partner abuse or foster care serves to protect child abuse and elder abuse victims. Rape crisis programs may send staff or volunteers to hospital emergency rooms to support victims through the rape exam and/or interview with police.

Grassroots support groups, such as Parents of Murdered Children (available on the web at *www.pomc.com*), Survivors Network of those Abused by Priests (SNAP) (available at www.snapnetwork.org) or Mothers Against Drunk Drivers (MADD) (available online at *www.madd.org*) have chapters available around the country to provide ongoing support to individuals recovering from these crimes. These and other support groups are now available via social media platforms such as Facebook and Twitter, etc.

The availability of specific types of crime victim services, or specialized services for certain types of crime victims, is dependent upon the local community. Services tend to evolve over time to respond to specific crime problems that exist in particular communities. Local politics, funding availability, and the initiative of local law enforcement and court officials, are often driving forces in the development of programs to meet the needs of crime victims. For example, specialized services for victims can even involve interaction with offenders.

Offender-Based Victim Services

In some communities, victims can be assisted through interaction with offenders. These special programs take a restorative approach to justice and recognize the importance of healing from the perspective of both the victim and the offender. For example, Victim-Offender Mediation (VOM) programs bring together offenders and victims, with a neutral third party, to discuss the crime incident, its impact on the victim, and to explore possible resolutions. With the assistance of a trained mediator, victims are given a unique opportunity to interact with the offender face-to-face and share their feelings regarding the criminal actions of the offender. Offenders come to realize that their behavior has real consequences to real people. Meetings between victims and offenders can occur at different points in the criminal justice system, depending on how the program is constructed. Some VOM programs operate as a form of pre-trial diversion, while others serve to inform the sentencing process. Regardless of where in the criminal justice system the VOM process occurs, victims and offenders jointly craft a resolution which often involves restitution to the victim, whether that restitution is monetary or more symbolic in nature. Some VOM programs are focused on juvenile offenders, while others involve adult offenders. In most cases, both victims and offenders voluntarily enter into the process, although there are some programs in which the offender may be required to participate (Umbreit and Greenwood, 2000). Research on the effectiveness of VOM programs, in terms of recidivism rates for offenders, is rather mixed; however, there is evidence that the process has some practical benefits for victims (Niemeyer and Shichor, 1996; Shichor and Sechrest, 1998). Umbreit and Greenwood (2000) identified 298 programs in the U.S. and note that such programs are now endorsed by the American Bar Association (ABA).

Another offender-based victim service is Victim Impact Panels (VIPs). Victim Impact Panels provide a forum for crime victims to share their experiences with a group of offenders. Unlike the VOM meeting where victims have an opportunity to meet face to face with the perpetrator who harmed them, Victim Impact Panels involve victims presenting to an audience of offenders who have committed similar crimes. The goal is to assist offenders in understanding the true impact crime has on victims, thus personalizing the impact crime has on victims, as well as the community at large. Offenders are generally required to attend a panel discussion as part of their sentence. Three or four victims comprise the panel and each takes a turn describing their experiences as a crime victim. Often, victims are encouraged to share even the most gruesome details of their experience in order to "educate" offenders on the human consequences of their criminal actions. Offenders are exposed to the pain and suffering they have caused others by virtue of the panel's experience (Fors and Rojek, 1999). Victim assistance staff is generally responsible for organizing the panel, moderating the discussion, and tracking offender participation. Law enforcement officials are often present to maintain order. At the conclusion of the panel, offenders are often asked for their written reflections of the session (Mercer, Lorden and Lord, 1999).

Victim Impact Panels are generally structured to pair specific types of offenders with victims such as, DWI or DUI, domestic violence, child abuse, assault, etc. A panel of victims may meet with offenders in prison or jail settings or in the community, depending on the specific type of offender the panel is intending to address. Over 200 Mothers Against Drunk Driving (MADD) chapters across the U.S. have developed VIPs to address about 400,000 DWI offenders per year (Polacsek, Rogers, Woodall, Delaney, Wheeler, and Rao, 2001). In most cases, bereaved victims are represented on DWI panels; however, police officers, emergency responders, and in some cases, remorseful offenders may also speak (Mercer et al, 1999). Research on the effectiveness of VIPs in reducing recidivism is mixed (Fors and Rojek, 1999; Polacsek et al, 2001; Shinar and Compton, 1995; Wheeler, Rogers, and Tonigan, 2004); however, victims have found the experience of speaking on a panel to be helpful in their recovery process (Mercer et al, 1999).

CRIME VICTIM SERVICES: FUTURE CHALLENGES AND PROMISING APPROACHES

Thanks to the tireless efforts of victim advocates and those directly impacted by crime, victim services have evolved to become institutionalized in many communities. As the previous section illustrates, a wide range of services, available to victims of a wide range of crimes, have been established. Crime victim services have become an important component of the criminal justice system and in many communities, law enforcement, court, and corrections officials have come to view such services in a positive light. Although tremendous gains have been made in the development of victim services and policies which support victims' rights, challenges do lie ahead for the future. Those challenges, however, can pave the way to innovation and promising new approaches to the delivery of victim services. Trauma-Informed Care, technology and adapting to crime trends is discussed here.

Trauma-Informed Care

One of the most important developments in recent years has been the recognition by health and behavioral health professionals of the role traumatic events play in the long-term physical and mental health of those who have experienced such events, especially when those events occurred in childhood. Child maltreatment, exposure to domestic violence, and various constructs of family dysfunction due to parental substance abuse, mental illness, or incarceration now have solid research grounding as factors associated with the leading causes of disease and death in adults. The initial study to bring this relationship into clear focus was conducted by the Centers for Disease Control and Prevention in partnership with Kaiser Permanente's Health Appraisal Clinic in San Diego. The study tracks the relationship between over 17,000 patients' ACE Score, which is represented by the total number of Adverse Childhood Experiences (ACE) reported as a proxy for childhood stress and has confirmed that "as the number of ACE increase, the risk for health problems increases in a strong and graded fashion"(CDC, 2015). Identified health issues include: substance abuse, chronic obstructive pulmonary disease, depression, fetal death, ischemic heart disease, liver disease, early initiation of sexual behavior, unintended pregnancies, and suicide attempts.

One of the first published reports of the study conducted by Felitti and associates (1998) recruited over 9,000 patients and examined the relationship between 7 ACE and 10 well known risk factors for disease and death in adults. Approximately 52% of the sample reported at least one ACE and 6.2% reported at least 4. As the number of exposures to ACE increased, so did the relationship to disease conditions such as ischemic heart disease, cancer, chronic bronchitis or emphysema, hepatitis or jaundice, skeletal fractures, and poor self-related health. Such findings strongly suggest that the relationship between early childhood traumatic events and long-term health status is a cumulative one.

Since 1998, over 50 published studies have been conducted exploring a breath of research exploring more in-depth the role of ACE to specific chronic diseases, sexual behavior and reproductive health, health risks, mental health, victimization and perpetration, and special populations of victims (CDC, 2015). For example, a recent study found longitudinal support that chronic exposure to ACE had an impact on health even for those as young as 18 (Thompson et al, 2015). The body of research related to ACE demonstrates clearly that an investment made early to prevent or intervene during critical traumatic events in childhood can perhaps prevent health related problems in the future.

The knowledge gained from this body of research has been instrumental in the recognition that previous trauma can play a significant role in the lives of adults who struggle with addiction, mental health related issues, and chronic interaction with the criminal justice system as a result of offending behavior. This recognition has helped to change the conversation and approach to services provided by behavioral health and social service practitioners and how they view their work. Trauma-Informed Care (TIC) is an approach that not only attends to the role of trauma in the clients served, but staff as well. The TIC approach can be utilized in any type of human service setting such as addictions treatment, housing/shelter services, schools, corrections, health care, etc. and is distinct from specific therapeutic interventions. Rather, it as an approach that involves shifting the paradigm for an entire organization or social service system at the community level to improve how services are rendered to eliminate practices or policies within an organization or system that can unintentionally re-victimize clients and staff.

According to the National Center for Trauma Informed Care (available at http://www.samhsa.gov/nctic/about) of the Substance Abuse Mental Health Services Administration (SAMHSA) suggests that "a program, organization, or system that is trauma-informed realizes the widespread impact of trauma and understands potential paths for recovery; recognizes the signs and symptoms of trauma in clients, families, staff, and others involved in the system; responds by fully integrating knowledge about trauma into policies, procedures, and practices; and seeks to actively resist re-traumatization" (NC-TIC,2015). The ultimate goal is to provide a cultural environment for both clients and staff that encourages healing and recovery (Harris and Fallot, 2001; Wolf et al, 2014).

The evolution of TIC is still yet to be determined; however, it is a very important advancement in the continuum of care in human services as it articulates and advocates for new approaches to service delivery to mitigate the "secondary victimization" or "secondary harm" survivors experience in their interactions with practitioners, fully acknowledges the impact victimization can have on child and adult development, and further validates the important role of victim assistance.

Technology

The advancement of technology in recent years has begun to revolutionize criminal justice agencies. Advancements in forensic science, investigative technology, computerized record keeping, surveillance, etc. have improved the ability of the police to fight crime and the courts to respond to high caseloads. Victim services have also benefited from technology, especially in the provision of services for victims of domestic violence (Roberts and Kurst-Swanger, 2002). Today, wireless technology, the Global Positioning System (GPS), and surveillance equipment can help to protect victims of violence.

In addition, the internet has been widely used by victim service agencies as a tool to communicate with their clients and the community at large. Through web pages, agencies and programs are able to provide critical information regarding the criminal justice process, compensation, civil court processes, issues regarding recovery, availability of services, upcoming events, publications, etc. In addition, the victim notification and information systems, discussed previously, have been found to be very beneficial to victims (Larsen and Year-wood, 2004). As noted above, social media platforms such as Facebook and Twitter also provide an opportunity for survivors to receive support and advocate for change.

It should also be noted however, that such technology has also provided a new opportunity for offenders to stalk and harass victims. Southworth and associates (2005) point out offenders use telephone, location and surveillance, and computer and internet technologies to locate, terrorize and control. Technology-enabled crime has provided opportunities for offenders to adapt their methods of committing ordinary crime, as well as creating new crimes that require the innovative use of technology to commit acts that are not necessarily illegal at the time (McQuade, 2006). Law enforcement and security officials will be challenged in the future to keep abreast of evolving technologies and their application in crime commission.

Responding to Crime Trends

Another challenge facing victim assistance programs is the changing nature of crime and the demographics in which it impacts. Planning for the future will require victim assistance programs to carefully monitor and track demographic changes and crime trends and adapt their programs to meet the diverse needs of their community. For example, the aging baby boomer population is likely to result in higher rates of elder abuse, neglect, and/or financial scams geared toward the elderly. Also, emerging crime trends such as identify theft, healthcare fraud, religion-related crime, technology-enabled crime, mass shootings, and domestic and international terrorism, etc. might require different types of victim assistance services than are currently available. Additionally, being able to respond to our citizens when victimized abroad is another important component to consider. Of course, it is also important that public policy is regularly updated to ensure the criminal justice system is equipped to deal with such trends.

Conclusion

Crime is a social phenomenon that exists today as a transnational problem. It is imperative that the needs of crime victims be recognized and dealt with as legitimate social concerns. The institutionalization of crime victim assistance services and programs in many communities is a positive step in the right direction. In fact, the crime victims' movement has enjoyed numerous accomplishments and successes that are worthy of celebration and recognition. Hopefully this chapter, in some small way, does just that.

References

Centers for Disease Control and Prevention (CDC) (2015). *ACE Study*. Injury Prevention and control: Division of Violence Prevention. Retrieved on December 27, 2015, from *http://www.cdc.gov/violenceprevention/acestudy/index.html*

Davis, L.V., Hagen, J.L., and Early, T.J. (1994). Social services for battered women: Are they adequate, accessible, and appropriate? Social Work, 39(6), 695–704.

Derene, S., Walker, S., and Stein, J. (2007). *History of the Crime Victims' Movement in the United States*. Participants' text. Washington D.C.: Office of Justice Programs, National Victims Assistance Academy. Office for Victims of Crime.

Elias, R. (1983). *Victims of the system: Crime and compensation in American politics and criminal justice*. New Brunswick, New York: Transaction Books.

Felitti, V., Anda, R., Nordenberg, D., Williamson, D.F., Spitz, A., Edwards, V., Koss, M.P., and Marks, J.S. (1998). Relationship of Childhood Abuse and Household Dysfunction to Many of the Leading Causes of Death in Adults: The Adverse Childhood Experiences (ACE) Study. *American Journal of Preventive Medicine*, 14(4), 245–258.

Fors, S., and Rojek, D. (1999). The Effect of Victim Impact Panels on DUI/DWI Rearrest Rates: A Twelve Month Follow-up. *Journal of Studies on Alcohol*, 60(4), 514–520.

Harris, M. and Fallot, R. (Eds.). (2001). Envisioning a trauma-informed service system: A vital paradigm shift. *New Directions for Mental Health Services*. 89, 3–22.

Irazola, S., Williamson, E., Niedzwiecki, E., Debus-Sherrill, S., and Stricker, J. (2013). *Evaluation of the Statewide Automated Victim Information and Notification Program: Final Report*, National Institute of Justice, Office of Justice Programs, U.S. Department of Justice. Retrieved on January 4, 2016 from https://www.ncjrs.gov/pdffiles1/nij/grants/243839.pdf

Jerin, R.A., and Moriarty, L.J. (1998). *Victims of Crime*. Chicago, Illinois: Nelson-Hall Publishers.

Kurst-Swanger, K., and Petcosky, J. (2003). *Violence in the home: Multidisciplinary perspectives*. New York, NY: Oxford University Press.

Larsen, C., and Yearwood, D.L. (2004). *Notifying and informing victims of crime: An evaluation of North Carolina's SAVAN system*. North Carolina Criminal Justice Analysis Center. Retrieved July 30, 2006 from http://www.nccrimecontrol.org.

Niemeyer, M., and Shichor, D. (1996). A preliminary study of a large victim/offender reconciliation program. *Federal Probation*, 60(3), 30–34.

McQuade, S. (2006). Technology-enabled crime, policing and security. *Journal of Technology Studies*. 32(1)32–42.

Mercer, D., Lorden, R. and Lord, J.H. (1999). Victim Impact Panels: A Healing Opportunity. *MADDvocate*, Winter. Retrieved on July 24, 2006 from http://www.madd.org/victims/2025.

National Center for Trauma-informed Care (NCTIC) (2015). *Trauma-Informed Approach*. Retrieved on January 7, 2015 from http://www.samhsa.gov/nctic/trauma-interventions

Office of Victims of Crime (OVC) (2015a). *Crime Victims Fund*. Office of Justice Programs, U.S. Department of Justice. Retrieved on December 26, 2015, from *http://www.ovc.gov/about/victimsfund.html*.

Office of Victims of Crime (OCV) (2015b). 2015 OVC Report to the nation: Fiscal years 2013–2104. Office of Justice Programs, U.S. Department of Justice. Retrieved on December 29, 2015 from http://ovc.gov/pubs /reporttonation2015/VOCA-compensation-and-assistance-statistics.html

Office of Victims of Crime (OVC) (2015c). *Landmarks in Victims' Rights and Services: Crime victims' rights in America, a historical overview* in 2015 NCVRW Resource Guide. Office of Justice Programs, U.S. Department of Justice. Retrieved on December 29, 2015, from http://ovc.ncjrs.gov /ncvrw2015/.

Polacsek, M., Rogers, E., Woodall, W., Delaney, H., Wheeler, D., and Rao, N. (2001). MADD Victim Impact Panels and Stages of Change in Drunk Driving Prevention. *Journal of Studies on Alcohol, 62(3),* 344–250.

Roberts, A.R. (1990). Helping crime victims. Newbury Park, California: Sage Publications.

Roberts, A.R. (2000). *Crisis Intervention Handbook: Assessment, treatment, and research.* New York, New York: Oxford University Press.

Roberts, A.R., and Kurst-Swanger, K. (2002). Police responses to battered women: Past, present, and future. In *Handbook of Domestic Violence Intervention Strategies* by A.R. Roberts (Ed), New York, New York: Oxford University Press.

Shichor, D., and Sechrest, D. (1998). A comparison of mediated and non-mediated juvenile offender cases in California. *Juvenile and Family Court Journal,* 49(2), 27–39.

Shinar, D., and Compton, R.P. (1995). Victim Impact Panels: Their Impact on DWI recidivism. *Alcohol, Drugs, and Driving,* 11(1), 73–87.

Southworth, C., Dawson, S., Fraser, C., and Tucker, S. (2005). A high-tech twist on abuse: Technology, Intimate Partner Stalking, and Advocacy. Safety Net Project at the National Network to End Domestic Violence Fund. Retrieved on January 10, 2016 from http://www.mincava.umn.edu /documents/commissioned/stalkingandtech/stalkingandtech.html

Thompson, R. Flaherty, E.G., English, D.J., Litrownik, A.J., Dubowitz, H., Kotch, J.B., and Runyan, D.K. (2015). Trajectories of Adverse Childhood Experiences and Self-Reported Health at Age 18. *Academic Pediatrics,* 15(50), 503–509.

Tutty, L.M., and Rothery, M. (2002). Beyond shelters: Support groups and community based advocacy for abused women. In A.R. Roberts (Ed.), *Hand-*

book of domestic violence intervention strategies: Policies, programs, and legal remedies (pp. 396–418). New York, New York: Oxford University Press.

Umbreit, M.S. and Greenwood, J. (2000*). National Survey of Victim-Offender Mediation Programs in the United States.* Center for Restorative Justice and Peacemaking, Office for Victims of Crime, U.S. Department of Justice, NCJ 176350. Retrieved on January 4, 2016 from http://www.mediate.com/articles/vomsurvey.cfm.

Walker, S. (2000). History of the victims' movement in the United States. *Perspectives, Journal of the American Association of Behavioral and Social Sciences*, 3. Retrieved on August 6, 2006 from *http://aabss.org/journal2000.*

Wheeler, D.R., Rogers, E.M., Tonigan, S.J., and Woodall, G.W. (2004). Effectiveness of customized Victim Impact Panels on first-time DWI offender inmates. *Accident Analysis and Prevention*, 36(1), 29–36.

Wolf, M.R., Green, S.A., Nochajski, T.H., Mendel, W.E., and Kusmaul, N.S. (2014). 'We're Civil Servants': The status of trauma-informed care in the community. *Journal of Social Service Research*, 40: 111–120.

Young, M., and Stein, J. (2004) *The History of the Crime Victims' Movement in the United States: A component of the Office for Victims of Crime Oral History Project.* Office for Victims of Crime, Office of Justice Programs, U.S. Department of Justice. Retrieved on August 1, 2006, from *http://www.ojp.usdoj.gov/ovc/ncvrw/2005/pg4c.html.*

CHAPTER 2

Evaluating the Effectiveness of Batterer Intervention Programs: Are We Asking the Right Questions?

Jill A. Gordon
Virginia Commonwealth University

Monica Leisey
Salem State University

Laura J. Moriarty
Monmouth University

Sara-Beth Plummer
Rutgers University

Introduction

"Batterer intervention programs are an integral part of any comprehensive approach to domestic violence" (Healey, Smith and O'Sullivan, 1998: 1). Batterer intervention may be either court-ordered or it may be part of a pre-trial situation where the offender seeks treatment before he is court-ordered to do so. The intervention or treatment focuses on changing behavior and attitudes that support violence as a means to solve issues.

As Healey and colleagues remind us, batterer intervention programs are part of an overall, comprehensive approach to domestic violence meaning that in order to reduce domestic violence a community approach must be invoked. All facets of the criminal justice system must be on board with bringing about this change, as well as treatment providers and the community-at-large. This comprehensive approach is a relatively new idea, and some authors, especially those working with the National Institute of Justice, are providing ways for criminal justice and treatment professionals to operate in a comprehensive manner. Two very important concepts in, or components of, this approach are changing batterers' behaviors and attitudes *and* raising cultural awareness of the problem. As Dr. Jeremy Travis, Director of the National Institute of Justice, summarized,

> *In the late 1970's, activists working with battered women realized that, although they might help individual victims, no real progress could be made against the problem of domestic violence unless actions were taken to reform perpetrators and challenge the cultural and legal supports for battering. Batterer intervention was initiated as a first step toward changing batterers and raising cultural awareness of the problem* (see Healey, et al., 1998, Forward).

It is through batterer intervention programs that we expect to see the changes in the batterers' actions and attitudes. Therefore, it is important to gauge the effectiveness of such programs, and to refine those programs that are not achieving an appropriate level of success. Many researchers have evaluated batterer intervention programs reporting mixed or inconclusive results.

The goal of this chapter then is to examine the batterer intervention programs evaluation literature to determine if the right questions have been asked when conducting said evaluations. In order to achieve our stated goal we will 1) summarize the evaluation literature, focusing on meta-analyses to provide an overall picture of the inconsistent results reported by various authors; 2) detail the methodological problems (e.g., weak research designs, conceptualization problems with the outcome variable, utilizing official data sources) associated with many of the research studies conducted to evaluate batterer intervention programs; 3) introduce the concept of treatment fidelity and question why it is missing from much of the batterer intervention programs evaluation literature; and 4) focus attention on the all too often missing component of the evaluations — the victim. We conclude with a discussion on how to better evaluate batterer intervention programs with more attention given to treatment fidelity and victim participation in the evaluations.

Overview of Batterer Intervention Programs

Batterer Intervention Programs emerged during the late 1970s in response to the large number of women seeking refuge in domestic violence shelters. These early programs were developed by domestic violence advocates, not the criminal justice system, and thus focused primarily on victim safety, not the criminality of the offender's behavior. Concomitantly, the programs were designed to change the attitudes and beliefs of men who had abused their wives and partners. An illustration of a batterer intervention program is *Emerge*, developed in 1977. The primary goal of *Emerge* is to emphasize offender accountability utilizing a psycho-educational process. Through counseling and group therapy sessions, the offender's motivation to change becomes the result of his own, internal, motivation for change, instead of changing because of external pressures, like the threat of incarceration or the spouse/partner leaving the relationship (Adams & Cayouette, 2002).

The 1980s marked President Reagan's "get tough" on crime policy agenda and domestic violence became one area of particular interest with get tough strategies emerging. During the Reagan administration, for example, behaviors that were considered criminal were being seen in the same light when the offender was a family member. Also, prosecutors began invoking "pro-arrest" and "no-drop" policies where police officers had to make an arrest in a domestic violence situation ("pro-arrest"), and where neither party could drop the charges when a domestic violence arrest was made ("no-drop").

At this time, batterer intervention programs became a more consistent option in terms of sanctioning because victims did not always support incarceration as the only option for convicted batterers (Jackson, Feder, Forde, Davis, Maxwell, and Taylor, 2003). Court-ordered treatment was utilized more frequently as a means to hold the batterer liable for his actions, while allowing the relationship to continue if the female so desired. There were no national standards during this time period; however, several themes or goals emerged including: (1) the importance of victim safety, (2) the recognition of domestic violence as a pattern of behavior, (3) the removal of the veil of privacy that had previously surrounded the behavior; (i.e., domestic violence was no longer a secret and batterers could no longer expect their behavior to be kept confidential), (4) the move to offender accountability, and (5) the emphasis on behavioral change (Healey, et al., 1998, Bennett and Williams, 2001, Austin and Dankwort, 1997).

The primary types of intervention utilized in batterer intervention programs over the last three decades include psycho-educational models, couples therapy, cognitive-behavioral approaches, and group processes/practice models. Psycho-educational models are linked to feminist theory and are a commonly recognized intervention primarily due to the Duluth model (Healey, et al., 1998; Pence and Paymar, 1993). The Duluth model seeks to change behavior through the use of group work targeted to confront a man's notion of power and authority over a woman in order to create an equitable relationship between the man and woman.

Couples therapy is often theoretically linked to family systems theory, which suggests that each individual contributes to the reduction of conflict; thus, the intervention focuses on enhancing interaction and communication to result in less conflict between the couple (Healey, et al., 1998). Many victims' advocates oppose the underlying premise of the approach, which suggests (if not outwardly claims) that the blame for the victimization (i.e., conflict) lies with the female (Jacobson, 1993), and opposition also results because this approach often leads to future violence (Lipchick, Sirles, and Kubicki, 1997). In support of this position, we find many states that will not allow such interventions (i.e., couples therapy) for court-ordered offenders (Healey, et al., 1998; Lipchick et al, 1998).

In the third model where cognitive behavioral approaches are utilized, the violence itself becomes the center of the intervention. Violence is considered to be learned behavior, and as such, it can be unlearned. The offender must learn to recognize the patterns that lead to such violent acts (i.e., behaviors) and to replace or re-learn non-violent responses (Adams, 1988). The focus then is on changing the way the offender thinks and reacts, teaching him new positive responses that become part of his routine.

The last model is group processes or group practice models. Here the intervention approach focuses on eliminating the violence by integrating two previously discussed intervention models: psycho-educational and cognitive-behavioral approaches (Jackson et al., 2003). The approach then attempts to change societal views as well as individual views and responses to the patterns of behaviors that lead to violence.

Overall, batterer intervention programs continue to be used as a court ordered sanction within the criminal justice system. And as such, there is a concerted effort to develop national standards for uniformity among these programs. While no national standards currently exist, we do find some commonalities among the programs that warrant inclusion in this chapter. For example, most batterer intervention programs provide intervention through the use of psycho-educational group models that are created around profeminist values and are based on social learning (Adams & Cayouette, 2002). Further, the interventions tend to educate abusers about the causes, dynamics, and consequences of domestic violence while also teaching abusers how to recognize and deal with anger and potentially violent situations. Often included in these intervention strategies are techniques that will either help abusers avoid emotionally charged situations where the violent behavior may result, or the strategies will provide mechanisms to help abusers resolve such situations.

EFFECTIVENESS OF BATTERER INTERVENTION PROGRAMS

Effectiveness can be measured in a number of ways and along a continuum of methods. Researchers often focus on the outcome of the treatment in terms of future violent behaviors. Some focus also on the treatment program itself and whether the offender completed the full program. When examining offender outcomes in terms of future violent offenses, researchers usually gather data from three sources: official reports of re-arrest, batterer self-reports of abuse, and victim reports of continued abuse. This next section of the chapter summarizes the literature in order to answer to the question, Are batterer intervention programs effective?

A few meta-analysis have been conducted to examine the overall impact of batterer intervention programs. A meta-analysis investigates the effect of a phenomenon by considering individual study results simultaneously; simply put it is the "analysis of analyses" (Glass, 1976 p. 3). A meta-analysis extracts data components from prior research, whether published or unpublished, and creates an individual dataset to examine the total effect of the variables being studied. This approach is more robust than a narrative review that chronologically discusses individual studies because a meta-analysis collection and analysis of the research provides a more objective and precise interpretation of the findings.

Meta-analysis typically provides an effect size of overall change. This can be conducted for each individual study and the overall analysis. The effect size characterizes the magnitude of a relationship; it portrays the relationship between the variables as big or small. The actual classification as to the degree of the effect size is varied based on the statistic utilized, for the d statistic an effect size of .20 is considered small, .50 considered medium, and .80 considered large.

BATTERER OUTCOMES

Do offenders who complete batterer intervention programs recidivate? An interesting and direct question yet there appears to be no conclusive answer found in the literature. What we do find is summarized here.

There have been three published meta-analyses (see Feder and Wilson, 2005; Babcock, Green, and Robie, 2004; and Aries, Arce, and Vilarino, 2013) and one synthesis of the literature with reported effect sizes (Davis and Taylor, 1999) on the impact of batterer intervention programs. The purpose of the four articles varies slightly and includes differing published and non-published reports on the impact of domestic violence programs.

Davis and Taylor (1999) set out to review several questions such as the general state of treatment effectiveness and whether outcomes vary by intervention type and/or offender characteristics. Although the goal was not to conduct a meta-analysis the authors calculated the *average* effect sizes among five studies and concluded "there is fairly consistent evidence that treatment works and that the effect of treatment is substantial" (Davis and Taylor, 1999, p. 69). However, Babcock et al. (2004) labels the reported average effect size ($h = 0.41$) as "small."

Babcock et al. (2004) conducted a meta-analysis using 22 studies which examined the impact of treatment as defined by victim-reported outcome and/or official statistics considering male batterers only. The goal was to determine the overall effect of intervention while moderating both study and treatment design. Specifically, the authors partitioned the effect size by type of outcome (police or partner report), quality of design (experimental and quasi-experimental), and type of intervention (Duluth model, cognitive-behavioral, or other). The study indicates that "regardless of reporting method, study design, and type of treatment, the effect on recidivism rates remains in the small range. In the best case scenario, using quasi-experimental designs based on partner report, the effect size is $d = 0.34$ . . ." (Babcock et al. 2004, p. 1044). More broadly, the effect sizes for the police reports ranged from 0.12 to 0.32 and for the partner reports from 0.03 to 0.34; such effect sizes interpret into no to modest values.

A meta-analysis conducted by Feder and Wilson (2005) who focused on males who were court-ordered into batterer intervention, and their study included 10 such studies. In general, the analysis considers the overall impact by type of design considering both official and victim reports. The authors report varying effects of domestic violence programs determined by research design type and outcome. To illustrate, experimental studies examining official reports show a "modest" impact but no effect appears with victim reports.

Among quasi-experimental no positive consequences are uncovered among studies using a "no-treatment comparison" and a large positive effect is established when considering those rejected from treatment (the implications of considering those rejected will be addressed latter).

The most recent meta-analysis included 19 English or Spanish studies from 1975–2013 that focused on measurement of recidivism from official accounts or couple reports (Aries et al., 2013). Overall the findings indicate higher recidivism when examining couple reports, no statistically significant difference in the impact of treatment, although the direction was positive, or on the type of treatment considering Duluth or cognitive behavioral intervention models in predicting offender outcome. That said, the authors uncovered a positive effect when considering "other treatment interventions" and also on long-term interventions, especially when examining official reports.

BATTERER OUTCOME: VICTIM'S PERSPECTIVE

While there are many studies that focus on offender outcomes using official and self-report data, there is a dearth of literature where the focus is on the victim and her views and experiences as they relate to the success or failure of batterer intervention programs. Once an abuser is arrested and referred to a batterer intervention program, little is known about how victims feel about such treatment. This is somewhat ironic since the inception of batterer intervention programs was in response to victims wanting to keep the family together. It seems like the victims should be part of the process and their views about the program should be assessed. For example, since victims often express ambivalence and confusion over current criminal justice reforms related to domestic violence (Bennett, Goodman, and Dutton, 1999; Bohmer, Brandt, Bronson, and Hartnett, 2002), then it is important that researchers inquire into how they view alternative types of punishment such as batterer intervention programs. Current research suggests that victims prefer alternative sanctions for abusive acts by their partners (Bennett et al.; Ford, 1983), however, few researchers have asked survivors to express their thoughts and opinions about these programs in terms of how well the victim feels the intervention is working (Austin and Dankwort, 1999; Gondolf, 1998; Gregory and Erez, 2002).

In an effort to narrow this gap, a few researchers have started to reach out to victims to gauge their views regarding batterer intervention programs. Three such articles were found in the literature (Austin and Dankwort, 1999; Gondolf, 1998; Gregory and Erez, 2002). These authors interviewed partners of batterers who had been mandated to a batterers' program after being arrested for abuse, and found that survivors responded optimistically about the future of their relationship with their abuser and the outcome of the batterer intervention programs (Austin and Dankwort, 1999; Gondolf, 1998; Gregory and Erez, 2002). In one study, over half of the survivors reported feeling safe while the batterer was in the program and almost half believed that it was very unlikely that the violence would continue once the intervention was complete (Gondolf, 1988).

The victims' optimism seems to not be misplaced as Gregory and Erez (2002) found the majority of victims (78%) reported a decrease in violence after a batterer's intervention. The caveat, however, is that the major reduction in violent behavior was related primarily to physical incidents, with only a small amount of victims reporting a decrease in verbal assaults. The authors remind the reader that abuse is not relegated to only physical assaults such as hitting and kicking. Rather, it is now widely known that emotional and verbal abuse is an integral part of power and control in a relationship, and as such, is considered abuse (National Coalition of Domestic Violence, 4).

Women tend to feel safe and express a sense of relief while their abuser is involved in batterer intervention programs (Austin and Dankwort, 1999; Gondolf, 1998; Gregory and Erez, 2002). The feeling of safety is correlated with a decrease or cessation in violent acts, the ongoing monitoring of the abuser's behavior, and a sense of validation of the victim's feelings about the abuse (Austin and Dankwort, 1999). Victims want to believe that an intervention program will work and that their partner will cease their violent ways. And although some victims, early on, fear an increase in reprisal by the abuser, many find a sense of relief and security as the perpetrator remains in the program (Gregory and Erez, 2002).

The more recent enhancements of batter interventions, such as the use of specialized caseloads, has created an additional opportunity to assess victim reactions. Klein and Crowe (2008) examined the effects of two case management strategies on both offender and victims. The assumption was that the use of Domestic Violence Unit to oversee probation supervision would yield higher rates of victim satisfaction than a traditional probation model. Victims of the specialized unit rated the probation personnel as supportive, interested in their well-being and empathetic of the situation compared to victim's associated with a traditional approach. Even so, the victims did not feel convinced, to a higher degree, that the sentence of probation would reduce further abuse.

INCONSISTENT RESULTS IN THE EVALUATION OF BATTERER INTERVENTION PROGRAMS: WHAT'S THE PROBLEM?

As indicated above, support for utilizing batterer intervention program varies by the conclusions drawn from the meta-analyses conducted. In other words, some researchers found effect sizes that would be considered acceptable, while others found effect sizes that were low. We offer two thoughts about why the results are not consistent across the authors who performed the analysis. The first focuses on methodological concerns or issues with the individual studies included in the meta-analysis; and the second focuses on treatment fidelity. Each is explained below.

METHODOLOGICAL CONCERNS

A number of factors influence the quality of an evaluation which has a snowball effect on the interpretation of effectiveness and the contribution to the field at large. It is important to recognize the influences on research when designing and implementing a program. There are four primary issues that influence the interpretation of the findings: design, sample, measurement of violence, and batterer retention. All of these facets impact the generalizability of the study results.

There are three types of research designs: non-experimental, quasi-experimental, and experimental, and each type of design has strengths and weaknesses. Each type of design has been implemented to evaluate batterer intervention programs. For example, the non-experimental designs were utilized early on to assess program participants, measuring change either in the form of a post-test only design, a pre-test and post-test design, or among treatment completers versus drop-outs (see Davis and Taylor, 1999 for tables of specific studies). Although such studies do little to assist in determining the true effectiveness of a program they can assist localities in determining who is most likely to be "ready" for treatment. However, it must be noted that such descriptions of "successful" participants are more likely a measure of motivation to change rather than a true outcome (i.e., real change in behavior) (Palmer, Brown, and Barrera, 1982).

Quasi-experimental designs were implemented strong force in the mid to late 1980s and such designs either employed a non-equivalent or equivalent matched group (i.e., Dutton 1986; Hamberger and Hastings, 1988). The stronger of the two design choices is the equivalent matched control group because the design helps alleviate internal validity concerns. We want to be sure that the impact of treatment is causing the change rather than a specific offender characteristic or difference between the two groups.

True randomized control group experiments were conducted in the early 1990s with the research agenda being pushed by evidence-based practices (i.e., Palmer, Brown, and Barrera, 1992; Feder 1996; Davis and Taylor 1997). True experimental designs, with control over randomization, reduce internal validity threats. The only problem is that experiments are difficult to conduct when society is your laboratory.

Understanding the type of research design is important in general; however, it is imperative when we realize that there is an inverse relationship between design rigor and program impact (Feder and Forde, 2000; Weisburd, Lum, and Petersino, 2001), meaning that less rigorous research designs fail to demonstrate appropriately treatment effects. Additionally, when conducting the quasi-experimental or randomized designs we must be cognizant to clearly articulate the delivery of services/punishment received among the comparison group. Concise verbalization of a programs target population, components of treatment, and release mechanisms will enable clarity in the comparability across studies. Currently, the literature is scattered in the consistency of reporting such information which limits the comparability between studies.

Study results are potentially overestimated when difficult subjects (i.e., substance use or prior batterer history) are removed from the sample (Rosenfeld, 1992). This point is further illustrated by Feder and Wilson (2005) who identified higher mean effects among program studies with limited samples. This suggests that such restrictions on the selection of participants "creams" the outcome to reflect more favorable results due to the inclusion of more motivated offenders. A similar parallel is drawn among the examination of treatment completers and treatment drop-outs. To summarize, the primary concern is to reduce selection bias in order to estimate the true impact of a batterer intervention program rather than selecting program participants that "cream" the selection process in favor of treatment.

In measuring program effectiveness there are three primary methods used: official reports, batterer reports, and victim reports. All have varying weaknesses that impact the reliability of the measures and validity of the results. To illustrate, police reports depend on the victim to call the police, and there are a number of obstacles to reporting, such as obstacles in the criminal justice system, the perception that the violent event was not serious enough, and/ or the assistance of police will require the victim to end the relationship (or the treatment intervention) (Fugate, Landis, Riordan, Naureckas, and Engel, 2005). Likewise, batterer self-report substantially underestimate the frequency and nature of an incident (Rosenfeld, 1992)

To overcome the above limitations, victim surveys, such as the Conflict Tactic Scale are a viable way to measure continued abuse. Logically, it makes sense that information obtained from victim self-reports are a more accurate reflection of abuse, however, the drawback is subject attrition (see Dunford, 2000, Feder and Dugan, 2002; Harrell, 1991). Research proposes women who do not complete the follow-up surveys are more transient and suffer from abuse more often and with a greater degree of harm (Sullivan, Rumpty, Campbell, Eby, and Davidson, 1996).

A final concern with batterer measures is the lack of standardization among follow-up time intervals. Davis and Taylor (1999) suggested such standardization would allow for comparability of short-term and long-term effects. Uniform guidance of time-interval points would also increase ease of comparability across studies. Davis and Taylor recommend monitoring batterer progress at six-month intervals up to one year but strongly advocate for a two-year follow up; we concur.

Across the batterer intervention literature one other factor is clearly considered, that of offender retention. As shown in Babcock et al. (2004) batterer retention varied from under 20% to over 80%; that is, about 80% of the participants *failed* to complete the required number of treatment sessions. This is an important point, because research indicates variation in the characteristics and abuse levels by program retention (Feder and Dugan, 2002). A number of factors should continually be measured due to the correlation with treatment retention, such as: employment stability, marital status, substance dependency, and motivation for change (DeMaris, 1988; Hamberger and Hastings, 1988; Gruszniki and Carrillo, 1988).

It is important to be aware of retention issues because the study outcome will be dependent upon the "quality" of participants. And while examining the treatment completers versus drop-outs does not fairly examine effectiveness or "address the broader issue of the likely reduction in domestic violence as a function of a policy to mandate such treatment" (Feder and Wilson, 2005, p. 256) we believe it does assist in defining broader policy development issues, such as the (1) identification/education of "marginal" communities and (2) identification/education of myths concerning various policy options (Fugate, Landis, Riordan, Naureckas, and Engel, 2005).

Treatment Fidelity

Although there are a modest number of batterer intervention programs evaluations available in the literature, limited attention has been given to the concept of treatment fidelity (Day, Chung, O'Leary & Carson, 2009; Scott, King, McGinn & Hosseini, 2011; Scott, Heslop, Kelly & Wiggins, 2015). Treatment fidelity is the accuracy to which intervention protocols are implemented (Cagle and Naleppa, 2005). It is related to two corresponding issues: how well treatment conditions are implemented, also referred to as *treatment integrity*, and how much treatment conditions differ due to the manipulation of independent variables, often referred to as *treatment differentiation* (Moncher and Prinz, 1991).

Outcome research treatment fidelity is a very important dimension. It provides a measure of the accountability of the intervention, therefore reflecting the congruency of the treatment/intervention provided to the treatment/intervention protocol. In research, implementing the treatment as intentioned and differentiating the independent variables across conditions will increases internal validity, minimize the influence of extraneous variables, increase rigor, enhance treatment clarity, and facilitate replication of the treatment and dissemination of the findings (Cagle and Naleppa, 2005). The ability to increase treatment fidelity boosts the confidence in the research outcomes, as changes in the dependent variables can be attributed directly to the manipulation of the independent variable (Borrelli et al, 2005).

Documentation of treatment fidelity in the research literature facilitates the translation of research findings to clinical practice (Bellg et al, 2004). The dimensions of treatment fidelity that have been identified as indicators that the treatment protocols have been followed and that the independent variables were manipulated as per the design include: clarity of treatment definition, identification of essential treatment components, service provider training, manualization or standardization of the treatment, supervision of service providers, and sampling of the intervention to ensure treatment consistency (Borrelli et al, 2005; Cagle and Naleppa, 2005; Moncher and Prinz 1991). Unfortunately, very few of these indicators are found in the batterer intervention programs evaluation literature.

Treatment fidelity is not clearly articulated in the batterer intervention programs evaluation conversation. The only consistent factor found in the literature is the dimension of the treatment definition as described by Borrelli et al. (2005). This is apparent through descriptions of treatment protocol (see Buttell and Pike, 2002; Dunford, 2000; or Buttell and Carney, 2005 for examples). Such descriptions commonly provide the underlying assumptions of the treatment, providing the reader with some understanding of what the intervention would include, along with many of the essential treatment components which were identified. However, it is often unclear whether or not a manual of the intervention was created to assist in standardizing the treatment. Unfortunately, in much of the batterer intervention programs evaluation literature there is little to no attention paid to the treatment protocol or to the essential treatment components. The lack of attention to information concerning the intervention provided implies that the intervention is not salient to the outcomes being measured — which is paradoxical considering the focus of much of the available literature is the effectiveness of the intervention.

More recently, the domestic violence literature integrates discussions about treatment efficacy in general and, at times, within an evaluative component. Suggesting multiple considerations regarding the integrity of a program to include not simply to what extent a program may or may not be meeting its treatment protocol but the monitoring for consistent delivery intervention over time and among varied staff to account for program drift or degradation (Day et al., 2009). Some current efforts do include varying insights for treatment efficacy through consideration of risk, need and responsivity of treatment delivery (Scott et al., 2015), examining resistant clients (Scott et al., 2011) and readiness for change among the offenders (Schmidt, Kolodinsky, Carsten, Schmidt, Larson & MacLachlan, 2007). Finally, we should not be surprised by a neglect to treatment fidelity since the policies and responses to domestic violence were created as a response to a system issue (Day et al., 2009). That is, the criminal justice system response is to provide an avenue for intervention with a wide amount of discretion remaining for non-compliance in terms of failure to attend the intervention or reoffending.

Concurrently, the training of the service providers or their philosophical position concerning the intervention being provided is scant or non-existent. Although the service providers perceptions are not explicit in the treatment fidelity literature, this component is important if no specific training has occurred, as it directly impacts the services being provided. Many service providers are concerned with the possibility of batterer intervention programs being provided by people who base their interventions on a feminist tradition of blaming and shaming the perpetrators for the actions that brought them to the intervention instead of treating each client with dignity while understanding that there are issues with the individual's behavior (S. Bachman, personal communication, October, 2005). It is important to know that batterer intervention programs are provided by individuals with the proper training and understanding of the treatment as well as the problem for which they are providing services.

Understandably, with so little attention paid to treatment fidelity in the literature, there is also no mention of any supervision of the treatment provided, or collecting samples throughout the intervention period to determine if there has been consistency in the provision of the intervention.

Lack of treatment fidelity information in batterer effectiveness literature may be indicative of the inherent problems with evaluating batterer intervention programs. Lack of clarity concerning the focus of the intervention and the change the intervention is attempting to facilitate, how outcomes are measured, and goals of the program may be real problems within the knowledge base. Most of the literature states that batterer intervention programs are only marginally effective. Based on the information provided in the literature, it is hard to know what that means. Effectiveness is based on measurements of recidivism, which is not the same as reducing domestic violence.

DISCUSSION

The research conducted on Batterer Intervention Programs reveals inconsistent findings in terms of the overall effectiveness of these programs. The reasons for these inconsistent findings range from the types of clients in the programs to methodological issues. More importantly, however, is what has not been addressed in these studies. And so we ponder whether the right questions have been addressed when designing research studies that evaluate batterer intervention programs effectiveness. We suggest it is time to reconsider the questions posed, and to change the direction and/or focus on the studies.

Primarily, we argue that the dependent variable — cessation of the behavior — is too limited in scope. If batterer intervention programs have as goals 1) victim protection, 2) offender responsibility, and 3) behavioral alteration, then why do the program evaluations only focus on recidivism? Arguably the most important outcome of a batterer intervention program is the cessation of the violence; however, it is rare that such results are achieved. What is more typically found is a reduction in the violence, not a total cessation. Therefore, if the outcome is cessation then many of the programs will fail. It is better in our opinion to focus on the multiple goals of the programs and to measure each goal as an indication of how well the program is doing.

We are not suggesting that a reduction in arrest rates is not a noble or satisfactory outcome rather, we advocate for outcome measurements to be aligned with what the program is supposed to achieve. Accordingly, there would be many outcome measures, and the outcomes would be specific to the programs being evaluated. The treatments also would be varied depending on the overall goals of the program. The cessation of the behavior appears to be firmly linked to societal attitudes about family violence, and for some programs changing attitudes in both areas is an important outcome. Thus, it would behoove researchers to measure societal attitudinal changes as well as offenders' attitudinal changes as a way to determine if the program is effective.

Since batterer intervention programs are supposed to protect the victim, then it makes sense to focus on the victims when evaluating overall effectiveness. Very little is known about the impact of batterer intervention programs on the victims themselves. We suggest that evaluation studies focus on the victim to determine 1) the victim's level of comfort with these programs, 2) any noticeable changes in the offender's behavior since entering the program, 3) whether the victim entered, maintained, or stopped attending any domestic violence related services when the offender started his program, and 4) whether any consideration was given to the victim's wishes in terms of the sanction (i.e., does she have a voice in the decision-making process?). As we pointed out in the previous sections of this chapter, some authors do advocate for inclusion of the victims in the evaluation; however, it is not a consistent involvement. Thus, we propose here that all evaluations include them.

Because victims have been involved in the evaluation process in limited ways, we don't really know much about their *perceptions* of batterer intervention programs. Their feelings of fear, frustration, and confusion have been connected to their satisfaction or dissatisfaction with the criminal justice system at large (Bennet, Goodman & Dutton, 1999). Moreover, if a woman is scared and perceives a lack of understanding and support from the very people expected to protect her, there will inevitably be dissatisfaction with individual agents of the system. Research indicates that satisfaction is expressed when the victim experienced support, sympathy, and encouragement from law enforcement and court officers, prosecutors, and judges (Buzawa, Austin, Bannon, and Jackson, 1992; Fleury, 2002). Several studies have shown that victims desire support, a sense of control (Fleury, 2002), and a voice in how the criminal course of action will proceed (Buzawa, et al., 1992). More specifically, victims expressed increased satisfaction when their preference was taken into account by police when deciding whether to arrest the abuser (Buzawa, et al. 1992). Additionally, research demonstrates that participation in the criminal justice decision-making process empowers a woman and increases her satisfaction (Erez and Bienkowska, 1993; Erez and Tontodonato, 1992).

Although this research was conducted on other aspects of the criminal justice system it suggests that victims may feel more secure and satisfied if administrators and agencies that conduct batterer intervention programs integrated their experiences and views on the success of these programs. Programs could not only increase individuals' satisfaction with the current system, but can also offer alternative ways to evaluate these programs (Gondolf, 1998). For example, the use of triangulation, in order to gain as much information from all parties involved, would improve the reliability of the results by comparing abuser self-reports with victim self-reports to counselor observations. In fact, Austin and Dankwort (1999) found that victims felt more empowered when counselors at the batterer intervention programs provided them with ongoing support, validation, and information about their partners' progress in the program.

Victim safety is the ultimate testimony of a successful program but as we have seen this is typically measured rather narrowly thus we really don't know much about the *impact* of batterer intervention programs on the victims. A few articles demonstrate the points that need to be expanded to encompass the true sense of victim safety. For example, Gondolf (2000) in a follow-up to his 1998 study, found that more than half of the women interviewed did not seek any additional counseling, advocacy or other supplementary support services for abused women once their partner started a batterer intervention program. This raises the question, if a woman is overly optimistic about the batterers' outcome in such a program, does she then become less likely to seek help? Is there a false sense of security when a batterer has been ordered into a batterer intervention program? Alternatively, this lack of follow-up by victims may have been a testament to the success of the intervention and an actual reduction in violence by the abuser. The point is, we don't know, until the focus of batterer invention programs becomes the victim.

Victim safety must also be conceptually examined through fear of reprisal since this is a well-known concern among victims (Bennett, et al., 1999; Bohmer, Brandt, Bronson & Hartnett, 2002). A facet of this was examined by Gregory and Erez (2002) research that reports victims were blamed by their abusive partners for the required attendance at weekly meetings of batterer intervention programs. Additional information on the level and types of reprisal towards victims may offer more answers to the overall "success" of such programs. In general, a broader framework of victim safety is needed that encompasses not just the physical but also economical and psychological control to adequately assess the success of batterer intervention programs.

Lastly, treatment fidelity must be addressed in program evaluations. Only a few studies have examined the treatment itself in terms of its delivery, and in terms of offender completion rates in these programs (see Gordon and Moriarty, 2003; Gross, Cramer, Forte, Gordon, Kunkel, and Moriarty, 2000).

As discussed above, without focus on treatment fidelity we are concerned about the overall knowledge base.

Batterer Intervention Programs: A decade later

Since publishing this chapter we are interested in knowing if research has improved to focus on more than just the cessation of violent behavior via the examination of official reports. Has the literature shifted to identify the impact of violence as seen through the lens of the victim, define domestic violence differently or examine or assess offender responsibility?

A review of the current literature finds mixed results. While a large amount of the literature still focuses on behavior cessation, there are several advances in the research that helps us understand the impact. Specifically, there are three general advances: (1) new approaches to case management, (2) consideration of accountability and/or identification of offender readiness to change, and (3) simultaneously treatment of substance use. In general, it appears that researchers are attempting to understand the cessation of domestic violence behavior by integrating theoretical perspectives from the general correctional intervention literature which seeks to determine for whom programming has the best impact.

Likewise, the purpose of batterer intervention programming remains an area of interest in the current literature with studies regarding intervention as simple punishment or intervention being an avenue to actually change behavior. The response by the criminal justice system classifies this, often court ordered, intervention as a punishment. The belief from courts, society and the victim is the program will educate the offender on the impact of violence, identify triggers or situations that can elicit a violent reaction and ultimately produce a reduction or elimination in such behaviors. Consequently, batterer intervention programming integrates a triad of somewhat incompatible concepts: punishment, education and treatment. As a result, the program components, duration, intensity and the assessment of effectiveness vary widely.

A case management strategy utilized in probation for several decades has recently been applied to domestic violence cases. In some jurisdictions, Domestic Violence Units (DVUs) that monitor only domestic violence cases have emerged. Not only are the caseloads specialized to a specific population but typically are smaller and attempt to move beyond the offender and integrate the concerns and needs of the victim as well. While DVUs vary by jurisdiction, there are some common themes of the probation unit (see Friday, Lord, Exum & Hartman, 2006; Klein & Crowe, 2008): achieving a reduction in offender violence; identifying and educating the offender on the primary sources of violence; developing a relationship with the victim; and assisting with the needs of the victim or family. Although few, the assessment of the impact of DVUs is mixed with some favorable outcomes reported. To illustrate, Klein & Crowe (2008) report an impact in victim satisfaction, offender responsibility and recidivism for certain offenders among DVU versus traditional probation case management strategies. Anderson (2014) reports the likelihood of recidivism for DVU clients was higher than domestic violence cases under traditional supervision. The author suggests the inequivalent design may have contributed to such a finding but also offers that specific predicting factors (i.e., age, positive drug screen, higher number of contacts) increased the likelihood of the DVU offenders to relapse.

An additional new management strategy applied to domestic violence offenders is the assessment and incorporation of risk, need and responsivity (RNR) to the intervention. While most probation units assess risk and assign the level of contact and programming based on this assessment, the integration or tailoring of appropriate levels and modalities of programming is lacking. That said, a recent application of RNR for matched intervention strategies was conducted. Specifically, Scott, Heslop, Kelly & Wiggins (2015) set out to identify the impact of a RNR approach on a law enforcement second responders program. Although this domestic violence assessment is not associated with a correctional entity, it is an important advancement in the understanding of effective cessation behavior or offender accountability. Specifically, Scott et al. (2015) identified those at a moderate to high risk of offending as a target for specialized services. The results of the quasi-experimental study indicate diminished involvement, overall, and for domestic situations, with law enforcement during the two year follow up. Such a finding is promising and as the authors recognize may be due to the matching of treatment protocol to the correct offender type or the immediacy of the intervention rather than a significant lag time from the precipitating event which is an inherent concern with BIPs.

Within the BIPs protocol, a desire exists for offenders to acknowledge their accountability with or responsibility for their actions and has, more recently, been included in the literature investigating domestic violence programming (Crockett, Keneski, Yeager & Loving, 2015; Lila, Oliver, Catala-Minana & Conchell, 2014; Schmidt, Kolodinsky, Carsten, Schmidt, Larson & MacLachlan, 2007; Scott, King, McGinn & Hosseini, 2013). Each study provided various treatment services, including resolution counseling intervention, psychoeducational programming and domestic violence offender treatment to measure the impact on accountability and reduction in violence. Although varying treatment and methodological approaches were utilized, all noted a realization and acceptance by the offender to take responsibility for prior and current actions. As noted by Lila et al. (2014) such a finding is truly significant especially in light of the fact that most domestic violence offenders do not view their actions as criminal.

While a goal of the BIP evaluations still remains understanding if, and to what extent, the program stopped violent behavior, the evaluations now seek to identify predictors resulting in reduced recidivism. Specifically, a number of important predictive factors, such as the relationship between client and therapist, compliance with treatment conditions (i.e., homework), readiness for change among the offender and motivational interviewing have resulted in recidivism reductions. To illustrate, similar to the responsivity principle but not as comprehensive is the establishment of a collaborative relationship between the treatment provider and client during batterer intervention programming (Eckhardt, Murphy, Black & Suhr, 2006). The literature suggests the development of a cooperative alliance between the offender and treatment specialists produces more favorable outcomes. That is, the impact on the offender is greatest when "a warm bond between therapist and client, agreement on the goals of treatment, and agreement on the tasks or strategies needed to attain those goals" (p. 374) exits. Such an approach requires a caring and responsive partnership even though the focus is on violent events.

Assessment of the offender's readiness to change appears to be a positive factor to consider on multiple definitions of success (Eckhardt et al., 2006; Levesque, Ciavatta, Castle, Prochaska & Prochaska, 2012). The stages of change model involves five phases from pre-contemplation (unable to recognize an issue, problem or need to change; simply not ready) to maintenance. Utilization of the stages of change model has been successful in predicting the effectiveness of many behaviors including smoking, weight loss and substance use. In general, the domestic violence research indicates that offenders who are beyond the pre-contemplation stage are more likely to be an engaged participant in the intervention, increase compliance with conditions of supervision and treatment and assist in reducing engagement in emotional and physical abuse (Eckhardt et al., 2006; Levesque et al., 2012; Murphy & Eckhardt, 2005). Similarly, the use of motivational interviewing techniques is promising in increasing recognition of responsibility for one's actions, compliance and program completion (Eckhardt et al., 2006; Scott, et al., 2013).

Lastly, a recent study examined the impact on offender cessation of violence with a more standard batterer intervention program compared to the standard intervention combined with substance intervention (Stuart, Shorey, Moore, Ramsey, Kahler, O'Farrell, Strong, Temple & Monti, 2013). The focus was on psychological and physical violence towards the partner measured across 3, 6, and 12 months. Overall, the authors report a short-term impact on psychological aggression toward their partner but no reduction in physical contact, additional charges or restraining orders in the current year time frame.

CONCLUSION

The purpose of this chapter was to examine the effectiveness of batterer invention programs. We examined the research where such programs were evaluated and found inconsistent findings in the meta-analyses. Some of the reasons for the inconsistent findings focus on methodological problems that we described within. In the discussion of previous research findings, we noted that most program evaluations have multiple goals for the program however, not every goal is assessed in the evaluation process. We noted that treatment fidelity and victim's views are not considered in terms of the effectiveness of the program in many studies. We advocate for a broader inclusion of variables that measure all the goals of the programs, in order to establish a better framework for understanding if a batterer intervention program is effective. And finally, we included a current assessment of how batterer intervention is being examined. The literature is still deficient in the inclusion of the victim's perspective but overall progress is being made in identifying predictors of success of program goals or behavior to include factors such as readiness for change and connection between the client and therapist. In addition, we discussed advancements in measuring offender accountability or acceptance in understanding that they are responsible for their violent actions.

REFERENCES

Adams, D. (1988). Counseling men who batter: A profeminist analysis of five treatment models. In M. Bograd and K. Yllo (Eds.), *Feminist perspectives on wife abuse* (p. 177–198). Beverly Hills, CA: Sage.

Adams, D., and Cayouette, S. (2002). Emerge — A group education model for abusers. In E. Aldarondo and F. Mederos (Eds.), *Programs for Men Who Batter* (chapter 3). Kingston, NJ: Civic Research Institute.

Anderson, L. (2014). Domestic violence: Contemporary interventions and the rise of specialized domestic violence units. Dissertation, Virginia Commonwealth University.

Austin, J. B., and Dankwort, J. (1999). The impact of a batterers' program on battered women. *Violence Against Women, 5*(1), 25–42.

Babcock, J., Green, C., and Robie, C. (2004). Does batterers' treatment work? A meta-analytic review of domestic violence treatment. *Clinical Psychology Review* 23, 1023–1053.

Bellg, A.J., Borrelli, B., Resnic, B., Hecht, J., Minicucci, D.S., Ory, M., Ogedegbe, G., Orwig, D., Ernst, D., and Czajkowski, S. (2004). Enhancing treatment fidelity in health behavior change studies: Best practices and recommendations from the NIH behavior change consortium. *Health Psychology, 23*(5), 443–451.

Bennett, L., Goodman, L., and Dutton, M., (1999). Systemic obstacles to the criminal prosecution of battering partner: A victim perspective. *Journal of Interpersonal Violence,* 14, 761–772.

Bennett, L. and Williams, O. (2001). Controversies and recent studies of batterer intervention program effectivness. *Applied Research Forum: National Electronic Network on Violence Against Women.* National Resource Center on Domestic Violence.

Borrelli, B., Sepinwall, D., Ernst, D., Bellg, A.J., Czajkowski, S., Breger, R., DeFrancesco, C., Levesque, C., Sharp, D.L., Ogedegbe, G., Resnick, B., and Orwig, D. (2005). A new tool to assess treatment fidelity and evaluation of treatment fidelity across 10 years of health behavior research. *Journal of Consulting and Clinical Psychology, 73*(5), 852–860.

Buttell, F.P., and Carney, M.M. (2005). Do batterer intervention programs serve African American and Caucasian batterers equally well? An investigation of a 26-week program. *Research on Social Work Practice, 15*(1), 19–28.

Buttell, F.P., and Pike, C.K. (2002). Investigating predictors of treatment attrition among court-ordered batterers. *Journal of Social Service Research, 28*(4), 53–68.

Bohmer, C., Brandt, J., Bronson, D., and Hartnett, H. (2002). Domestic violence law reforms: Reactions from the trenches. *Journal of Sociology and Social Welfare, 29*(3), 71–87.

Buzawa, E. S., Austin, T. L., Bannon, J., and Jackson, J. (1992). Role of victim preference in determining police response to victims of domestic violence.

In E.S. Buzawa and E. Buzawa (Eds.), *Domestic violence* (pp. 255–269). Westport, CT: Auburn House.

Cagle, J.G. and Naleppa, M.J. (2005, January). Treatment fidelity and the independent variable in social work intervention research. Paper presentation at the Society for Social Work and Research Conference. San Antonio, TX.

Crockett, E. E., Keneski, E., Yeager, K. and Loving, T. J. (2015). Breaking the mold: Evaluating a non-punitive domestic violence intervention program. *Journal of Family Violence, 30,* 489–499.

DeMaris, A. (1989). Attrition in batterers' counseling: The role of social and demographic factors. *Social Science Review*, March, 142–154.

Davis, R., and Taylor B. (1999). Does batterer treatment reduce violence? A synthesis of the literature. *Women and Criminal Justice*, Vol. 10(2), p. 69–93.

Davis, R. and Taylor, B. (1997) A proactive response to family violence: The results of a randomized experiment. *Criminology* 35, (2) 307–333.

Day, A., Chung, D., O'Leary, P. and Carson, E. (2009). Programs for men who perpetrate domestic violence: An examination of the issues underlying the effectiveness of intervention programs. *Journal of Family Violence, 24,* 203–212.

Dunford, F.W. (2000). The San Diego navy experiment: An assessment of interventions for men who assault their wives. *Journal of Consulting and Clinical Psychology, 68*(3), 468–476.

Dutton, D. (1986). Wife assaulter's explanation for assault: The neutralization of self-punishment. *Canadian Journal of Behavioral Science*, 18 (4) 381–390.

Eckhardt, C., Murphy, C., Black, D. & Suhr, L. (2006). Intervention program for perpetrators of Intimate Partner Violence: Conclusions from a clinical research perspective. *Public Health Reports, 121,* 369–381.

Erez, E., and Bienkowska, E. (1993). Victim participation in proceedings and satisfaction with justice in the continental systems: The case of Poland. *Journal of Criminal Justice, 21,* 47–60.

Erez, E., and Tontodonato, P. (1992). Victim participation in sentencing and satisfaction with justice. *Justice Quarterly, 9*(3), 393–415.

Feder, L. (1996). A test of the efficacy of court mandated counseling for domestic violence offenders: A Broward County experiment. National Institute of Justice: Washington D.C.

Feder, L. & Dugan, L. (2002). A test of the efficacy of court mandated counseling for domestic violence offenders: The Broward Experiment. *Justice Quarterly*, 19 343–375.

Feder, L. & Forde, D.R. (2000). Test of the efficacy of court-mandated counseling for domestic violence offenders: The Broward experiment. (NCJ report #184752). Washington, DC: author.

Feder, L. and Wilson, D. (2005). A meta-analytic review of court-mandated batterer intervention programs: Can courts affect abusers' behavior? *Journal of Experimental Criminology*, 1 (2), 239–262.

Fleury, R. E. (2002). Missing voices: Patterns of battered women's satisfaction with the criminal legal system. *Violence Against Women*, 8(2), 181–205.

Ford, D.A. (1983). Wife battery and criminal justice: A study of victim decision-making. *Family Relations, 32*, 463–475.

Friday, P.C., Lord, V.B., Exum, M.L., and Hartman, J.L. (2006). *Evaluating the impact of a specialized domestic violence unit*. Washington, D.C: National Institute of Justice, U.S. Department of Justice.

Fugate, M., Landis, L., Riordan, K., Naureckas, S., and Engel, B. (2005). Barriers to domestic violence help seeking: Implications for intervention. *Violence Against Women, 11 (3) 290–310.*

Glass, G. V. (1976). Primary, secondary, and meta-analysis of research. *Educational Researcher, 5,* 3–8.

Gondolf, E.W. (2000). A 30-month follow-up of court-referred batterers in four cities. *International Journal of Offender Therapy and Comparative Criminology,* 44 (1), 111–128.

Gondolf, E. W. (1998). The victims of court-ordered batterer: Their victimization, help seeking, and perceptions. *Violence Against Women,* 4(6), 659–676.

Gordon, J.A. & Moriarty, L.J. (2003, February). The effects of domestic violence batterer treatment on domestic violence recidivism: The Chesterfield County experience. *Criminal Justice and Behavior,* 30 (1), 118–134.

Gregory, C. and Erez, E. (2002). The effects of batter intervention programs: The battered women's perspective. *Violence Against Women,* 8(2), 206–232.

Gross, M., Cramer, E.P., Forte, J., Gordon, J.A., Kunkel, T., and Moriarty, L.J. (2000). The Impact of Sentencing Options on Recidivism Among Domestic Violence Offenders: A Case Study. *American Journal of Criminal Justice,* 24 (2), 301–312.

Grusznksi, R., and Carillo, T. (1998) Who completes batterer's treatment groups? An empirical investigation. *Journal of Family Violence, 3,* 141–150.

Hamberger, L., and Hastings, J. (1988) Skills training for treatment of spouse abusers: An outcome study. *Journal of Family Violence, 3,* 121–130.

Harrell, A. (1991). *Evaluation of court ordered treatment for domestic violence offenders.* Final Report, Washington DC: Urban Institute.

Healey, K., Smith, C., and O'Sullivan, C. (1998). *Batterer Intervention: Program Approaches and Criminal Justice Strategies.* (NCJ report #168638). Washington, DC: author.

Jackson, S., Feder, L., Forde, D.R., Davis, R.C., Maxwell, C.D., and Taylor, B. (2003). Batterer Intervention Programs: Where Do We Go From Here? (NCJ report #195079). Washington, DC: author.

Jacobson, N.S., (1993). *Domestic violence: What are the marriages like?* Annual meeting of American Association of Marriage and Family Therapy, Anaheim, CA.

Klein, A. R., and Crowe, A. (2008). Findings from an outcome examination of Rhode Island's specialized domestic violence probation supervision program. *Violence Against Women, 14,* 226–246.

Levesque, D. A., Ciavatta, M. M., Castle, P. H., Prochaska, J. M., and Prochaska, J.O. (2012). Evaluation of a stage-based, computer-tailored adjunct to usual care for domestic violence offenders. *Psychology of Violence, 2,* 368–384.

Lila, M., Oliver, A., Catalá-Miñana, A., and Conchell, R. (2014). Recidivism risk reduction assessment in batterer intervention programs: A key indicator for program efficacy evaluation. *Psychosocial Intervention, 23,* 217–223.

Lipchik, E, Sirles, E., and Kubicki, A. (1997). Multifaceted approaches in spouse abuse treatment. In R. Geffner, S. Soenson and P. Lundberg-Love (Eds.) *Violence and sexual abuse at home: Current issues in spousal battering and child maltreatment* (p. 131–148). New York: Haworth Press.

Moncher, F.J., and Prinz, F.J. (1991). Treatment fidelity in outcomes studies. *Clinical Psychology Review, 11,* 247–266.

Murphy, C., and Eckhardt, C. (2005). *Treating the abusive partner: An individualized cognitive- behavioral approach.* New York: Guilford Press.

National Coalition of Domestic Violence (2006). The problem: What is battering. Retrieved from http://www.ncadv.org/learn/TheProblem_100.html on August 16, 2006.

Palmer, S. Brouwn R., and Barrera, M. (1992). Group treatment program for abusive husbands: Long-term evaluation. *American Journal of Orthopsychiatry, 62*(2), 276–283.

Pence, E., and Paymar, M. (1990). *Power and Control: Tactics of Men who Batter, an Educational Curriculum.* MN: Duluth Abuse Intervention Project.

Rosenfeld, B. (1992). Court-ordered treatment of spouse abuse. *Clinical Psychology Review*, 12, 205–226.

Scott, K., Heslop, L., Kelly, T., and Wiggins, K. (2015). Intervening to prevent repeat offending among moderate- to high-risk domestic violence offenders: A second-responder program for men. *International Journal of Offender Therapy and Comparative Criminology, 59*, 273–294.

Scott, K., King, C., McGinn, H., and Hosseini, N. (2011). Effects of motivational enhancement on immediate outcomes of batterer intervention. *Journal of Family Violence, 26*, 139–149.

Scott, K., King, C., McGinn, H., and Hosseini, N. (2013). The (dubious?) benefits of second chances in batterer intervention programs. *Journal of Interpersonal Violence, 28*, 1657–1671.

Schmidt, M., Kolodinsky, J., Carsten, G., Schmidt, F., Larson, M., and MacLachlan, C. (2007). Short term change in attitude and motivating factors to change abusive behavior of male batterers after participating in a group intervention program based on the pro-feminist and cognitive-behavioral approach. *Journal of Family Violence, 22*, 91–100.

Stuart, G. L., Shorey, R. C., Moore, T. M., Ramsey, S. E., Kahler, C. W., O'Farrell, T. J., Strong, D. R., Temple, J. R., and Monti, P. M. (2013). Randomized clinical trial examining the incremental efficacy of a 90-minute motivational alcohol intervention as an adjunct to standard batterer intervention for men. *Addiction, 108*, 1376–1384.

Sullivan, C.M., Rumptz, M.H., Campbell, R., Eby, K.K., and Davidson, W.S. (1996). Retaining participants in longitudinal community research: A comprehensive protocol. *Journal of Applied Behavioral Science, 32* (3) 262–276.

Taylor, B.G., Davis, R.C., and Maxwell, C.D. (2001). The effects of a group batterer treatment program: A randomized experiment.

Weisburd, D., Lum, C., and Petersino, A. (2001). Does research design affect study outcomes in criminal justice? *Annals of the American Academy of Political and Social Science*, 578, 50–70.

Website: http://www.duluth-model.org/

CHAPTER 3

Electronic Monitoring of Domestic Violence Offenders: Is It Working?

Laura J. Moriarty and Matthew E. McDermott
Monmouth University

Recently, the governor of New Jersey, Chris Christie, vetoed a bill that would advocate for the use of electronic monitoring of domestic violence offenders. The bill known as Lisa's Law (Hoffman, 2013) would have required domestic violence offenders to wear electronic monitoring, GPS devices, to electronically track convicted domestic violence offenders using this GPS technology to alert victims via their cell phones regarding the offenders' whereabouts. The governor vetoed the bill, in part, because Attorney General Hoffman's analysis stated that electronic monitoring is ineffective in preventing domestic violence and creates a false sense of safety for victims. Nevertheless, many states have approved similar bills into law as there is evidence that electronic devices serve as a deterrent for further criminal activity in general, and perhaps further abuse during the pretrial time period.

The purpose of this chapter is to provide an overview of electronic monitoring of domestic violence offenders with the intent of determining the overall effectiveness of such devices as a crime deterrent. The chapter begins with an overview of electronic monitoring devices relative to cost, effectiveness, and victims' satisfaction with these devices. We then move into a discussion about electronic monitoring devices focusing on one specific crime: domestic violence. We conclude with general support for the use of electronic monitoring devices in that the cost is relatively inexpensive, some victims feel better knowing the whereabouts of the offenders, and there is some evidence that the devices serve as a deterrent to domestic violence when part of a larger coordinated response especially in the pretrial phase of the case.

Overview of Electronic Monitoring

Electronic monitoring of defendants is a type of technology used to track offenders either by radio frequency (RF) or global positioning systems (GPS). Offenders are under such surveillance with restricted movement by sending an electronic signal indicating the whereabouts of the defendant. Electronic monitoring devices include ankle and wrist bracelets, field monitoring devices (GPS), and voice verification systems (Sklaver, 2010). In general, there are advantages and disadvantages associated with electronic monitoring programs. Included in the advantages are financial savings, decreased recidivism, and monitoring and pinpointing offenders' locations in real time (Sklaver, 2010). The disadvantages include discrimination against indigent families/offenders, violations and false positives, flight risks, and emotional effects (Sklaver, 2010). This chapter focuses primarily on GPS monitoring systems in relationship to crimes in general and domestic violence in particular.

According to a report by the DC Crime Policy Institute (Roman, et al. 2012) describing the costs and benefits of electronic monitoring compared to standard probation, on average, GPS electronic monitoring was found to reduce arrests by 24% for program participants. Said another way, offender recidivism declined for offenders in the program. Further, Roman and his colleagues (2012) concluded, "We find that there is an 80 percent chance that an EM program for 800 offenders would yield benefits that exceed its cost" (pg 4). These studies looked at all types of crimes including domestic violence.

Decades of data from states and jurisdictions across the country were analyzed by Roman and his colleagues to estimate how spending decreased in response to reductions in arrests. They found that, on average, electronic monitoring reduced per participant costs to local agencies by $580 and saved federal agencies $920. Likewise, the average number of arrests prevented per participant was expected to generate $3,800 in societal benefits per participant. Societal benefits refer to reduced victimization. Based on these findings, they hypothesized that there is an 80 percent chance that a new GPS program in Washington, DC, would be cost effective, that is, that the combined agency savings and societal benefits are greater than the cost of implementing the program. Furthermore, they assert that the average expected net benefit in averting offenses and arrest by using EM is $4,600 per person with a median net benefit of $4,800 per person (Roman, et al., 2012).

According to the leading and most recent evaluation study conducted on GPS monitoring and domestic violence (Erez et al. 2012, 37), the average cost to agencies implementing GPS programs per day is $9.80, and the cost to the defendant is an average of $8.80. These numbers can vary greatly between states where different funding sources are available (or not) to agencies. As more programs are carried out and the technology becomes more readily available to agencies, prices will naturally go down.

The cost associated with GPS monitoring is also available outside the United States. For instance, Spain has been a leader in bringing GPS technology to the rest of Europe, and as such has lower daily costs than other European countries. As of 2013, Spain had 1,746 people being electronically monitored on early release programs at a daily cost of 5.5 euros (or approximately $6.30). Other countries had higher rates. The Netherlands placed GPS monitoring devices on 94 people who were part of pretrial bail program with the daily cost being 75 euros. Portugal had 105 people placed specifically on GPS for domestic violence with a daily cost of 21.2 euros. Most other European nations as well as Australia and New Zealand use electronic monitoring as a condition of pretrial bail or an early release program (Graham & Melvor, 2013) with specific costs in about the same range as reported above. Thus, from the available cost information, electronic monitoring is relatively inexpensive. Where the cost increases is when it becomes part of a well-coordinated response to criminal activity in that in order to protect victims, law enforcement must be able to respond immediately when offenders have breached the boundaries associated with the off limit areas.

Another benefit of electronic monitoring is that it allows law enforcement to know whether defendants are adhering to terms and conditions of the program. Such knowledge presents some reassurance to victims that offenders are not anywhere near the victim. It can also establish an alibi for a defendant if accused of another crime and such knowledge can also be used to gather information about another crime, if the detection indicates that the offender was at the scene of a crime.

Likewise, there is some evidence that electronic monitoring devices reduce recidivism especially in the pretrial phase of the crime. Thus, the benefits or advantages of electronic monitoring promote the usage of electronic monitoring especially when we factor in the cost of incarceration.

DOMESTIC VIOLENCE AND GPS

A review of state websites reveals that 35 states currently have enacted legislation or are piloting legislation where domestic violence offenders use electronic monitoring of some sort, most often GPS. Likewise, Erez and colleagues

(2012) published the results of their comprehensive, NIJ-funded evaluation study of GPS monitoring technologies and domestic violence where they report that 21 states and the District of Columbia have enacted legislation that supports either ordering, or recommending, offenders' use of electronic monitoring, GPS devices, under specific conditions. With more than one half of the states either having legislation requiring the use of electronic monitoring or piloting the use of such technology, the researchers reported that the "trend is toward increased adoption of GPS for domestic violence offenses" (Erez, et al, 2012, 1).

These researchers also report that the states (and District of Columbia) with GPS mandates have demonstrated success in protecting victims, and this is leading to more states considering similar mandates (Erez et al, 2012). This protection of victims comes from the enhanced technology which is more versatile and allows for a broader detection range and multiple zone coverages. The technology also allows for law enforcement and/or sponsoring agencies to track the offender in real time, thus giving the victim the ability to set up exclusion zones beyond their home. If the offender breaches these zones, the police response system would be initiated.

GPS monitoring in domestic violence cases has also been implemented overseas. In Spain, the defendant and victim are equipped with a GPS system that monitors their position which is archived in a database (passive GPS monitoring), making it possible to consult with the offender at any time about his movements. The device is also prepared to work as a cellular telephone with the Control Center, so the victim and the aggressor can be in touch with the Control Center at any time and vice versa. When an alarm is detected, the Control Center contacts with the aggressor and the victim to check the incidence before they call the police. In case the Control Center cannot make contact with one of the users, the police are called immediately (EUCPN, 2010).

In most states, the abuser must be recommended to the program by the court; however, not all who are recommended for the monitoring program are accepted. Defendants often do not meet certain requirements. A lack of cooperation may exist from either the defendant or the victim, or defendants might be unable to pay fees required to participate in the program.

Agency sponsored GPS programs may be perceived as centering more on defendants, in terms of resources and services provided during the pretrial period. However, as Erez and colleagues (2012) position, the tools the program can offer are extremely victim-centric, meaning that it is the victim who benefits from an alert that a victim would receive immediately after an exclusion zone was broken. Thus, such programs provide benefits to both victims and offenders.

Erez et al. (2012) found victims reporting that they have greater "peace of mind" and relief from harassment and abuse when offenders are part of GPS programs. These same victims report that although they do not fully understand how the technology works and they know there are limitations with the technology as it does not "guarantee" their safety, they feel that the technology allows them to resume some normalcy in their lives. Others reported that the programming involved with GPS in identifying exclusion zones and home addresses when a victim moves, results in a lack of privacy, which often is associated with fear as well. The fear, or anxiety, can manifest when the victim has the ability to track the offender. Therefore, although one would expect relief for a victim knowing the whereabouts of the offender, for some victims, the opposite is found.

Rhodes (2013) examined the use of GPS surveillance to enforce domestic violence protection orders. As Rhodes explains, "despite its benefits, a civil protective order in a domestic violence case can be particularly difficult to enforce, given the intimate relationship between both parties" (page 11). Offenders are very familiar with the victim's regular routines and are acquainted with both friends and family, thus making it very easy for the offender to harass or intimidate the victim. GPS surveillance allows for detection of the offender attempting to engage in behavior that violates protective orders before the order is violated. As a result, victims report that such surveillance technologies allow them to establish a sense of control over their own lives, leading to less fear in their own homes. As one victim reported, "once [the abuser] was put on the GPS and couldn't contact me, I felt free" (Rhodes, 2013: 142).

Effectiveness of Electronic Monitoring

According to Peter Thompson (2011) who looked at using GPS as a comprehensive strategy to reduce crime, he reports:

> Today (2011), more than 120 federal, state, county and local law enforcement organizations have implemented GPS systems (many pilot programs) to track offenders short-term who are on pretrial supervision, serving terms of probation or parole, or as an alternative to prison. The technology is being used to track . . . persons convicted of domestic violence. . . . Jurisdictions have found ways to leverage GPS technology to create a wide range of structured offender monitoring programs for various types of needs. As one example, a Massachusetts law grants authority to judges to require domestic

abusers to wear GPS transmitters where they have violated restraining orders and been determined to be dangerous after undergoing an assessment. The movements of these offenders are monitored by several centers. If an offender crosses an "exclusion zone" mapped digitally around the victim or her children, the police are instantly notified. In fact, the use of GPS to reign in domestic abusers appears to be catching on. Twelve other states have passed similar legislation, and, as a result, about 5000 domestic abuse offenders are being tracked nationwide.

Our research found as of May 2016, at least 35 states have either passed legislation authorizing the use of GPS monitoring in domestic violence cases or were in the process of doing so. It is important to note that legislation is not required to allow for GPS monitoring; however, it is required to obtain funding to run pilot programs. This is generally met with bipartisan, unanimous support.

As with all crime deterrents, we find similar results when looking at the effectiveness of GPS as a deterrent to domestic violence in that research has shown mixed results. Most often researchers look at several variables to gain a sense about the effectiveness of the sanction. Cost, rearrest or recidivism, victims' views/perceptions, and criminal justice personnel views are often the main variables reviewed when making judgements about the effectiveness of the technology.

Results have been published in the media of successful pilot programs throughout the country. The main issue currently is that the pilot programs are being completed with better than expected results, but are not being renewed or expanded due to the lack of funds within certain states' budgets. A report in the Hartford Courant (2012) reflects this trend in Connecticut (Kovner, 2012). Three court districts were funded to run a GPS program with sponsorship provided through the federal stimulus packages. When the program ended in 2011, 119 offenders had been tracked without a single incident to any victim. The program was kept alive for the next year due to a surplus which was found to exist in the probate-court administrator's office. However, there is no evidence that the program will continue on a statewide basis due to the estimated cost of $2 million required to implement it; despite the preliminary successful results.

Another pilot program in Minnesota has received national attention for its promising outcomes during its first year in operation from 2012–2013. The program is voluntary with both the victim and offender agreeing to participate. The defendant wears an ankle bracelet and the victim gets a "stalker alert" device, indicating if the defendant gets too close to the victim and does not leave the area. As reported by Forliti:

> 19 of 170 eligible defendants participated (in the pilot program), and 12 finished with successful results . . . The data set is small, but looks promising. Defendants who participated in the GPS pilot demonstrated greater overall compliance with court orders and (had) significantly lower rates of recidivism than the comparison group . . . Seven participants were unsuccessful for several reasons, including not following program rules or violating a no-contact order. One defendant cut off the bracelet. In that case, both victim and monitoring center got alerts. The dispatch center immediately sent police to the victim's house and the defendant's house. The defendant had fled, but was arrested later (Forliti, 2014).

In a case study of U.S. GPS programs, Cotter and Delint (2009) focused on the rehabilitation of offenders on GPS monitoring systems of domestic violence offenses looking at recidivism and reintegration/rehabilitation. The study was conducted in order to determine what we should consider a successful program and what turned out to be the largest contributing factors to a successful program. The authors found a positive correlation with reduced recidivism and increased rehabilitation of defendants in programs that actively managed its surveillance technology and specifically targeted clients individually.

Erez and colleagues (2012) found that after a one-year follow up defendants on GPS were less likely to be rearrested for a domestic violence offense, as well as any other new offense, than those who were not monitored by GPS. Indications are that the long term effect of the program leads to an overall reduction in recidivism and increased compliance with the law.

GPS monitoring provides benefits to defendants placed into these programs. Such programs allow defendants to enter as part of their court bond, in lieu of spending time in jail, where the cost to the taxpayer is high. The GPS technology also allows for protection against false accusations. However, the best result of the technology in preventing crime results when treatment is provided to the offender along with the use of the technology. Such treatment focuses on engaging in more constructive pursuits such as returning to school, securing employment, building relationships with family, and reorienting life without the victim in it. The biggest benefit of GPS programs outside recidivism is the ability of the offender to stay employed instead of being incarcerated (Erez et al, 2013).

Lastly, the use of GPS monitoring in domestic violence cases, as well as other violent crimes, during the pretrial stage continues to show promising outcomes no matter where it is implemented, and no matter the demographics. Erez (2012) found the technology to be a deterrent in the short and long term in relation to recidivism rates and contact with the victim throughout the multiple regions of the country in which they conducted their research. In order for the program to work, all parties must be able to buy into the arrangements that are made. The parties include the defendant, victim, agency, and police. The research presented demonstrates that when this happens, the program is overwhelmingly successful in achieving its goals.

Conclusion

According to the National Network to End Domestic Violence website (2016), "It is critical to understand that GPS monitoring of offenders is only effective as part of a larger coordinated system. If not enough trained officers can respond quickly when an offender approaches a victim and if courts lack resources to hold offenders accountable, the monitoring devices will not be effective."

As was presented in this chapter, surveillance of offenders is a good deterrent for future domestic violence crimes at the pretrial level. But, as just stated, there needs to be a coordinated effort by many parts of the criminal justice system for this technology to work. Victims tend to feel better having the knowledge about where the offender is at any given time; but this information can also cause anxiety and fear, especially if the offender somehow sidesteps the technology and is able to come in contact with the victim.

At present, there is really no consensus about the effectiveness of electronic monitoring of domestic violence offenders. Some studies have indicated moderate success on several dimensions (i.e., variables under review); but a full scale advocacy for adoption of GPS to prevent domestic violence has not been forthcoming. Perhaps Governor Christie is correct; until the state has a coordinated response to domestic violence where enough officers are available to track offenders, it might not be in the best interest of the victim to rely solely on GPS monitoring. We certainly do not advocate such a response. We support the position cited above, and advocate for a well-coordinated response to domestic violence incidents where GPS is part of this coordinated system.

References

Cotter, R. & De Lint, W. (2009). GPS-Electronic Monitoring and Contemporary Penology: A Case Study of US GPS-Electronic Monitoring Programmes. *The Howard Journal.* Vol 48 No 1. (2009): p 76–87. Web. 15 March, 2016. http://onlinelibrary.wiley.com/doi/10.1111/j.1468-2311.2008.00545.x /abstract.

Erez, E., Ibarra, P.R., Bales, W.D. & Gur, O.M. (2012). GPS Monitoring Technologies and Domestic Violence: An Evaluation Study. Washington, DC: National Institute of Justice. (2012): p 1–218. Web. 1 Feb. 2016. https://www .ncjrs.gov/pdffiles1/nij/grants/238910.pdf.

European Crime Prevention Network (EUCPN). (March 2010). Domestic Violence and Implementation of Technical Measures- Situation in the Member States. Web. 4 April, 2016. http://eucpn.org/sites/default/files/content /download/files/09._overviews_wc_of_i rene_winter_-_domestic_violence _technical_measures.pdf.

Forliti, A. (2014). For Domestic Violence Victims, Promise in GPS. The Washington Times. March 9, 2014. Web. 15 Feb. 2016. http://www.washingtontimes .com/news/2014/mar/9/for-domestic-violence-victimspromise-in-gps/ ?page=al.

Graham, H. & McIvor, G. (2015). Scottish and International Review of the Uses of Electronic Monitoring. Scottish Crime Centre for Crime & Justice Research No. 8: p 1–137. Web. 24 April, 2016. http://www.sccjr.ac.uk /wp-content/uploads/2015/08/Scottish-and-International-Review-of-the -Uses-of-Electronic-Monitoring-Graham-and-McIvor-2015.pdf.

Hoffman, J.J. (2014). Report on the Availability of Appropriate Technology to Monitor Domestic Violence Offenders and their Victims. (Pursuant to P.L. 2013, c. 229). Web. 15 Feb. 2016. http://www.nj.gov/lps/Final-DV -Monitoring-Report-2014.pdf.

Kovner, J. (2012, June 23) "Domestic Violence Offenders to be Tracked Again." The Hartford Courant. Web. 15 March. 2016. http://articles.courant.com /2012-06-13/news/hc-domestic-violence-gps-0614-20120613_1_gps-device -alvin-notice-tiana-notice.

National Network to End Domestic Violence (NNEDV). (2016). Fact Sheet. Web. 3 June, 2016. http://nnedv.org/resources/safetynetdocs/154-organizational -technology-capacity-development/1021-gps-monitoring-of-offenders .html.

Rhodes, A. (2013). Strengthening the Guard: The use of GPS Surveillance to Enforce Domestic Violence Protection Orders. *Tennessee Journal of Race, Gender & Social Justice.* Vol 2 (2013): P 120–144. Web. 1 Feb. 2016. http://trace.tennessee.edu/cgi/viewcontent.cgi?article=1031&context=rgsj.

Roman, J., Liberman, A.M., Taxy, S., and Downey, P.M. (2012). "The Costs and Benefits of Electronic Monitoring in Washington DC." District of Columbia Crime Policy Institute. Web. 15 March, 2016. <http://www.urban.org/sites/default/files/alfresco/publication-pdfs/412678-The-Costs-and-Benefits-of-Electronic-Monitoring-for-Washington-D-C-.PDF>.

Sklaver, S.L. (2010). The Pros and Cons of Using Electronic Monitoring Programs in Juvenile Cases. (Juvenile Justice Committee Newsletter, No.5). Washington, DC: American Bar Association.

Thompson, P. (2011). A Comprehensive Strategy Targeting Recidivist Criminals with Continuous Real-Time GPS Monitoring: Is Reverse Engineering Crime Control Possible? *Engage,* Vol 12 Issue 3. Web. 1 May, 2016. http://www.fed-soc.org/publications/detail/a-comprehensive-strategy-targeting-rediVist-criminals-with-continuous-real-time-gps-monitoring-is-reverse-engineering-crime-control-possible.

CHAPTER 4

IMPROVING POLICE RECORDS OF REPEAT DOMESTIC VIOLENCE: A CASE STUDY

Marie Mele
MONMOUTH UNIVERSITY

INTRODUCTION

This chapter reports on a collaborative effort between researchers and police officials, generated by a common interest in assessing the nature and extent of repeat domestic violence in one U.S. city. This collaboration was informed by the understanding that because domestic violence is repetitive by nature, greater understanding and prevention of this crime can be achieved by studying the pattern of repeat victimization. Research on repeat victimization has fostered better understanding and prevention of crimes such as burglary, robbery, and vehicle theft. Research on repeat domestic violence similarly suggests that the analysis of repeat victimization may enhance our efforts to prevent domestic violence.

Among the first to study repeat domestic violence was Lloyd, Farrell & Pease (1994) who found that a small proportion of domestic violence victims accounted for a disproportionate number of reported cases. This finding led to an innovative police response to domestic violence, which included the improved transfer of information from courts to police regarding civil protection orders, and the distribution of neck-pendant alarms to repeat victims. An initial assessment of the project revealed a reduction in repeat victimization, as well as increased confidence and a greater sense of security among victims (Lloyd et al., 1994). Similar findings were reached by Hanmer, Griffiths & Jerwood (1999) who studied a three-tiered program of police intervention designed to reduce repeat domestic violence by protecting victims and demotivating offenders. The three-tiered program was based on the number of police visits: the higher the number of visits, the higher the level of intervention. Interventions ranged from an information letter to the victim and an official warning for the offender, to the issuance of a panic button for the victim and incarceration without bail for the offender. In one year, the project made possible the identification and assessment of repeat offenders, and reduced repeat offenses by responding more appropriately to victims who needed immediate assistance and offenders who required firm action from the police (Hanmer et al., 1999).

These innovative approaches to the prevention of repeat domestic violence served as the genesis for the present case study, in which an existing partnership between one city's police department and a local university allowed for an analysis of repeat domestic violence. When this study began, domestic violence was a considerable drain on police resources. Each year, the police processed thousands of domestic violence incident reports and responded to thousands more calls for service. The most prevalent domestic violence crimes reported were physical assaults and harassment (i.e., threatening or controlling behaviors such as repeated unwanted contact). While efforts were made to reduce these crimes (via mandatory arrest policies), the problem was one that evaded an easy solution.

With this in mind, a collaborative effort was initiated between the domestic violence unit of the police department and criminal justice researchers from a local university. Of primary interest was the identification of repeat domestic violence victims, with an ultimate goal of assessing the nature and extent of repeat domestic violence, and offering suggestions on how the police could protect repeat victims from further victimization.

IDENTIFYING REPEAT VICTIMS

When the study began, police responded to roughly 45,000 domestic violence calls for service each year; representing roughly 11% of all calls for which an officer was dispatched. In addition, police processed between 5,000 and 6,000 domestic violence incident reports annually. This was a significantly large caseload; especially considering the domestic violence unit consisted of four detectives who processed all domestic violence cases reported in the city.

It was believed that preventing repeat victimization could reduce the incidence of domestic violence. However, the police had a limited ability to identify repeat victims, since case information was primarily maintained using 3×5 index cards. Each index card contained the names of a victim and an offender, their demographic information (race, age, gender), and the date and type of offense. Index cards were categorized by the first letter of the victim or offender's last name and stored in a file cabinet in the domestic violence unit. When the project began, there were roughly 1,500 index cards stored in filing cabinets. With such a large number of cards, locating reports was a time-consuming task, and previous reports of domestic violence were often overlooked. In some cases, cards were not filed correctly and detectives failed to find previous cases involving repeat victims. This resulted in the creation of a second (or third) file card for victims and an inaccurate account of their victimization history. The same problem occurred for repeat offenders. It was common for offenders to have several cards, leading to an inaccurate account of their offense history.

In order to address this issue, the primary researcher assisted an officer from the management information systems unit of the police department in designing a computerized database that helped to improve record keeping practices. The database was created using Microsoft Access, which allowed detectives to create and maintain electronic files for victims and offenders. The database was designed so that duplicate files could not be created once a victim or an offender was entered into the system. The database also provided drop down lists for several data elements, including crime type, victim/offender relationship, and case outcome, which helped to reduce the number of errors that were made when entering this information into the database.

Shortly after the database was created, it was installed on all computers within the domestic violence unit, and detectives were briefed on how to enter case information and extract data. At first, detectives were wary of learning a new record keeping process, but they soon realized the benefits of computerized files. Locating a repeat victim or repeat offender became a much simpler and less time-consuming task. Detectives only needed to enter the victim or offender's last name to find existing records, instead of sifting through hundreds of index cards. The collection, storing, and retrieval of data became a more organized operation, so that detectives were better able to track repeat cases.

COLLECTING DATA ON REPEAT DOMESTIC VIOLENCE

Once detectives were able to identify repeat victims, the task became assessing the nature and extent of repeat victimization. What percentage of domestic violence victims were repeat victims? How many times were they victimized? What were the correlates of repeat victimization? These were all questions that detectives and researchers sought to answer. In order to answer these questions, information was extracted from the database. One year after the database was installed, there were electronic files for 4,424 domestic violence victims. Information on victim/offender demographics, victim/offender relationship, offense type, and case outcome was extracted and converted into SPSS for statistical analysis.

ANALYSIS

Demographics

Women accounted for 84% of victims in the database. Victims had a median age of 29, and ranged in age from 14 to 88. The majority of victims (70%) were African American. Offenders' demographic characteristics were similar to victims. The median age of offenders was 30, and they ranged in age from 14 to 83. The majority of offenders (72%) were also African American.

Repeat Victimization

Repeat victims were identified as any victim listed on more than one domestic violence incident report within one-year. Analysis revealed a great deal about the nature and extent of repeat domestic violence. Perhaps the most interesting finding was that repeat victims made up a small proportion of the victim population, yet they accounted for a large proportion of cases: repeat victims represented 19% of domestic violence victims, but accounted for 37% of the domestic violence caseload. This finding was also noted in previous studies of repeat domestic violence (i.e., Lloyd et al., 1994; Hanmer et al., 1999).

Out of the 4,424 victims, 823 were victimized more than once. Out of 823 repeat victims, 562 (68%) were victimized twice, 158 (19%) were victimized three times, 49 (6%) were victimized 4 times, 26 (3%) were victimized 5 times, and 16 (2%) were victimized 6 times. It is likely that if analysis had been extended beyond one year, additional victimizations would have been reported.

Victim/Offender Relationship

In order to qualify as domestic violence, the parties involved had to be current or former spouses, dating partners, cohabitants or co-parents. Roughly half of all victims in the database were in a current or former dating relationship with the offender at the time they reported their victimization. Sixty-five percent of one-time victims and 56% of repeat victims identified the offender as a current or former dating partner (boyfriend/girlfriend). One major difference between repeat and one-time victims was the percentage victimized by a co-parent. Almost twice as many repeat victims (29% v. 16%) were victimized by co-parents, suggesting that victims who had children in common with the offender were more likely to be repeatedly victimized than victims who did not have children in common with the offender.

A larger proportion of repeat victims (46%) than one-time victims (34%) reported having dependent children. However, out of the 1,590 victims who reported having children, only 374 (24%) were repeat victims. In other words, a large majority (76%) of victims with children were not repeat victims. In addition, there was little difference in employment and cohabitation between one-time and repeat victims. About half of all victims in the sample were unemployed, and about half were living with the offender at the time of their victimization.

Offense Type

Domestic violence was defined as one of six offenses: simple assault, aggravated assault, terroristic threats, criminal mischief, harassment, and violation of a restraining order. The most common offense reported by victims in the database was simple assault (54%), followed by harassment (11%), terroristic threats (11%), aggravated assault (10%), criminal mischief (7%) and restraining order violation (4%). The types of offenses reported by repeat victims were similar to those reported by one-time victims. The one exception to this was violations of restraining orders, with 3% of one-time victims, 7% of repeat victims (at the first victimization) and 32% of repeat victims (at the fifth victimization) reporting such violations. It was unclear, however, whether repeat victims were more likely to obtain restraining orders (because of past victimizations), or whether restraining orders created an opportunity for further victimization (via restraining order violations).

Case Outcome

Analysis also revealed that cases involving repeat victims were more likely to result in a court summons (56% v. 49%), while cases involving one-time victims were more likely to result in arrest (41% v. 36%). Case outcome for repeat victims, however, changed over the course of multiple victimizations: the percentage of cases that resulted in arrest increased as the number of victimizations increased. This may reflect an increasing willingness of the police to arrest in cases involving repeat victims, or an increasing willingness of repeat victims to report their victimization to police.

Time Course of Repeat Victimization

Analysis also revealed that the median number of days between successive victimizations declined steadily as the number of victimizations increased. This finding lends support to the time course of repeat victimization, which suggests that as victimizations increase in frequency, the time intervals between successive incidents decrease. This finding has important implications for prevention policy, as timely responses to an initial victimization may prevent further victimizations from occurring. The police response to repeat domestic violence was the next focal point of this project.

POLICE RESPONSE TO DOMESTIC VIOLENCE

In addition to measuring repeat victimization, insight was sought on how police handled repeat cases, and how this process could be improved to better identify repeat victims. For this purpose, detective interviews and patrol ride-alongs were conducted in order to: (1) provide further information on how domestic violence incident reports developed from calls for service; (2) assess the factors that influenced an officer's decision to file (or not file) an incident report; and (3) determine whether repeat cases were less likely to be properly recorded by police, as suggested by Laycock (2001).

Patrol Ride-alongs

The primary researcher conducted ride-alongs with patrol officers for a period of two months. A total of 18 ride-alongs were conducted, during which 50 domestic violence calls for service were observed. Ride-alongs were scheduled with patrol officers in order to observe how calls for service resulted in the filing of incident reports. Ride-alongs were scheduled during evening hours (4:00pm — 12:00am) between Thursday and Saturday, when domestic violence incidents were most likely to be reported.

Qualitative interviewing techniques were used to gain an understanding of how patrol officers handled domestic violence calls for service. An interview guide was used to provide a framework within which questions were asked to explore various topics of interest. The interviewer was free to develop conversations with officers within particular subject areas (i.e., repeat offenders). This technique allowed for flexibility in interviewing, and enabled the interviewer to be responsive to individual differences and situational changes, as suggested by Patton (1990). All questions were open-ended to allow officers to respond in their own terms. Also, potentially threatening questions (i.e., why incident reports were not filed) were worded in such a way as to inquire *how* officers made decisions, not *why*. Questions were worded in this way to avoid the impression that judgment was being passed on the officers' decision-making process.

It was believed that the more time spent with patrol officers, the more likely their typical behavior would be observed. As officers became accustomed to the presence of an observer, the less their behavior would be influenced, thereby reducing researcher bias. After several observations, it became apparent that officers were at ease with the presence of an observer. They encouraged questions and did not object to note taking. They were also forthcoming with information about what they did on patrol and the factors that influenced the decisions they made.

DECISIONS TO "TAKE ACTION"

Patrol ride-alongs provided a greater understanding of the factors that influenced officers' decisions to file (or not file) domestic violence incident reports. In many cases, aside from offense severity, the most important factor was the victim's desire to file (or not file) a report. In cases where the victim wanted to file a report, officers would often comply and file a report. In cases where the victim did not want to file a report, officers would often comply and not file a report. The victim also influenced the officer's decision to arrest or not arrest the suspect. When asked what factors they took into consideration when deciding to arrest a suspect, officers cited the victim's level of cooperation in providing information that would support the arrest. However, officers also noted that if there was visible injury to the victim, they had to "take action" (i.e., make an arrest).

Despite mandatory arrest laws, which required officers to arrest and file a criminal complaint against a suspect if there was probable cause to believe a domestic violence offense took place, officers typically considered the severity of the alleged offense when deciding whether or not to file an incident report and/or make an arrest. As a result, officers were less likely to "take action" in cases involving harassment or simple assault than they were in cases involving terroristic threats or aggravated assault. Officers justified these decisions by citing a large caseload and the victim's desire not to press charges. Officers freely admitted that they did not view mandatory arrest as the most realistic or efficient way of processing domestic violence cases, especially in situations of limited resources and overwhelming demand for police assistance.

Response to Repeat Victims

When asked if cases involving repeat victims were handled differently than cases involving first-time victims, all officers agreed that they were more likely to file an incident report or make an arrest if the victim had been previously victimized. However, several officers made reference to the fact that the paperwork associated with a domestic violence report was very time-consuming. One officer commented that even when he did file a report and/or make an arrest in a repeat case, "It's discouraging, because even when you arrest someone, they're back out on the street in no time committing another crime."

As a general rule, officers had to account for their time while on patrol by making an entry in their logbook approximately every 20 minutes. They were discouraged by their superior officers from spending long periods of time on any one call for service. This may have deterred patrol officers from filing a report, making an arrest, or pursuing a suspect who had fled the scene, as these actions required additional paperwork and time.

Talking with patrol officers also revealed that the discrepancies between the number of calls for service received by police and the number of incident reports processed by detectives was not unique to domestic violence. As one supervising officer reported, "Only about 20% of all calls for service result in an incident report." He added, "If we wrote a report for every call we got, we wouldn't be able to do our job." This coincides with the practice of "load-shedding" (Maxfield, Lewis & Szoc, 1980), which suggests that police reduce their workload by not recording an incident as a verified crime.

Patrol ride-alongs also revealed that not all calls for service warranted the filing of an incident report, regardless of officer discretion. In some cases, the incident did not qualify as domestic violence, as in the case of a woman who was harassed by someone with whom she got into a car accident. In other cases, no crime was committed, as in the case of a man who was left at the side of the road by his girlfriend after an argument. Neither of these cases qualified as a criminal offense, nor did they warrant the filing of a domestic violence incident report.

In addition, calls were not always coded correctly when they were dispatched to patrol. Some calls were coded as domestic violence, but were subsequently changed to reflect the true nature of the incident. This often occurred when police learned that the parties involved did not have an intimate relationship. Also, many calls were downgraded, from domestic violence in progress to a family dispute, after police learned that the incident was not as serious as the dispatcher was led to believe.

All of these factors helped to explain the discrepancy between calls for service received by police and incident reports processed by detectives. While preliminary analysis suggested that this discrepancy was substantial (only 15% of domestic violence calls resulted in an incident report), this supplemental fieldwork revealed that not all calls categorized as domestic violence were, in fact, domestic violence, and not all calls met the requirements of a criminal offense.

Detective Interviews

In addition to patrol ride-alongs, interviews were conducted with all detectives in the domestic violence unit. Detective interviews provided enhanced understanding of how repeat cases were handled once incident reports were filed, and how the handling of repeat cases could be improved to better identify repeat victims. When the project began, there were four detectives and one lieutenant who handled all domestic violence cases in the city. All five officers were interviewed. Similar to patrol ride-alongs, an interview guide was used to provide a framework for interview questions. All questions were open-ended to allow detectives to respond in their own terms, and potentially threatening questions were worded in such a way as to ask *how*, not *why* detectives made decisions on repeat cases.

Detective interviews provided a wealth of information on how the police could better handle repeat cases. Each of the detectives admitted there was very little difference between the way they handled cases involving one-time victims or one-time offenders, and the way they handled cases involving repeat victims or repeat offenders. Detectives agreed, "more could be done" to address the problem of repeat domestic violence, and several detectives gave suggestions on how to accomplish this goal.

Case Management

Among the suggestions made by detectives was a proposal to reorganize the domestic violence unit so that social services (i.e., counseling) and emergency resources (i.e., shelter) were readily available to victims. Detectives believed that reorganizing the unit so that victim services were more centralized would allow them to improve case management and ensure that victims were not "lost in the shuffle." It was also suggested that the domestic violence unit have more contact with the victim/witness unit of the prosecutor's office. All of the detectives agreed that there was "very little contact, if any" between the two agencies.

Centralized Database

Another suggestion made by detectives involved the creation of a centralized database to track all domestic violence cases reported in the county. Since victims frequently moved in and out of the city, it was difficult for police to track offenses that took place in neighboring jurisdictions. A centralized database would allow police to determine whether someone had offended or been victimized in another jurisdiction. This information could then be used to facilitate investigations and inform decisions on arrest and bail.

Victim Assistance

Detectives made several other suggestions regarding the handling of domestic violence cases, including the provision of more advanced training for domestic violence detectives and patrol officers. Several detectives identified in-service domestic violence training as a "step in the right direction," and further suggested that the pre-service (academy) training they received did not prepare them for the challenges of domestic violence cases.

Additional Resources for Domestic Violence Unit

Something every detective mentioned during the interview was the need for more resources. As one detective noted, "One of our main problems is that we are understaffed. We don't have enough detectives to handle the number of cases we get. If we had more people, we could do a lot more." As suggested by detectives, a lack of resources significantly hindered their ability to address the complexity of domestic violence. With four detectives handling 400 to 500 cases each month, it was difficult for them to do anything but "the bare minimum." From talking with detectives, it was clear that they wanted to do more. They wanted to collaborate with other agencies, they wanted to follow-up with victims, they wanted to arrest repeat offenders, but they were ill equipped to do so because they were overworked and understaffed. Detectives agreed that before any steps could be made to address the problem of repeat domestic violence, they would need additional resources (i.e., more detectives) to reduce their workload. A reduced workload would give detectives more time to follow up with victims, arrest offenders (instead of issuing summons), conduct more detailed investigations, and collaborate with other criminal justice and social service agencies to address the variety of victims' needs.

POLICY RECOMMENDATIONS

One of the goals of this project was to develop recommendations for the police to consider in their efforts to reduce repeat domestic violence. Upon analysis of incident reports and information gathered from patrol ride-alongs and detective interviews, several recommendations were offered.

Prioritize Domestic Violence at Compstat Meetings

The first recommendation was to make domestic violence a priority at weekly Compstat meetings. It was clear throughout the project that domestic violence was not given nearly as much attention by police administrators as other repeat crimes. While efforts were routinely made by police (via the establishment of specialized task forces) to prevent other types of repeat crime, including robbery and car theft, very little effort was given to address repeat domestic violence. After the installation of the electronic database, the domestic violence lieutenant was required to report the number of repeat offenders at Compstat meetings. However, according to the lieutenant, "nothing was ever done with the information." The development of an electronic database made the identification and analysis of repeat cases possible. The next step is to use Compstat meetings as a platform to discuss the analysis of these cases and develop innovative ways to protect repeat victims and deter repeat offenders.

Interagency Communication and Collaboration

Another recommendation was to improve communication and collaboration between police officers who have knowledge of repeat cases, judges who grant restraining orders, and prosecutors who process criminal charges. Practitioners within each of these agencies have access to information that is vital to case disposition. What was lacking at the time of this study was a formal system of information sharing to equip the police, prosecutors and judges to make decisions on the best way to handle repeat cases. Likewise, patrol officers who responded to domestic violence calls for service needed to share information with social service agencies, in order to address victims' immediate needs. In many cases, responding officers had knowledge of the victims' needs (i.e., shelter, money, advocacy), which social service providers did not become aware of until after the case went to court (several weeks after the incident occurred). If patrol officers made contact with social service providers on the same (or next) day, appropriate steps could be taken to provide victims with the assistance they need to protect themselves from further victimization.

Repeat Victimization as a Performance Indicator

Finally, it was recommended that police officials consider using repeat victimization to assess the effectiveness of any domestic violence prevention strategy implemented in the future. As suggested by Farrell and Buckley (1999), where policing is a response to victimization, it might be preferable to look for a crime prevention effect in the level of repeat victimization. The current study revealed that a small proportion of domestic violence victims accounted for a disproportionate number of reported cases. It follows logically, then, that by focusing police resources on repeat victims, who represent a fraction of the victim population, a disproportionate number of domestic violence offenses could potentially be prevented. One way to measure the effectiveness of a victim-focused response to domestic violence is to look for a reduction in the number of cases involving repeat victims.

Of course, better measures of repeat victimization are needed before it can be used as a performance indicator for police. While the implementation of an electronic database has improved the ability of police to identify repeat cases, what is still needed is an effort by the police to track these cases and maintain better records on repeat victims and repeat offenders. This would allow police to determine the effectiveness of an intervention aimed at reducing repeat victimization.

Conclusion

This chapter describes a collaborative effort between researchers and police officials, generated by a common interest in addressing a complex social problem. The key to the project's success was collaboration in a way that helped both the researcher and the host organization. The researcher benefited from access to vital case information, while the host organization benefited in several important ways.

First, domestic violence detectives recognized how a data file that identified repeat offenders produced information that could aid their investigations of domestic violence incidents. Prior to the implementation of an electronic database, it was very difficult for detectives to keep track of repeat cases. The database, created largely as a result of this project, significantly altered the way detectives collected and stored case information, hence improving their ability to conduct more thorough and informed investigations.

Second, recognizing that implementing a new data system is especially difficult in a tradition-bound organization, the transition was eased somewhat by having a researcher enter data initially to get the system up and running. One intentional by-product of this was the establishment of quality-control procedures. The researcher, aware that the reliability of data gathering was important, was able to establish reliable data entry routines for the entire domestic violence unit.

The unit benefited in another important way. Each week, the domestic violence lieutenant was required to present a summary of the unit's activities at Compstat meetings. Before the database was developed, the lieutenant spent several hours preparing for these weekly meetings. After the database was operational, preparation time was reduced to minutes. In addition, the lieutenant was able to introduce new performance measures (repeat offenders and repeat victims) that came to be valued by the department's chief. If a victim-focused response to domestic violence were to be developed, this information could be used to assess a reduction in the number of cases involving repeat victims.

Perhaps one of the most significant outcomes of this project, from both a researcher and practitioner standpoint, was the knowledge generated on repeat domestic violence. Not only did this project create new ways for police to share this information, but it also enabled researchers to explore previously unanswered questions about repeat victims and repeat offenders. It is anticipated that the findings and recommendations of this project will be utilized by police personnel to consider new ways of preventing domestic violence by focusing on repeat cases. Protecting repeat victims from further victimization may prove to be an effective way to reduce the incidence of domestic violence, as has been shown with other repeat crimes. An innovative approach such as this is particularly important for departments with limited resources and a substantial domestic violence caseload. As this case study suggests, repeat victims account for a large proportion of domestic violence cases. Further study is needed to determine whether focusing prevention efforts on repeat victims is a more efficient way to allocate police resources with the ultimate goal of reducing domestic violence.

REFERENCES

Farrell, G. & Buckley, A. (1999). Evaluation of a UK Police Domestic Violence Unit Using Repeat Victimisation as a Performance Indicator. *The Howard Journal*, 38 (1), 42–53.

Hanmer, J., Griffiths, S. & Jerwood, D. (1999). Arresting Evidence: Domestic Violence and Repeat Victimization. Police Research Series Paper 104. London: Home Office.

Laycock, G. (2001). Hypothesis-Based Research: The Repeat Victimization Story. *The International Journal of Policy and Practice*, 1 (1), 59–82.

Lloyd, S., Farrell, G. & Pease, K. (1994). Preventing Repeated Domestic Violence: A Demonstration Project on Merseyside. Police Research Group, Crime Prevention Unit Paper 49, London: Home Office.

Maxfield, M., Lewis, D. & Szoc, R. (1980). Producing Official Crimes: Verified Crime Reports as Measures of Police Output. *Social Science Quarterly*, 61 (2), 221–236.

Patton, M. Q. (1990). Qualitative Evaluation and Research Methods, 2nd Edition. London: Sage Publications.

CHAPTER 5

REPEAT VICTIMIZATION AND PROBLEM-ORIENTED POLICING: A RECIPROCAL APPROACH TO ADDRESSING CRIME

Elizabeth Quinn
MIDDLE TENNESSEE STATE UNIVERSITY

INTRODUCTION

Just as a small proportion of all offenders represent a large amount of crime committed (Moffitt, 1997), so too do a small proportion of victims represent a surprisingly large (and therefore disproportionate) amount of victimizations (Farrell, 1992; Farrell and Pease, 1993; Farrell and Bouloukos, 2001; Farrell and Pease, 2001). Recent research by Frank, Brantingham and Farrell (2012) found that when using a crime estimator called the Recorded Repeats Adjustment Calculator (RRAC), repeat victimization accounted for half of recorded burglaries in Metro Vancouver. Furthermore, severe repeats (5 or more burglaries in a household) accounted for 20% of recorded burglaries. Even more compelling is that this pattern of disproportionality of major offenders and repeat victims is found across crime types and methods of research (Farrell, 1992). In terms of a crime prevention strategy numerous authors have suggested that in order to curb the crime problem, police should focus on repeat victimizations (or better, repeat victims) to decrease the amount of crime committed (Farrell and Pease, 1993; Farrell, 1995; Taylor, 1999). In effect, "if repeat or multiple victimization can be prevented, a large proportion of all crime might be prevented" (Farrell, 1992, p. 85). Additionally, Johnson et al.

have created and refined a method by which they can predict "near repeats," defined as crime events, tested on burglaries, happening within close proximity to a primary location within a specified period of time. Johnson et al. (2007) differentiate between "exact-repeats" — consecutive events at the same crime location — and "near-repeats" to demonstrate the pattern of crimes in a particular area, thereby deeming it a vulnerable area, versus singular place. Therefore, not only are primary victims at risk for repeated victimizations, but those close to the primary victim may be at heightened risk when compared to the general public. Given this information, that repeat victims account for a disproportionate amount of crime, and that risk increases for victimization for both the same victim and those within close proximity to the primary victim, it makes sense that crime prevention strategies may be effective at reducing additional crime by focusing on repeat victims and near-repeats.

One major problem for best understanding repeat victimization lies in the way it is reported. According to Ellingworth, Farrell and Pease (1995) "[a]ll official sources of crime information are misleading ... police recording systems ... have been more or less inadequate in identifying repeated victimization of the same dwellings or the same people," whereas, "victimization surveys ... underestimate repeat victimization by limits placed upon the number of victim forms completed, and upon the maximum number of incidents in a series of victimizations" (p. 360). This chapter will focus on repeat victimization and the problems associated with identifying it and defining it, and will discuss the utilization of problem-oriented policing as a technique to decrease its occurrence.

Definition

Definitions of repeat victimization range from using repeat victimization as a catch-all phrase to include victimizations of multiple crime types by multiple offenders to the obvious, repeated victimization of the same crime type by the same offender (Farrell, 1992). Other researchers suggest that repeat victimization and multiple victimization should be used to define the two markedly different experiences (Outlaw, Ruback and Britt, 2002). They suggest that the term repeat victimization be used only when the victim experiences the same crime type by the same offender (or maybe was "referred" by that offender) (Outlaw et al., 2002). Multiple victimizations, therefore, exist when a victim experiences multiple types of crime victimizations by multiple offenders, so repeat victimizations and multiple victimizations are separate events. Ratcliffe and McCullagh (1998) raise the question at what point in time do repeat victimizations become new initial victimizations . . . six months, one year, two years . . . and according to what criteria? They suggest that looking at the initial crime might help to answer that question, such as, is the modus operandi the same as the original event, is the point or method of entry the same or different, and is the time of day of the crimes similar or different. Findings from one jurisdiction under investigation by Ratcliffe and McCullagh (1998) suggested that if the repeat victimization shared point of entry and method of entry OR occurred around the same time of day, it could be considered a repeat victimization and not a new 'initial' victimization.

Probably the most prolific writers on repeat victimization, Graham Farrell and Ken Pease, propose that repeat victimization includes the following: "multiple criminal incidents experienced by either a person or place" (Farrell, 1992, p. 86; Farrell and Pease, 2001) and suggest that it can be called by any of the following names — multiple victimization, repeat victimization, recidivist victimization or multi-victimization (Farrell, 1992). This paper will rely on Farrell and Pease's definition when discussing repeat victimization overall. The discussion on the definition of repeat victimization is important for the reason that researchers and police departments alike may label victims differently depending on their own definition of repeat victimization; therefore, accurate accounts of the prevalence of repeat victimization both through research and police records may vary according to the person or agency responsible for the collection of information. This will be especially important when discussing crime prevention of repeat victimization as addressed by problem-oriented policing. Crime reduction strategies have evolved to rely increasingly on evidence-based practices, therefore having a consistent definition and measurement plan for repeat victimization is paramount to addressing it through effectively (Frank, Brantingham & Farrell, 2012).

Prevalence

The majority of the public will not be victimized in their lifetimes (Ellingworth, Farrell and Pease, 1995). For instance, findings from the 1982–1992 British Crime Surveys suggest that overall 6% of people are victims of property crime and 3% of people are victims of personal crime (Ellingworth et al., 1995). However, for those people who are victimized it is estimated that between 24% and 38% of crime "is suffered by people who experience five or more such offences . . . over a year" (Ellingworth et al., 1995, p. 362). Farrell (1992) reports that in the 1982 wave of the British Crime Survey only 14% of all victims experienced over 70% of all offences it covered. Additionally,

Williams (1999) reports that those who are members of already disadvantaged groups are at even higher risk of becoming repeat victims. Though repeat victimization has been studied since the late 1970s, it appears that the representation of it may not have been done for the purpose of focusing on the problem of repeat victimization, but as an instrumental purpose to illustrate a theory or as an addition to an article or book on victimization overall. Sparks, Genn and Dodd (1977) found that a substantial proportion of the population in their study of three London boroughs experienced a great deal of victimization over all types of crime. Hindelang, Gottfredson, and Garofalo (1978) observed some patterns of repeat victimization in their study of victimization in eight United States cities. Essentially, they found that if a place or person was previously victimized the likelihood of subsequent victimization was greater than that by chance, and that individuals who lived in a household where someone else was victimized were also likely to be victimized, and finally that people who lived in a household that experienced a victimization had a higher risk of experiencing a personal crime than those who lived in non-victimized households (Hindelang et al., 1978). From his analysis of the United States National Crime Victimization Survey, Reiss (1980) concluded that repeat victimization was not a random occurrence and that those victimized were more likely to experience the same type of victimization repeatedly.

When one thinks of personal crimes such as domestic violence and/or assaults this may seem obvious. Oftentimes in those instances the victim and perpetrator know each other or have personality characteristics that may precipitate acts of violence (in the case of the assaulter who is both victimized and offends). This may be the case for the findings of Sherman et al.'s 1989 study of domestic violence in Minnesota. As reported by Farrell (1992), Sherman et al. (1989) found that 50% of all calls to police came from only 3% of locations. As will be elaborated upon later, Farrell (1992) suggests that this may illustrate a connection between crime prevention and hot spot analysis. Farrell and Bouloukos (2001) assessed repeat victimization internationally by focusing on the 1989, 1992 and 1996 versions of the International Crime Victims Survey. They found that repeat victimization was widespread in the industrialized countries surveyed. They found that personal crimes had a higher rate of revictimization than property crimes (40–60% of sexual incidents perpetrated against the same women and 30–40% of assaults and threats were found to be against the same persons) (Farrell and Bouloukos, 2001). Even in countries with notoriously low crime rates (Japan) it appeared that for those people or places that were victimized they were repeatedly victimized . . . so whatever mechanism contributed to low crime rates did not contribute to low rates of repeat victimization (Farrell and Bouloukos, 2001). Planty and Strom (2007), in examining the role of repeat victims in our estimation of victimization rates in the United States, found that officially represented victimization statistics within the National Crime Victimization Survey (NCVS) distort the actual incidence of repeat victimization, or series victimizations as they are called in the NCVS. They do not include all victimizations included within a series incident and thus present a false picture of victimization and risk. The authors suggest this may be done for an understandable reason, but that figuring out how to adjust the problems these offenses present is a better solution than eliminating them from reported estimates.

TIME FRAME FOR REPEAT VICTIMIZATION

It appears that with property crime once a person or place has been victimized the next victimization, if any, will occur quite soon after the initial victimization (Farrell, 1992; Bridgeman and Hobbs, 1997; Ratcliffe and Mc-Cullagh, 1998; Kleemans, 2001; Mawby, 2001; van Dijk, 2001). This presents a very short time frame when taking into consideration crime prevention efforts of victims and/or police departments, "the greatest risk of a repeat is the time immediately after a burglary" (Ratcliffe and McCullagh, 1998, p. 657). Additionally, Ratcliffe and McCullagh state that Anderson et al. (1995) found that 40 percent of repeat calls occurred within one month of the initial victimization and Burquest et al. (1992) "found an even greater figure of 79 per cent of revictimization incidents occurring within one month for school burglaries" (Ratcliffe and McCullagh, 1998, p. 657). In their own study, Ratcliffe and McCullagh (1998) found that 27.8% of revictimizations occurred within one year of the preceding victimization. Overwhelmingly in the Ratcliffe and McCullagh study, the victims were non-residential locations, including sports centers, schools and building sites. Van Dijk (2001) found similar findings in his analysis of the International Crime Victims Survey. Van Dijk (2001) found that across developed, transitional and developing nations repeat victimization was common all over and approximately 20% of repeat victimization occurred within months of the initial incident. Additionally, he found that 24% of burglary victims and 41% of women victims of violence experienced repeat victimizations within one year of the initial victimization. Mele (2009) reports that the time between repeat victimizations decreases as time goes on, so not only are victims experiencing additional victimizations but the time between them for recovery becomes less and less for each subsequent victimization. Mele (2009) suggests further that the more exposure one has to the perpetrator the more opportunities arise for repeated victimization, thus affecting the time between victimizations. In her analysis of domestic violence victims, Mele (2009) found that "the median number of days between successive victimizations declined as the number of victimizations increased" (p. 621). The resulting time lapse was 62 days between the 1st and 2nd victimizations with a steady decrease to a reported 15 days between subsequent victimizations at the 9th and 10th abuse occurrence (Mele, 2009).

Property and Personal Crimes: Is There a Difference?

The bulk of the literature conducted on repeat victimization has focused on better understanding repeat victimization of burglaries (Farrell, 1992; Ratcliffe and McCullagh, 1998; Farrell and Pease, 2001; Chenery, Henshaw, and Pease, 2002) — property crimes. However, a good deal of literature also exists on the revictimization of women with sexual offenses and domestic violence, as well as repeat victimization of children who experience child abuse and neglect (Lynch, Berbaum and Planty, 1998; Messman-Moore and Long, 2000; Breitenbecher, 2001). Breitenbecher (2001) reports that the literature on sexual revictimization of women suggests that between 24% and 67% of women with sexual abuse or assault pasts are revictimized. Additionally, Messman-Moore and Long (2000) report that "few empirically sound studies have investigated revictimization" of the occurrence of adult sexual, physical or psychological abuse of child sexual abuse survivors (p. 490). Often in these types of crime the offender and perpetrator are known to each other, so it makes sense that within an intimate relationship proximity of the victim and offender will be close and constant and more instances of crimes may likely occur. Messman-Moore and Long (2000) report that child sexual assault survivors (CSAS) individuals were more likely to experience adult sexual abuse, physical abuse and psychological maltreatment than nonvictims of child sexual abuse. Finally, Lynch, et al. (1998) examined repeated victimizations using the National Crime Victims Survey (NCVS) collected from 1992 through 1995. They found that prior victimizations of burglary and assault indeed were positively related to subsequent victimizations of the same type. Additionally, they found evidence that certain victim characteristics were good predictors of repeat victimization as well, such as age of head of household, location of household, and marital status of head of household (Lynch et al., 1998).

Repeat Victimization and "Hot Spots"

Ratcliffe and McCullagh (1998) suggest that because there are so many problems with identifying repeat victims (both places and persons) through police records because of the problems mentioned above, the use of geographic information systems (GIS) might be a good alternative to identifying repeat victimization. The purpose for this is that GIS can eliminate the address text-based system of police agencies and that GIS locations are static, as opposed to reliant on the individual who inputs the data.

Farrell and Sousa (2001) suggest a need to "examine overlap between repeat victimization and hot spots in relation to high-crime areas and repeat offending for different crime types" (p.221). They indicate that repeat victimization may be more likely to occur in hot spots and may vary by crime time. Additionally, they state that hot spot policing might prevent a range of crimes from repeating. Aside from policing hot spots for new crimes, the prevention of repeat victimization within hot spots may be more effective than policing hot spots for new crimes themselves and for the prevention of repeat victimization alone (Farrell and Sousa, 2001). They suggest that offenses at hot spots may be more frequent and more serious. For the repeat victim, this may mean that victimizations become more intense and may have profound psychological, physical and economical effects on the target or individual. Additionally, in terms of allocation of policing duties, if police are most useful at spots where there is high-crime activity, focusing policing efforts in hot spots with high repeat victimization is "administration-friendly." Farrell and Sousa (2001) further suggest that targeting repeat victims may also help to detect offenders, and in particular "super-predators." Indubitably, the placement of police officers in hot spot areas with the purpose of preventing new crime, repeat crime and detecting chronic offenders can lead to a decreased crime rate. Additionally, if problem-oriented policing tactics are utilized to address repeat victimizations within hot spots new performance indicators could be created to indicate effectiveness in the reduction of repeat victimizations. Levy and Tartaro (2010) examined the phenomenon of both repeat auto thefts in hot spots within Atlantic City with an environmental indicator technique called the Watchers, Activity Nodes, Location, Lighting and Security indices (WALLS). The crux of the WALLS indices is that locations, and conditions within those locations, may make places and the people that frequent them vulnerable to victimization. This makes the location particularly vulnerable to being a hot spot for repeated criminal activity. Environmental conditions within those locations can work to decrease or increase the vulnerability of an area and ultimately the chance of victimization. Levy and Tartaro (2010) found that places with lower pedestrian traffic (Watchers and Activity) and fewer security mechanisms (Security) were particularly vulnerable to repeat auto theft.

As noted earlier, not only are primary victims at risk of repeat victimizations, but those within close proximity to the primary victim may also be at risk. Bowers, Johnson, and Pease (2003) call this phenomenon "near repeats," meaning that those nearest to a victimized target are more at risk of becoming victims as well because of their proximity to the primary victim. Their study focuses on burglary victimizations, but other research suggests that the same phenomenon can be found for personal victimization as well (Hindelang et al., 1978). Short, D'Orsogna, Brantingham, and Tita (2009) found a similar pattern of predicting repeat and near repeat burglary in their study of residential areas in Long Beach, CA. They suggest that an area becomes particularly vulnerable surrounding each crime event as the offender is knowledgeable about the primary target and surrounding residences. These findings help us to be able to focus on problem areas and predict future risks of primary victims and proximity-oriented victims. They suggest that in addition to focusing on where initial victimizations occur police departments should also look at prospective victimizations, specifically near repeats. In this sense a problem-oriented policing approach to addressing repeat victimization could include addressing prospective victimizations, and crime prevention could be truly a community effort. Bowers et al.'s spatial analysis technique highlights the most vulnerable predicted areas of victimization and has been highly successful, predicting 90% of future burglaries, which was better than focusing on traditional hot spot analysis (Bowers et al., 2003).

Victim's Call for Service — Expectations of the Police and Victim Satisfaction

According to van Dijk (2001) repeat victims contact the police more often and with greater demands than singular victims. In a comparison of developed versus poor countries it was found that those in developed countries were more likely to report victimizations than those in transitional or developing nations. The motivation for reporting also differs by country. In developed countries, van Dijk (2001) suggests that motivation for reporting lies in a belief that crimes should be reported and to comply with insurance purposes. In transitional and developing countries victims report crimes in order to recover items, to see the perpetrator caught and sentenced, and to request help to stop what is happening (van Dijk, 2001). It appears that overall repeat victims are less certain that police can meet the needs of the victims and are hence, often less satisfied with police. Additionally, dissatisfaction occurs because of the lack of ability to find the perpetrator or solve the crime, but also from mistreatment by police officers. Though those in developed nations report greater satisfaction van Dijk (2001) suggests this may be not only because of better services, but also because of lower expectations of victims. Van Dijk (2001) found that burglary victims were two times more likely to report to police than women victims of violence. He suggests that perhaps financial considerations as well as wanting protection from the offender were the reasons for reporting. For women victims of violence, he suggests that the victimization is reported because the woman wants the offender caught and punished.

Van Dijk (2001) presents an interesting juxtaposition, however. He reports that although repeat victims are less satisfied with police and at times may feel neglected by the police because of the inability to solve the crimes, repeat victims tend to demand more protection, and/or services, than other callers. This makes sense if one considers that fact that each call by a repeat victim may be treated as an initial offense and could ignore the impact of repeat victimizations. In this sense, perhaps a shift needs to occur to better address repeat victimization.

In spite of the problems with defining repeat victimization and thus, the problems associated with garnering a "true" estimate of its occurrence, it is clear that there is an opportunity to reduce crime through addressing repeat victimizations (Pease, 1998). Because research suggests that reactive policing doesn't seem to be reducing repeat victimizations a new approach may be needed, and problem-oriented policing has shown to be effective at reducing repeat victimization in the United Kingdom (Chenery, et al., 2002; Pease, 1998).

PROBLEM-ORIENTED POLICING

Before one can discuss the benefit of utilizing a problem-oriented policing approach to addressing repeat victimization, there must be some background given on the problem-oriented policing approach. The object of problem-oriented policing is to address crime through "recogniz(ing) the relationships between incidents . . . and . . . tak(ing) a more in-depth interest in incidents by acquainting themselves with some of the conditions and factors that give rise to them" (Goldstein, 1990, p. 33). This definition speaks directly to repeat victimization as the term repeat implies multiple incidents. In problem-oriented policing police officers are asked to take a more proactive than reactive approach to solving community problems (Goldstein, 1990). Additionally, problems to be addressed by the police are determined collaboratively with community residents and the police. Residents can include actual residential inhabitants of the community, business owners, and service delivery personnel (which can include judges, prosecutors, church representatives, and other service providers). In essence, the focus of problem solving in a community includes working together with community partners to assess community problems that will be addressed by both the police and the community.

POLICE RESPONSE TO VICTIMIZATION

Hirschel, Lumb, and Johnson (1998) found that burglary crime victims, in general, responded well to perceived interest and helpfulness of officers in a problem solving/community policing approach to responding to crime victims. Above all other indicators, crime victims were most satisfied with police when they believed the police were actually concerned about the victimization and were significantly more likely to be satisfied when they were offered information on how to prevent future victimizations. Russell and Light (2006) found a similar result in satisfaction of victims of domestic violence. The more police showed interest, belief, and concern, the higher the rates of satisfaction of victims. Because of how repeat victimizations are recorded (and the problems associated with it discussed previously), it is easy to see that the police response to repeat victimizations may remain reactive and focused on each incident as not connected. What seems evident from the Hirschel et al. (1998) study, however, is that repeat victimizations may be prevented through the simple introduction of useful crime prevention information, which may not be dependent upon police knowing that a particular call for service is in response to a victim who has never been offended upon before or is a repeat victim. This shift from reactive, information gathering only, to a more problem-solving approach could work to improve victim satisfaction for both single and repeat victims. No doubt police officers are well aware that the same places and/or people are being victimized, but internal policing policies do not always address the need to focus on repeat victimizations in the problem-oriented approach as discussed above. Furthermore, Bracey (1996) states, oftentimes the police response to a crime is merely symbolic because in a great deal of cases there is not a lot the police can do after the fact without good leads to the perpetrator. This is especially true for burglaries, for without information on the perpetrator the most the police can do is acknowledge that things were stolen from a home or an establishment and collect identifying information on those items. The expectations for police may be a bit different for repeat victimization, however. Because we know that repeat victimizations occur relatively soon after the initial victimization, the visitation of the police to the crime scene may result in a crime prevention discussion in addition to collecting information about the items stolen and the symbolic role of acknowledging that something has been taken. Bridgeman and Hobbs (1997) suggest a graded response to repeat victimization that includes the following framework:

- base future risk on prior victimizations, not on individual victims' characteristics;
- early intervention is key because of the high risk period following an initial victimization;
- interventions remain familiar (and less expensive), though the officer should heighten the level of security needed when appropriate;
- continual effort to alleviate the problem as it becomes more difficult;
- the plan is simple and clear — officers are aware of their duties and victims feel they are getting some help.

The Bridgeman and Hobbs (1998) scheme fits well with a problem-oriented police response as it appears to follow the SARA model of scan, analyze, respond, assess. Additionally, Chenery et al. (2002) suggests that when a report is taken on a burglary there needs to be a place on the incident form requesting information about any previous victimizations. In this sense, Chenery et al. (2002) propose that the assessment phase of SARA is prolonged with no real end to the assessment. Furthermore, Chenery et al. (2002) suggest an additional graded response they call "The Olympic Model" which suggests that responses to victims be done so on a need-based level with those suffering repeated victimizations receiving greater services/attention by police officers. This type of a response was found to be greatly accepted by police in the Huddersfield "Biting Back" project in which this response scheme was implemented. Not only did it better inform officers as to actual crime events occurring (but not always reported) in their jurisdictions, but also it gave the police officers a boost in morale as they indicated that they felt like they were actually doing something for their customers (Chenery et al., 2002). In a similar vein, Russell and Light (2006) found that concerted efforts of law enforcement agencies to coordinate with other agencies in their response to domestic violence victims resulted in elevated satisfaction of victims. The coordination effort required officers to participate in a SARA-like approach, and thus though not called problem-oriented policing per se, it appears that one was utilized.

PROBLEM-ORIENTED POLICING AND REPEAT VICTIMIZATION

It makes sense that if analysis for problem-oriented policing exists to focus on individuals likely to commit crime and areas in which they will commit crime (Goldstein, 1990) that a combination focus on both "offenders" and "victims" could be helpful. After all, Goldstein (1990) states that "the objective . . . is to develop tailor-made responses: to fashion a response that holds the greatest potential for eliminating or reducing the specific problem" (pg. 44). The beauty of addressing repeat victimization with problem-oriented policing is that problem-oriented policing is already geared to look at both the place and person involved in repeat victimizations (Goldstein, 1990). This speaks directly to the finding by Outlaw et al. (2002) that it was not adequate enough to address repeat victimization by dealing with the victimized person or place, but that more often it was necessary to look at the neighborhood or community as a whole in order to cause *real* change. Though written after Goldstein's (1990) seminal work on problem-oriented policing this idea seems tailor-fit to the objective of problem-oriented policing as suggested in the following quote:

> In the range of postures that the police can assume, there is ample room for them to take greater initiative in dealing with community problems. In calling for the police not simply to resign themselves to living with recurring problems, problem-oriented policing urges the police to be more aggressive partners with other public agencies. (Goldstein, 1990, pg. 47)

Key to this quote is the phrase "with other public agencies," which addresses the concern voiced by Outlaw et al. (2002). Scott (2003) suggests that though it appears that policing agencies have been slow to integrate problem-oriented policing into their routine operations, an overwhelming benefit of doing so is that:

> the police, and those who oversee their actions, would insist that the broad community interest in these problems, as well as the larger community's response to them, be explored, rather than more narrowly looking at what the police are doing to solve the problems. The police would be held more accountable for addressing problems, but less responsible for addressing them alone (pg. 51).

This understanding might help to make the idea of incorporating POP practices into daily routines more appealing. This could hold particularly true for agencies that find particular neighborhoods or segments of their jurisdictions continually problematic. If the responsibility is not completely on the shoulders of the police, but shared with the community, then police effectiveness may have a different meaning. To hold the police completely responsible for reducing or eliminating a community's problems is like holding a doctor *completely* responsible for the health of his or her patient.

EFFECTIVENESS OF PROBLEM-ORIENTED POLICING AS A CRIME PREVENTION APPROACH TO REPEAT VICTIMIZATION

Goldstein (2003) and Scott (2003) suggest that problem-oriented policing may not be utilized, and therefore studied, by police departments for three main reasons: 1) many police officers do not completely understand the basic elements of POP and how it fits into their roles as police officers, 2) that the skills and knowledge needed to implement POP are not yet held by police officers in general, and 3) the incentives for integrating POP as a policing strategy are insufficient. In this sense it is difficult to address the effectiveness of problem-oriented policing approaches because they may not be implemented in agencies to the degree originally set forth by Goldstein (1990).

However, multiple studies of police responses to repeat victimization have occurred in the United Kingdom (U.K.). One such experiment utilizing problem-oriented policing as an approach to repeat victimization occurred in Kirkholt, England. Using the SARA approach (though not named as such) investigators identified a burglary problem in the Kirkholt Estate with particular attention focused on the relative quickness of repeated attacks following an initial victimization (Laycock and Farrell, 2003). Burglaries were found to be concentrated on particular targets and a goal was set to reduce repeat victimization in the Estate. The results of the police effort include zero burglaries after seven months and a total reduction of 75% fewer burglaries over a period of 3 years. A graded approach dealing with repeat victimization was taken to address the problem (Laycock and Farrell, 2003). The Kirkholt Estate project is identified as a problem-oriented policing approach as it first scanned the area for crime problems, analyzed the results, formulated a response and assessed the effect of the response. Laycock and Farrell (2003) suggest that utilizing this same approach with other jurisdictions would be beneficial. Indeed, so did the Home Office of the U.K. government, so much so that they launched replications of the project in 20 cities within the U.K. and supplied the cities with extra resources to address repeat victimizations. Though the results were mixed, the Home Office funded even more projects utilizing the Kirkholt approach and it was determined that repeat victimizations were to be dealt with within a range of possible alternatives for dealing with each community's particular repeat victimization problems. Ultimately, a graded response was determined allowing for flexibility in response to repeat victimization by officers (Laycock and Farrell, 2003). Though initial replications of the problem-oriented policing approach exercised in Kirkholt had varying responses, Pease (1993) suggests that the variation was due more to the proper implementation of the program (i.e., methodological problems) as opposed to *real* levels of success. When applied appropriately in the follow-up replications the problem-oriented policing approach proved effective (Laycock and Farrell, 2003). Some more recent projects in the U.K. have included the concept of risk vulnerability in their assessment of problem-oriented policing approaches to repeat victimization. Millie (2008) suggests that due to a lack of consistent definition of vulnerability, and attempting to run a multi-level project of both repeat victims and the "perceived" most vulnerable within the group, may not result in the same type of crime reduction as focusing solely on repeat victims in a larger framework.

In response to the U.K. POP experiments on repeat victimization, Laycock and Farrell (2003, p. 217) suggest seventeen reasons why police should address repeat victimization that could have benefits aside from crime prevention alone.

1. Repeat victimization is one means of addressing crime prevention, which is one of Robert Peel's original policing principles;
2. addressing repeat victimization is a smart administrative move for allocation of officers' time in the field and departmental funds as repeat victims often account for a substantial amount of victimizations;
3. repeat victimization is found in all crimes;
4. repeat victimization can be used as an evaluation measure to assess officer and/or program effectiveness;
5. police resources are naturally allocated to hot spot or high crime areas thereby serving a great number of repeat victims;
6. prevention of repeat victimization allows officers to respond only when new victimizations occur;
7. near-repeats and virtual repeats can also be "protected" by addressing repeat victimization;
8. prevention of repeat victimization is more focused than general prevention and may be a better means of preventing displacement;

9. preventing crime through addressing repeat victimization may improve crime prevention environmentally, thereby confusing offenders by changing vulnerable and/or attractive targets;

10. cooperation between police and communities (businesses, residents, faith-based personnel . . .) can be improved as prevention of repeat victimization will necessitate heightened communication and cooperation between multiple parties; this point is also echoed by research conducted by Russell and Light (2006), illustrating that an integrated approach between police and other community organizations both raises satisfaction of repeat victims and helps to decrease repeated victimizations;

11. police officers may feel more satisfied with their jobs as they will be able to do something tangible for crime victims;

12. feedback from victims may become increasingly positive because of the reorientation of police to victim service;

13. repeat victimization issues can be addressed without a technical assessment by the police department as officers can include a question in their crime scene interview about previous victimizations;

14. sometimes, repeat victimization does not require a full inventive problem solving session, techniques that have been used in the past may be referred to and utilized for new cases of repeat victimization;

15. detection of prolific and serious offenders may be done through treatment of repeat victimization;

16. eliminating vulnerable targets that are repeatedly victimized may eliminate organized crime and terrorism opportunities;

17. previously perceived "victimless" crime activities targeted toward the state or nation can be addressed through treatment of repeat victimization.

These same justifications are consistent for implementing problem-oriented policing approaches in the United States.

Conclusion — Why Study Repeat Victimization and Why Use Problem-Oriented Policing?

Laycock and Farrell (2003) argue that problem-oriented policing should not replace incident-driven policing, but should work in conjunction with it. (Because a small percentage of victims 'person or place' report repeat victimizations this means a larger percentage experience little to no victimizations; therefore, an incident-driven approach may work best with certain elements of the general population.) This is particularly necessary in the case of repeat victimization in which the same "target" receives multiple calls for service (or if calls are not carried through the "target" remains highly victimized). Repeatedly responding to the same "target" for victimization after victimization is not an effective crime prevention strategy so incident-driven policing for repeat victimization is ineffective, basically. Laycock and Farrell (2003) suggest "the problem-oriented policing approach would be to deal with the problem as efficiently and fairly as possible, ideally without recourse to the criminal justice system" (pg. 231). Additionally, as research continues to develop in the area of repeat victimization, it is becoming increasingly evident that problem-oriented policing techniques (whether they are named that or not) are what lead to higher degrees of victim satisfaction overall.

It has been shown that repeat victimization is an important issue to study within the field of policing. The potential for crime prevention and crime reduction utilizing approaches to address repeat victimization can have markedly grand effects (Laycock and Farrell, 2003). It appears that the best approach to dealing with repeat victimization is problem-oriented policing as the degree of understanding needed to identify repeat victimization can be found only within the problem-oriented policing strategy. Compelling evidence exists from our neighbors "across the pond" that should stimulate our own interest in responding to crime through studying repeat victimization and police and community responses through the utilization of problem-oriented policing.

References

Bowers, K., Johnson, S., and Pease, K. (2003). Prospective hotspots: Some preliminary findings. Paper presentation at the American Society of Criminology annual meeting, Denver, CO.

Bracey, D. (1996). Assessing alternative responses to calls for service. In L. Hoover (Ed.), *Quantifying quality in policing* (pp. 153–166). Washington, D.C.: Police Executive Research Forum.

Breitenbecher, K.H. (2001). Sexual revictimization among women: A review of the literature focusing on empirical investigations. *Aggression and Violent Behavior,* 6(4), 415–432.

Bridgeman, C., and Hobbs, L. (1997). *Preventing repeat victimisation: the police officers' guide.* Police Research Group: London, England.

Chenery, S., Henshaw, C., and Pease, K. (2002). Repeat victimisation and the policing of communities. *International Review of Victimology, 9*(2), 137–148.

Ellingworth, D., Farrell, G., and Pease, K. (1995). A victim is a victim is a victim? Chronic victimization in four sweeps of the British Crime Survey. (Symposium on Repeat Victimization). *British Journal of Criminology, 35*(3), 360–365.

Farrell, G. (1992). Multiple victimization: Its extent and significance. *International Review of Victimology, 2,* 85–102.

Farrell, G. (1995). Preventing Repeat Victimization. In M. Tonry and D.P. Farrington, (Eds.), *Building a safer society: Strategic approaches to crime prevention,* pp. 469–534. Chicago, IL: University of Chicago Press.

Farrell, G., and Bouloukos, A.C. (2001). International overview: A cross-national comparison of rates of repeat victimization p. 5–26. In G. Farrell and K. Pease (Eds.), *Repeat Victimization, Crime Prevention Studies, Volume 12* (pp. 5–26). Monsey, NY: Criminal Justice Press.

Farrell, G., and Pease, K. (1993). *Once bitten, twice bitten: repeat victimization and its implications for crime prevention. Police Research Group Crime Prevention Unit Series Paper no. 46.* London, England: Home Office Police Department.

Farrell, G., and Pease, K. (2001). Why repeat victimization matters. In G. Farrell and K. Pease, (Eds.), *Repeat victimization, Crime Prevention Studies, Volume 12,* (pp. 1–4). Monsey, NY: Criminal Justice Press.

Farrell, G., and Sousa, W. (2001). Repeat victimization and hot spots: The overlap and its implications for crime control and problem-oriented policing. In G. Farrell and K. Pease, (Eds.), *Repeat victimization, Crime Prevention Studies, Volume 12,* (pp. 221–240). Monsey, NY: Criminal Justice Press.

Frank, R., Brantingham, P.L., and Farrell, G. (2012). Estimating the True Rate of Repeat Victimization from Police Recorded Crime Data: A Study of Burglary in Metro Vancouver. *Canadian Journal of Criminal Justice and Criminology, 54*(4), 481–494.

Goldstein, H. (1990). *Problem-oriented policing.* New York, NY: McGraw-Hill, Inc.

Goldstein, H. (2003). On further developing problem-oriented policing: The most critical need, the major impediments, and a proposal. In J. Knutsson, (Ed.),

Problem-oriented policing: From innovation to mainstream, Crime Prevention Studies, Volume 16, (pp. 13–47). Monsey, NY: Criminal Justice Press.

Hindelang, M., Gottfredson, M.R., and Garofalo, J. (1978). *Victims of personal crime: An empirical foundation for a theory of personal victimization*. Cambridge, MA: Ballinger.

Hirschel, D., Lumb, R., and Johnson, R. (1998). Victim assessment of the police response to burglary: The relative effects of incident, police action, outcome and demographic variables on citizen satisfaction. *Police Quarterly, 1*(4), 1–20.

Johnson, S. D., Bernasco, W., Bowers, K. J., Elffers, H., Ratcliffe, J. H., Rengert, G. F., and Townsley, M. (2007). Space–time patterns of risk: A cross national assessment of residential burglary victimization. *Journal of Quantitative Criminology, 23*(3), 201–219.

Kleemans, E.R. (2001). Repeat burglary victimization: Results of empirical research in the Netherlands. In G. Farrell and K. Pease, (Eds.), *Repeat victimization, Crime Prevention Studies, Volume 12*, (pp. 53–68). Monsey, NY: Criminal Justice Press.

Laycock, G., and Farrell, G. (2003). Repeat victimization: Lessons for implementing problem-oriented policing. In J. Knutsson, (Ed.), *Problem-oriented policing: From innovation to mainstream, Crime Prevention Studies, Volume 16*, (pp. 213–248). Monsey, NY: Criminal Justice Press.

Levy, M.P., and Tartaro, C. (2010). Repeat victimization: A study of auto theft in Atlantic City Using the WALLS Variables to Measure Environmental Indicators. *Criminal Justice Policy Review, 21*(3), 296–318.

Lynch, J.P., Berbaum, M.L., and Planty, M. (1998). *Investigating repeated victimization with the NCVS, executive summary*. National Institute of Justice/NCJRS (See NCJ-193414).

Mawby, R.I. (2001). The impact of repeat victimization on burglary victims in East and West Europe. In G. Farrell and K. Pease, (Eds.), *Repeat victimization, Crime Prevention Studies, Volume 12*, (pp. 69–82). Monsey, NY: Criminal Justice Press.

Mele, M. (2009). The time course of repeat intimate partner violence. *Journal of Family Violence, 24*, 619–624.

Messman-Moore, T.L., and Long, P.L. (2000). Child sexual abuse and revictimization in the form of adult sexual abuse, adult physical abuse, and adult psychological maltreatment. *Journal of Interpersonal Violence, 15*(5), pp. 489–502.

Millie, A. (2008). Vulnerability and risk: Some lessons from the UK Reducing Burglary Initiative. *Police Practice and Research, 9*(3), 183–198.

Moffitt, T.E. (1997). Adolescence-limited and life-course persistent offending: A complementary pair of developmental theories. In T. Thornberry, (Ed.), *Developmental theories of crime and delinquency,* (pp. 11–54). New Brunswick, CT: Transaction Publishers.

Outlaw, M., Ruback, B., and Britt, C. (2002). *Repeat and multiple victimizations: The role of individual and contextual factors. Violence and victims, 17(2),* 187–204.

Pease, K. (1998). *Repeat victimisation: Taking stock.* Crime detection and prevention series, paper 90. London: Police Research Group.

Planty, M. & Strom, K.J. (2007). Understanding the role of repeat victims in the production of annual US victimization rates. *Journal of Quantitative Criminology, 23*(3), 179–200.

Ratcliffe, J.H., and McCullagh, M.J. (1998). Identifying repeat victimization with GIS. *British Journal of Criminology, 38(4),* 651–662.

Reiss, A.J., Jr. (1980). Victim proneness in repeat victimization by type of crime. In S.E. Feinberg and A.J. Reiss, Jr. (Eds.), *Indicators of crime and criminal justice: Quantitative studies.* Washington, D.C.: U.S. Department of Justice, Bureau of Justice Statistics.

Russell, M., and Light, L. (2006). Police and victim perspectives on empowerment of domestic violence victims. *Police Quarterly, 9*(4), 375–396.

Scott, M.S. (2003). Getting the police to take problem-oriented policing seriously. In J. Knutsson, (Ed.), *Problem-oriented policing: From innovation to mainstream, Crime Prevention Studies, Volume 16,* (pp. 49–77). Monsey, NY: Criminal Justice Press.

Short, M.B., D'Orsogna, M.R., Brantingham, P.J., and Tita, G.E. (2009). Measuring and modeling repeat and near-repeat burglary effects. *Journal of Quantitative Criminology, 25,* 325–339.

Sparks, R., Genn, H., and Dodd, D. (1977). *Surveying victims.* London: Wiley.

Taylor, G. (1999). Using repeat victimization to counter commercial burglary: The Leicester experience. *Security Journal,* 12(1), 41–52.

van Dijk, J.J.M. (2001). Attitudes of victims and repeat victims toward the police: Results of the International Crime Victims Survey. In G. Farrell and K. Pease, (Eds.), *Repeat victimization, Crime Prevention Studies, Volume 12,* (pp. 27–52). Monsey, NY: Criminal Justice Press.

Williams, B. (1999). *Working with victims of crime: Policies, politics and practice.* London: Jessica Kingsley Publishers.

Ybarra, L.M.R., and Lohr, S.L. (2002). Estimates of repeat victimization using the National Crime Victimization Survey. *Journal of Quantitative Criminology, 18*(1), 1–21.

CHAPTER 6

WHO IS SHE? THE INVISIBILIZATION AND DEHUMANIZATION OF BLACK WOMEN VICTIMIZED BY POLICE

Breea C. Willingham
PLATTSBURGH STATE UNIVERSITY OF NEW YORK

Kimberle Crenshaw asked the attendees of the *Race and Resistance: Against Police Violence* conference at UCLA Law School to stand and remain standing until she called a name they did not recognize. Crenshaw began her roll call: Mike Brown. Freddie Gray. Eric Garner. No one sat down. By the time Crenshaw finished saying the names of Black women — Sandra Bland. Rekia Boyd. Eleanor Bumpurs — only three of roughly 100 people remained standing. Crenshaw then asked, "How are you going to stand for justice when you don't even know their names?" This one-minute exercise painted a powerful illustration of the invisibility of Black women and girls who routinely fall victim to state-sanctioned violence. The three women Crenshaw named are only a small fraction of the more than 60 Black women and girls who have been killed or brutalized by police, or died under suspicious circumstances while incarcerated. They include:

Miyekko Durden-Bosley. LaTanya Haggerty. Eula Love. Margaret Mitchell. Chuniece Patterson. Brenda Williams. Barbara Lassere. Kyam Livingston. Keara Crowder. Jacqueline Nichols. Patricia Thompson. Vernicia Woodard. Martina Brown. Tyisha Miller. Janisha Fonville. Yvette Henderson. Eleanor Bumpurs. Darnisha Harris. Shelley Frey. Latandra Ellington. Natasha

McKenna. Alesia Thomas. Sheneque Proctor. Aura Rosser. Meagan Hocka-day. Erica Collins. Monique Jenee Deckard. Anna Brown. Sharmel Edwards. Karen Day Jackson. Michelle Cusseaux. Miriam Carey. Tanisha Anderson. Yvette Smith. Malissa Williams. Alberta Spruill. Shantel Davis. Rekia Boyd. Shereese Francis. Aiyana Stanley-Jones. Tarika Wilson. Kathryn Johnston. Kendra James. Marlene Pinnock. Rosan Miller. Pearlie Golden. Lucinda Batts. Alexia Christian. Venus Green. Starr Brown. Barbara Floyd. Sandra Bland. Ralkina Jones. Raynetta Turner. Joyce Curnell. Dajerria Becton. Jacqueline Allen. Denise Stewart. Sonji Danese Taylor. Danette Daniels. Frankie Perkins. Keyarika Diggles. Princola Shields. Dominique Worrell.

The #SayHerName movement, created by the African American Policy Fo-rum, has helped to bring more attention to the Black women victimized by police, but these women's experiences are still too often pushed so far into or deleted from the margins of society that their stories go unnoticed or are over-shadowed by those of Black men victims like Eric Garner and Mike Brown. Black men become the face of the racial and social justice movements while those of Black women are obliterated. The cases of Black men killed by police are certainly important, but these movements continually fail Black women while uplifting the causes of Black men.

Take, for instance, the story of 22-year-old Rekia Boyd. Boyd was killed by an off-duty Chicago police officer on March 21, 2012, in Chicago. She was walking with four friends when Detective Dante Servin got into a verbal al-tercation with one of her friends. According to media reports, Servin said he thought he saw one of the men in the group pull a gun from his pants and point it at him. Servin, claiming he feared for his life, fired five rounds over his left shoulder through his car window. One of the bullets hit Boyd, who was unarmed, in the back of the head. Police charged Servin with involuntary manslaughter; he was acquitted on April 20, 2015. On April 22, a rally orga-nized by Black Lives Matter New York in honor of Boyd and other Black women and girls killed by police drew a modest crowd of approximately 100 people, a pale comparison to the thousands who gathered in support of Mike Brown.

The purpose of this chapter is to critically examine Black women's experi-ences with state-sanctioned violence and find out why they are often neglected. The primary question I am seeking to answer is: Why do the cases of Black women and state-sanctioned violence go unnoticed? I argue that what is hap-pening with Black women and police violence is significantly more than simply ignoring these women's stories. Instead, it is a manifestation of the continued social exclusion of Black women. As Johnson (2003) contends in *Inner Lives: Voices of African American Women in Prison*, this exclusion "highlights the importance of narrative to inform and critique existing social structures, legal doctrine and embedded biases in institutions such as the criminal justice system" (p. 8). Further, hooks (1981) says in *Ain't I A Woman*, "No other group in America has so had their identification socialized out of existence as have Black women. When Black people are talked about, it's Black men. When women are talked about, it's white women" (p. 7).

As it particularly relates to Black women and police violence, Savali (2014) makes an important distinction in her article *Black women are killed by police, too*:

> It is understandable, though not acceptable, that Black women often find ourselves on the fringes of these conversations. Even when we are front and center it is usually to prove our fidelity to Black men and their unique struggles. Very seldom is the violence inflicted upon Black, female bodies by law enforcement positioned as pivotal to justice movements; rather our lived experiences as victims of the state tend to be peripheral and anecdotal (Savali, 2014, para. 9).

Black women's experiences with state-sanctioned violence is not a new phenomenon. The horrors of women and girls being brutalized by police that are playing out in social media are examples of modern-day lynchings. The tree has been replaced by white police officers with guns standing over dead Black bodies. Social media has become the platform for which voyeurs can view the lynchings instead of gathering in a crowd to gawk at Black bodies hanging from a tree. Social media has made police violence more visible in the same way the media made the brutality against Black people in the South salient to people in the North during the 1950s and 1960s. Perhaps what is most disturbing about these modern day lynchings is Black girls are under siege too. They are being seen as threats and treated as such, as seen in the McKinney, Texas, case when 15-year-old Dajerria Becton was slammed to the ground by a cop after which, she said, he pulled her hair and twisted her arm. The incident, caught on video that has gone viral, happened on June 5, 2015, after a fight broke out between white adults and Black teens during a graduation party at a community pool. Police claim after they showed up, partygoers refused to follow orders. The video shows McKinney police Cpl. Eric Casebolt yanking the bikini-clad Becton onto her stomach by her head then kneeling on her back with his right knee. Black girls are not even safe from police brutality in school, as evidenced by the Spring Valley High School incident on October 26, 2015 when Richland (S.C.) County Sheriff's Deputy Ben Fields grabbed the 16-year-old girl from her desk, slammed her to the floor, and dragged her across the classroom before handcuffing her. Fields has been fired.

Theoretical Framework

I use Black Feminist Thought and Black Feminist Criminology as my theoretical frameworks to provide relevant contexts for understanding the intersections of race and gender in the invisibilization of Black women and the role these oppressions play in their dehumanization. While this study is primarily about Black women's experiences with police violence, it is also about all Black women in America who continue to struggle with the multi-marginalizations associated with being a Black woman. These marginalizations require Black women to navigate the race, gender and class oppressions in a society that continues to relegate them to a social standing of non-existent.

In *Feminist Theory*, hooks (2000) argues that one of the flaws in feminist thought has been the assertion that all women are oppressed; it implies all women share common experiences with class, race, religion, sexuality and other oppressions, and there is no diversity in these experiences. Similarly, because criminal justice issues are still primarily viewed from a male's perspective, researchers, scholars, and activists tend to neglect to tell stories of women's experiences with the criminal justice system. As a result, the women's experiences are dismissed, leaving the impression the injustices committed against them are to be accepted or that the women are OK.

But there is a difference in how Black women experience these oppressions in the criminal justice system, so race needs to be critically examined in this context. Black feminist criticism grew, in part, from the notion that Black women's experiences were seen as deviant while those of Black men, white men and white women were regarded as the norm. Black women's experience is at the core of Black Feminist Thought; the overarching theme of Black feminist theories is the desire to find a voice that can express a self-defined Black women's standpoint. Collins (2004) defines Black Feminist Thought as specialized knowledge created by Black women, which clarifies the "experiences and ideas shared by Black women and provides a unique angle of vision on self, community and society" (p. 22) and which is situated in Black women's struggle against systems of oppression. However, in an important qualification, Collins (2004: 25) contends that while Black women may share similar challenges resulting from "living in a society that historically and routinely derogates" (p. 25) them, this does not mean that they have all had the same experiences. Simply acknowledging that a legacy of struggle exists does not make the meaning of the struggle the same for all Black women. In a similar context, Black feminist criminologist Hillary Potter argues that it is crucial to include race, sexuality and economic status into any examination of women's experiences with crime. Black feminist criminology, then, "extends beyond traditional feminist criminology to view African American women . . . from their multiple marginalized and dominated positions in society, culture, community and families" (Potter, 2006, p. 107). Potter further argues that,

> Although gender is certainly important and crucial to considering women's (and men's) involvement in crime either as victims or as offenders, for Black women, and arguably for all women, other inequities must be considered principal, not peripheral, to the analysis of women. This includes incorporating key factors such as race and/or ethnicity, sexuality, and economic status into any examination (p. 107).

Including Black women's experiences in the discourse about police violence authenticates their experiences with state-sanctioned violence. Furthermore, I argue that placing these women's experiences at the center of the discourse, and not treating them as an afterthought, constitutes a form of active Black feminism that seeks to respond to race, gender and sexual oppression of Black women, as well as address political and social topics.

METHOD

I began with a Google search of "Black women killed by police" and "Black women police violence" to find stories of shootings and assaults of Black women by police. I also asked some of my former journalism colleagues to search their newspaper archives for any related stories. The searches ultimately yielded 64 cases dating back to as early as 1984 to 2015. Finding these cases proved to be a challenge because law enforcement agencies typically do not keep track of police killings by gender and race. Websites such as www .mappingpoliceviolence.com and www.killedbypolice.net have started to keep track of these deaths. However, mappingpoliceviolence.com does not track by gender; killedbypolice.net tracks shootings by race and gender but only goes back as far as May 1, 2013. What was also challenging is because women's cases do not get as much media coverage as men's, the women's cases are not as easily accessible. This leads me to believe there are many more cases that have yet to be uncovered. Finally, it is important that I explain how my researcher positionality has impacted this study and created an unexpected challenge. I found myself identifying with the victims, not because I have been a victim of police violence, but as a Black woman, I am fully aware that the privileges of my Ph.D. do not leave me any less vulnerable to being shot, body slammed, kicked in the groin, choked, killed or raped by police. The May 2014 case of Arizona State University English Professor Ersula Ore serves as a stark reminder of this. Ore was walking home from classes on the evening of May 20 when campus police officer Stewart Ferrin stopped her, alleging she was in violation for walking in the middle of the street. A dash cam video shows a verbal altercation between Ore and Ferrin quickly escalated and resulted in Ferrin handcuffing and throwing Ore to the ground. Balancing the subjective and objective is why, according to Giddings (1984):

> For a Black woman to write about Black women is at once personal and an objective undertaking. It is personal because the women whose blood runs through my veins breathe amidst the statistics. . . . Writing such a book is also an objective enterprise because one must put such experiences into historical context, find in them a rational meaning so that the forces that shape our own lives may be understood (p. 5).

I navigated the hyphen between subjective-objective while writing this chapter, fully aware that being a Black woman means I can be killed or brutalized by a cop at any time for no justifiable reason, or found dead in a jail cell and my death written off as a suicide.

RESULTS

The website www.mappingpoliceviolence.com reports that more than 100 unarmed Black people were killed by police since 2014; six of them were Black women. According to a report by the Mint Press News Desk, out of the 776 people killed by police in 2015 (the latest number at the time of this writing), 745 were men and 161 unarmed. Though police killed more White than Black people, Black people are killed at a higher rate disproportionate to their population. For instance, police killed almost five Black people per every million Black residents in the United States in 2015, compared to 2 million for both White and Hispanic people (776 People Killed By Police, 2015, para. 5). Furthermore, the Center for Disease Control's cause-of-death data reveals that for more than 40 years, police killed Black people at disproportionate rates (as cited in Lee, 2014, para. 6).

> Between 1968 and 2011, Black people were between two to eight times more likely to die at the hands of law enforcement than whites. Annually, over those 40 years, a Black person was on average 4.2 times as likely to get shot and killed by a cop than a White person (Lee, 2014, para. 6).

While the numbers of Black women killed by police are not as high as those of Black men, women appear to be killed at similar rates as Black men. For instance, within a month (March-April 2012) three Black women were killed by police. Four Black men were killed by police in July-August 2014 and in July 2015, five Black women were found dead in jail cells in New York, Texas, Ohio and Alabama.

The women in this study were daughters, sisters, grandmothers, mothers of young children. Some suffered from mental illness, were victims of domestic violence or were collateral consequences of drug busts gone wrong. Their deaths are glaring reminders of how Black women have always been regarded as "less than," or simply disposable. As Malcolm X said in 1962, "The most disrespected person in America is the Black woman. The most unprotected person in America is the Black woman. The most neglected person in America is the Black woman." Through the use of anecdotal evidence, the remainder of this chapter will detail some of the ways in which Black women suffer from physical violence at the hands of police.

History Repeats Itself

The contemporary police violence perpetrated against Black women is rooted in the enforcement of such historical state-sanctioned practices as slave codes and Jim Crow segregation laws and is merely a reflection of the continual victimization of Black women at the hands of the state. I include this brief discussion in my analysis as historical context to illustrate the specific violence Black women have historically endured as subjects of terror or objects for white men, and how this violence is perpetuated in the same way today through interactions with police. The slave owner who beat and raped his enslaved Black women is today's White cop beating, killing and raping Black women. For instance, consider the case of former Oklahoma City police officer Daniel Holtzclaw who stood trial this fall for the rape and sexual assault of 13 Black women who, prosecutors said, Holtzclaw targeted because they are poor with criminal records. After four days of deliberation, the jury found Holtzclaw guilty on December 10 of 18 of the 36 charges, which included rape and sexual battery. Holtzclaw is scheduled to be sentenced on January 21; he faces up to 236 years in prison.

Given the historical context of Black women and rape, Tomlinson and the organizations Black Women's Blueprint and Women's All Points Bulletin (2014) conclude in their report *Invisible Betrayal: Police Violence and the Rapes of Black Women in the United States* that "the long-standing legacy and continued devaluing of Black women as legitimate victims of rape and assault generally compound Black women's continued victimization and likelihood to get a conviction against a police officer, no less" (Tomlinson, 2014, para. 10).

McGuire (2010) describes some of that legacy in her book *At the Dark End of the Street: Black Women, Rape, and Resistance — A New History of the Civil Rights Movement from Rosa Parks to the Rise of Black Power.* McGuire recounts stories of brutal sexual assaults police committed against Fannie Lou Hamer and other women of the Student Non-Violent Coordinating Committee after they were arrested at a rest stop in Winona, Mississippi, on June 9, 1963. "Once in custody, each activist received a savage and sexually abusive beating by the Winona police" (McGuire, 2010, p. 193).

The Association of Black Women Historians released a statement on July 28, 2015, admonishing today's state-sanctioned violence against Black women. In the announcement titled "ABWH Statement on the Modern-Day Lynching of Black Women in the U.S. Justice System," the group describes the deaths of Black women and girls as "a modern-day Red Record of anti-Black female violence" (Duncan et al., 2015, para. 3).

> From the earliest days in the colonies when laws failed to punish the rape of Black women, the antebellum era where Black women were brutally punished for resisting rapists-enslavers, to the post-emancipation period when the sexual and physical assault of Black women went unabated, and right up through the Civil Rights Movement, the judicial system failed us (Duncan et al., 2015, para. 2).

Black women's bodies were never meant to be protected primarily because they were considered property, not people. Slave owners often used the concept of seduction as a source of power. Rape was defined in the nineteenth century as the illegal "forcible carnal knowledge of a female against her will without consent," but as Hartman (1997) explains, this law did not apply to enslaved women. Instead, the concept of seduction was used to mask the actual violence committed against enslaved women. Any sexual relations between master and slave were assumed to be consensual bonds of affection, not crimes (Hartman, 1997, p. 86). Black women are also seen as threats and police are responding by physically attacking them. Several such cases happened in 2014. The July 1, 2014, brutal attack of 50-year-old Marlene Pinnock by California Highway Patrol Officer Daniel Andrew serves as a good example. The attack, caught on video, shows Andrew straddling and repeatedly punching Pinnock in her upper torso and head. On June 29, 2014, Clayton County, Georgia, off-duty officer Thomas Sheats followed 27-year-old Michele Griffith for several miles in a fit of road rage. When Griffith pulled into a parking lot at a pizza restaurant, Sheats reportedly spit in her face and called her a nigger. Even pregnant women are not off limits, as evidenced by the following four cases.

Nicola Robinson accused a Chicago police officer of punching her in her stomach on May 15, 2015, when she was eight months pregnant. In a Fox 32 News Chicago television interview, Robinson explained that she laughed at officers who were not able to catch a suspected drug a dealer they were chasing. Robinson said that's when one of the officers punched her on the right side of her stomach. The incident was caught on tape.

Charlena Michelle Cooks was also eight months pregnant when police assaulted her on January 26, 2015, at her daughter's elementary school in Barstow, California. The incident happened after a woman who works at the school told police Cooks "sped through the parking lot, cut her off then confronted her" (Lohr, 2015, para. 5). Two officers wrestled Cooks to the ground after she refused to give her name. Cooks is heard on the dash cam video screaming, "I'm pregnant. Please stop this."

Another video shows a New York City cop placing Rosan Miller in a chokehold on July 27, 2014, just ten days after Eric Garner died after another NYPD cop put him in a chokehold. According to a *New York Daily News* report, police alleged Miller was grilling on a public sidewalk and asked her to move the cookout to the back. The altercation happened after she asked officers why she had to move (Moore, 2014).

On September 18, 2009, Baltimore police hurled a pregnant Starr Brown to the ground following an argument between Brown and Officer Andrew Galletti. According to Brown's court testimony detailed in The Baltimore Sun's investigative report *Undue Force*, she grabbed the iron railing and screamed that she was pregnant. Galletti ignored her pleas, grabbed her arms and "slammed me down on my face. The skin was gone on my face.... I was tossed like a rag doll. He had his knee on my back and neck. [Officer Karen Crisafulli] had her knee on my back trying to put handcuffs on me." (Puente, 2014, paras. 61, 62) Brown was charged with obstruction, disorderly conduct, resisting arrest and assault, but a judge dismissed the charges. She sued in April 2010 and settled in March 2011 for $125,000.

"You promised you wouldn't kill me": Black Women Dying in Custody

When deputies dressed in hazmat suits and gas masks pulled 37-year-old Natasha McKenna from her Fairfax County jail cell, the first thing she said was, "you promised you wouldn't kill me." Officers tasered McKenna, who suffered from schizophrenia, four times while trying to restrain her so she could be transported to Alexandria. McKenna stopped breathing several minutes later; officers attempted CPR in the garage of the jail. McKenna died five days later at an area hospital. Fairfax County Sheriff Stacy Kincaid released the 48-minute video of the February 3, 2015, incident to, she said, show the officers followed procedure. The officers will not face criminal charges.

Seven other Black women have died in jails across the country following McKenna's death, all victims of apparent suicides. Princola Shields was less than a month away from being released from the Indiana Women's Prison when the 20-year-old was found unresponsive in her cell on September 22, 2015. Shields was due to be released on October 15 after serving nearly a year for battery, resisting arrest and disorderly conduct (Chan, 2014).

Officials at the Southern Correctional Institute in Troy, North Carolina, found 26-six-year-old Dominique Worrell hanging in her cell on August 26, according to North Carolina Department of Corrections officials. Worrell had been serving a four-year sentence for assault with a deadly weapon inflicting serious injury, felony breaking and entering and larceny following an incident at a Raleigh bar on September 29, 2014 (Overton, 2015).

Perhaps the most recognizable case happened on July 10, 2015, when 28-year-old Sandra Bland was arrested for failing to signal a lane change in Hempstead, Texas. Bland's case made national headlines after she was found hanging from a noose made of a plastic trash bag in her jail cell at the Waller County Jail, just three days after her arrest. The dashcam video of Bland's arrest released a week after her death shows Trooper Brian Encinia aiming a Taser at Bland and yelling, "I will light you up." Bland stepped out of her car and minutes later she can be heard telling Encinia, "You a real man now. You just slammed me, knocked my head into the ground. I have epilepsy . . . ," to which Encinia responds, "Good" (Ortiz, 2015).

Prior to her death, Bland spoke passionately and publicly about police brutality against Black people, and often posted to Facebook using the #SandySpeaks hashtag. In an April 8, 2015, video, Bland challenged White people to stand with Black people in the Black Lives Mater Movement. "At the moment, Black Lives Matter. I'm not calling all white people racist because y'all not, but for the ones who wanna get on my page talking about All Lives Matter, show me in American history where all lives have mattered."

The day after Bland's death, 18-year-old Kindra Chapman committed suicide in an Alabama prison. Ten days later, Joyce Curnell was found dead in her cell (Townes, 2015, para. 4). Ralkina Jones, who told Cleveland Heights officers "I don't want to die in your cell," (Danylko, 2015, para. 1) was found dead in the Cleveland Heights City Jail on July 26. The next day Raynetta Turner, a mother of eight, was found dead in a Mount Vernon jail cell after alerting officers of her hypertension and other health issues (Lewis, 2015, para. 2).

The fear of dying in jail is also evident in the 2014 case of Latandra Ellington. According to a report by the *Miami Herald*, Ellington, a 36-year-old mother of four, wrote her aunt a letter on September 21 describing how an officer at the Lowell Correctional Institution had threatened to beat and kill her. Ellington died 10 days later. An autopsy revealed she "suffered blunt-force trauma to her abdomen consistent with being punched and kicked in the stomach" (Brown & Klas, 2014, para. 5).

"I do not trust you!": Black Women's Fear of Police

On August 6, 2015, a video showing a White cop gripping the wrist of a Black woman and trying to pull her outside surfaced on social media. The woman had allegedly left her daughter and son in the car while she went inside a post office, and someone called the police. It is unclear in what city this happened or what the woman's name is, but the fear the woman exhibits is painstakingly obvious. The following is an excerpt from the 6:39 cell phone video recording:

The officer asks the woman to step outside and give him her identification. The woman refuses and he grabs her arm. The woman, pulling away, then says, "I'm not trying to attack you. I simply want to call my mom so she can come get my kids. That's all I want to do, sir. Can you let go of my arm, sir?" The officer begins to pull the woman towards the front door and she begs, "Please, sir! Get off of me," then screams, "I do not trust you! I do not trust you!"

The officer replies, "I know you don't." He continues to pull the woman towards the door; she continues to beg him to release her arm. "Get off of me! Get off of me!" she screams. Her children are crying and yelling, "Let go of my mom!"

This encounter happened just two-and-a-half weeks after Sandra Bland's death. This video represents an ominous reality: that a Black woman is afraid to step outside in broad daylight with a cop speaks volumes about the severity of the level of violence between Black women and police.

CONCLUSION

The relationship between society and Black women has always been a rapacious one grounded in a history of gendered injustices against Black women's bodies. Black women continue to battle the intersecting oppressions of race, gender and justice while living in a society that routinely derogates them. Black men are typically stereotyped as violent thugs while Black women are stigmatized as crazy, angry or sexually aggressive. The intersection of race and gender, as well as what Earl Ofari Hutchinson calls the "feminization of racial stereotyping" (Hutchinson, 2014, para. 4), contributes to the violence Black women experience at the hands of police and operates as a function of the systemic racism that permeates through the American injustice system.

The details of Black women's encounters with police that I have provided further illustrate the ways in which Black women are marginalized, thus contributing to their invisibility, and address how impossible it is for them to survive in a criminal justice system that not only victimizes them, but was not designed to protect them. Initiatives like #SayHerName are beginning to raise awareness about Black women's and girls' brutal encounters with police, but more advocating on their behalf needs to be done. The lack of attention to the police brutality against Black women not only reflects their history of social exclusion, it also sends two messages: one, in many cases police can get away with murder when it comes to Black women because the community often does not advocate for Black women victims the way they do for Black men and two, Black women remain vulnerable and unprotected by this nation's criminal justice system and their communities.

References

Brown, J., and Klas, M.E. (2014, October 7). Inmate reports threats by guard, turns up dead. Miami Herald. Retrieved from http://www.miamiherald .com/news/state/florida/article2564576.html

Chan, M. (2015, September 22). Indiana inmate, 20, dies of apparent suicide less than a month from prison release. *New York Daily News*. Retrieved from http://www.nydailynews.com/news/national/indiana-inmate-20 -dies-apparent-suicide-release-article-1.2370058

Collins, P. H. (2004). *Black feminist thought: Knowledge, consciousness and the politics of empowerment*. New York, NY: Routledge.

Danylko, R. (2015, August 10). 'I don't want to die in your jail cell': Police release video of Ralkina Jones taken prior to death. *Northeast Ohio Media Group*. Retrieved from http://www.cleveland.com/cleveland-heights/index .ssf/2015/08/i_dont_want_to_die_in_your_cel_1.html

Duncan, N., Garret-Scott, S., Gross, K. N., LeFlouria, T., Randolph, S.M., Simmons, L.M., and Williams, R.Y. (2015, July 28) *ABWH statement on the modern-day lynching of black women in the U.S. justice system.* Retrieved from http://www.abwh.org/index.php?option=com_content&view=category&layout=blog&id=3&Itemid=27

Hartman, S. (1997). *Scenes of subjection: Terror, slavery, and self-making in nineteenth-century America.* New York, NY: Oxford University Press.

hooks, b. (2000). *Feminist theory: From margin to theory.* (2nd Ed.) New York, NY: South End Press.

_____. (1981). *Ain't I a woman: Black women and feminism.* Cambridge, Mass.: South End Press.

Hutchinson, E. O. (2014, July 6). California highway patrol freeway beating casts ugly glare on assault of black women. *Huffington Post Black Voices.* Retrieved from http://www.huffingtonpost.com/earl-ofari-hutchinson/california-highway-patrol_b_5560090.html

Johnson, P.C. (2003). *Inner lives: Voices of African American women in prison.* New York, NY: New York University Press.

Killed by police. Retrieved from http://www.killedbypolice.net/

Lee, J. (2014, September 10). Here's the data that shows cops kill black people at a higher rate than white people. *Mother Jones.* Retrieved from http://www.motherjones.com/politics/2014/08/police-shootings-ferguson-race-data

Lewis, T. (2015, July 29). Black mother found in jail cell after alerting officials of her health problems. *Essence.* Retrieved from http://www.essence.com/2015/07/29/black-mother-found-dead-jail-cell-after-alerting-officials-health-problems

Lohr, D. (2015, May 28). Pregnant mom Charlena Cooks 'please stop' as cop wrestles her to the ground. *Huffington Post Crime.* Retrieved from http://www.huffingtonpost.com/2015/05/28/charlena-michelle-cooks_n_7461894.html

Mapping police violence. Retrieved from http://mappingpoliceviolence.org/aboutthedata/

McGuire, D. L. (2010). *At the dark end of the street: Black women, rape and resistance — a new history of the civil rights movement from Rosa Parks to the rise of black power.* New York, NY: Vintage Books.

Mint Press News Desk (2015, September 1). 776 people killed by police so far in 2015, 161 of them unarmed. *Mint Press News.* Retrieved from http://

www.mintpressnews.com/776-people-killed-by-police-so-far-in-2015-161
-of-them-unarmed/209127/

Moore, T. (2014, July 28). Pregnant woman apparently put in chokehold by NYPD cop during dispute over illegal grilling. *New York Daily News*. Retrieved from http://www.nydailynews.com/new-york/nyc-crime/pregnant -woman-apparently-put-chokehold-article-1.1882755

Ortiz, E. (2015, July 22). Newly released dashcam video shows Sandra Bland traffic stop. *NBC News*. Retrieved from http://www.nbcnews.com/news/us -news/newly-released-dashcam-video-shows-sandra-bland-arrest-n396191

Overton, R. (2015, August 26). Woman convicted in Raleigh sports bar stabbing found dead in NC prison. *WNCN News*. Retrieved from http://wncn .com/2015/08/26/raleigh-woman-found-dead-in-nc-prison/

Potter, H. (2006). An argument for black feminist criminology. *Feminist Criminology*, 2, 106–124.

Puente, M. (2014, September 28). Undue Force. *The Baltimore Sun*. Retrieved from http://data.baltimoresun.com/news/police-settlements/

Savali, K.W. (2014, August 18). Black women are killed by police, too. *Dame*. Retrieved from http://www.damemagazine.com/2014/08/18/black-women -are-killed-police-too

theGrio. (2015, May 19). Pregnant woman claims Chicago cop punched her in the stomach. *The Grio*. Retrieved from http://thegrio.com/2015/05/19/ pregnant-woman-chicago-cop-punched-stomach/ and https://www.you tube.com/watch?v=yySUN89I6Sw

Tomlinson, Y. M. S. (2014). *Invisible betrayal: Police violence and the rapes of black women in the United States*. Retrieved from http://www.ushrnetwork .org/sites/ushrnetwork.org/files/36-police-wapb.pdf

Townes, C. (2015, July 28). At least five black women found dead in jail since mid-July. *Think Progress*. Retrieved from http://thinkprogress.org/justice /2015/07/28/3685435/fourth-black-woman-found-dead-jail-cell-since -mid-july/

CHAPTER 7

Hate Crimes Victimization: A Legal Perspective

Stephanie Manzi and Kathleen Dunn
Roger Williams University

Introduction: Defining Hate Crime

A hate crime is a criminal offense, e.g., assault, murder, vandalism, that is *motivated by the perpetrator's bias* against some group, identified by race, religion, ethnic origin, disability, sexual orientation, or gender identity; and the victim's real or perceived membership in that group. Hate crimes can be perpetrated against people and property. Hate crime victims can be individuals, businesses, institutions, or society in general.

Because hate crimes are motivated by prejudice toward an entire group of people, these crimes have the potential to impact more victims and inflict greater harm than crimes not motivated by such bigotry. Hate crimes are far more likely to involve assaults than other crimes. Such hate-motivated assaults are also significantly more likely to result in serious bodily harm to the victim (Meli, 2014). Moreover, a bias crime assaults a victim's very identity, stigmatizing him or her, causing emotional harm, and creating a sense of vulnerability that is greater than that created in victims of crimes not motivated by such prejudice. Also, the harm caused by hate crimes is not limited to the direct victim or victims. In a very real sense, hate crime victimizes all members of the group targeted by the bias-motivated perpetrator. Members of the "target community" will not only empathize with the victim, but may even perceive the crime as a personal threat or attack. Finally, hate crime victimizes society as a whole in that it may incite violence and threaten the security of entire groups of individuals, thereby undermining society's interest in preserving the peace and protecting its citizens from harm. Thus, bias crimes are distinguishable from non-bias motivated rimes both in terms of the perpetrator's motivation, and the nature and extent of harm caused by such crimes (Meli, 2014; Lawrence, 1999).

HATE CRIME VICTIMIZATION: MEASURING HATE CRIME

By the late 1980s twenty-four states had enacted laws addressing the problem of hate crime. Congress then enacted the first federal mandate, the Hate Crimes Statistics Act of 1990 (HCSA), requiring the Attorney General to establish guidelines and collect data on "crimes that manifest evidence of prejudice based on race, religion, sexual orientation or ethnicity." Prior to the enactment of the HCSA, no official national hate crime data existed. The goal of the HCSA was to gather information on hate crimes, including the nature of a given offense, the type of bias motivating the offender, and the number and types of victims and offenders. Data collection was to begin in the calendar year 1990 and continue for four years, under the purview of the Federal Bureau of Investigation (FBI) and its Uniform Crime Report (UCR) program.

During the past several years the criteria used by participating law enforcement agencies to submit hate crime data has been changed. The most significant changes follow the passage of the Matthew Shepard and James Byrd, Jr., Hate Crimes Prevention Act of 2009. This Act expands data collection to crimes motivated by gender (male and female) bias and gender identify (transgender and gender nonconforming) bias, hate crimes committed by or against a juvenile, and expands the categories for sexual orientation bias, race and ethnicity, making each category more exhaustive.

The Uniform Crime Report

The FBI's Uniform Crime Report Program compiles reported offenses from more than 18,000 law enforcement agencies nationwide. Each month participating agencies aggregate the number of Index and Non-Index Offenses that have been reported, the number of offenses that have been cleared, and the characteristics of individuals who have been arrested in connection with those offenses (FBI, 2015a). Since 1992 the UCR has included a supplemental report, *Hate Crime Statistics* that chronicles hate crime incidents reported to law enforcement agencies. For UCR purposes, a hate crime incident is defined as an act "motivated by offenders' bias against race, gender, gender identity, religion, disability, sexual orientation, and ethnicity" (FBI, 2015b). A bias crime is recorded only when an investigation reveals "sufficient objective facts to lead a reasonable and prudent person to conclude the offenders' actions were motivated, in whole or in part, by bias" (FBI, 1999).

Collection data differentiate between single bias and multiple bias incidents. A single bias incident occurs when "one or more offense types within the incident are motivated by the same bias." A multiple bias incident occurs when "more than one offense type occurs in the incident and at least two offense types are motivated by a different bias" (FBI, 2005b).

In 2014, eighty-four percent of the law enforcement agencies submitting data to the UCR Program included, in their reports, one to twelve months of hate crime data. Of these 15,494 agencies, 1,666 jurisdictions submitted bias-motivated incident reports for examination. These data indicate that 5,479 hate crime incidents, involving 6,418 offenses occurred; of these, 5,462 represented single-bias incidents, while only seventeen were classified as multiple-bias incidents. The majority of offenses (3,303) were committed against persons or society, with the remaining committed against property. Intimidation and the destruction, damaging or vandalizing of property ranked as the highest reported crimes (25.5% and 31%, respectively), followed by simple assault (24%) and aggravated assault (11%) (FBI, 2015b).

The majority (48.3%) of reported single–bias hate crimes were motivated by racial bias. Within racially motivated offenses, the majority (63.5%) were motivated by bias towards blacks, while approximately twenty-three percent were motivated by bias towards whites, five percent by bias towards American Indians/Alaskan natives, four percent by bias towards multi-racial individuals, and less than one percent by bias towards Native Hawaiian or other Pacific Islander.

The remainder of the reported single-bias hate crimes was motivated by religion (17.1%), sexual orientation (18.4%), ethnicity (12.4%), and disability (1.5%). Of hate crimes motivated by religious bias, the majority (58.2%) of the 1,092 reported offenses were motivated by bias toward Jews, with the remainder motivated by bias towards Muslims (16.3%), Catholics (6.1%), Protestants (2.6%), other religions (11%), multiple religions (4.7%), and atheists or agnostics (less than 1%) (FBI, 2015b).

The majority (60.1%) of crimes based on sexual orientation was motivated by bias towards male homosexuals, with approximately fourteen percent motivated by bias towards homosexuals in general, fourteen percent by bias towards female homosexuals, two percent by bias towards heterosexuals and slightly more than two percent by bias towards bisexuals. Of the 109 crimes based on gender identity, approximately sixty-three percent were motivated by bias towards transgender individuals. Approximately thirty-seven percent were motivated by bias towards those who identify as 'gender non-conforming' (FBI, 2015b).

Forty-eight percent of the 790 offenses motivated by ethnicity or nationality were motivated by bias towards Hispanics or Latinos, and fifty-two percent by bias towards some other ethnicity or nationality. Of the very small number of offenses (95) motivated by bias towards those with disabilities, approximately twenty-seven percent were motivated by bias toward individuals with physical disabilities and almost seventy-three percent by bias towards individuals with mental disabilities (FBI, 2015b).

For the seventeen multiple bias incidents no further breakdowns are available because they include more than on offense type and/or motivation by two or more biases (FBI, 2015b).

Although the FBI's UCR program remains the main conduit for collecting hate crime data, an additional system of data collection, the National Crime Victimization Survey which is sponsored by the Bureau of Justice Statistics, has been collecting data on crimes motived by hate since 2003. The main difference between the two data sources is that the UCR collects data on crimes known to the police while the NCVS collects data on crimes that are known to the police as well as those that go unreported to the police.

The National Crime Victimization Survey (NCVS)

The National Crime Victimization Survey (NCVS) is an annual data collection in which interviewed persons are asked to self-report the number and characteristics of victimization within a sixth month time frame. Respondents, who must be 12 years of age or older, come from a national representative sample of households from within the United States. Data is collected on five nonfatal personal crimes and three household property crimes, which may or may not have been reported to a law enforcement agency (Bureau of Justice Statistics, 2014).

For 2012, it was reported that 1.2% of all victimizations and 4.2% of violent victimizations were hate crimes. Victims' perception of the offender's bias in hate crimes was 51% based on ethnicity, 46% based on race, 27% based on religion, 26% based on gender, 13% based on sexual orientation, and 11% based on disability. Victims of the violent hate crime victimization tend to be male, white, between the ages of 12 and 17, and live in a household with an annual income of $24,999 or less. A more detailed examination shows that in 2011, white non-Hispanics, black non-Hispanics, and Hispanics shared similar violent hate crime victimizations rates. However, in 2012, Hispanics experienced higher ratios of victimization than whites and a slightly higher rate than blacks. Also, the rates of violent hate crime victimization increased for persons ages 18 to 24 and 50 to 64 (Bureau of Justice Statistics, 2014).

Offender characteristics, as reported by victims, show that the majority of violent hate crimes are committed by a single offender, males, those 30 years of age and older, and by someone known to the offender Victims also reported that their offender had a weapon in at least 24% of the violent hate crime victimizations. Approximately 60% of hate crime victimizations were not reported to the police (Bureau of Justice Statistics, 2014).

Limitations of Hate Crime Data Collection Methods

Concerns with the accuracy of hate crimes statistics, for both the UCR and NCVS, stem from two general sources, victim reporting and law enforcement reporting. Regarding victim reporting, research indicates that victims of hate crimes may not report their victimization for several reasons, including fear of reprisal by the offender, embarrassment, or a belief that the police are unable to do anything. Crime victims may also experience difficulty recalling significant details of an incident, undermining the chances of apprehending an offender. Victims may not recognize that hate was the motive in the crime committed against them, and may not be aware that bias motivation may be a factor in determining how an offense is handled (Bureau of Justice Assistance, 2000, Shively, 2005).

Law enforcement agencies face several barriers to the accurate reporting of hate crime data. State-by-state variations in hate crime statutes, collection efforts, reporting provisions and law enforcement training result in uneven reporting across jurisdictions and wide variation in the quality of data collected. Moreover, the lack of consensus across law enforcement agencies regarding the legitimacy of treating hate crimes as distinct offenses means that some officers may be unable to recognize a hate crime, and some may be reluctant to acknowledge the role of hate as the motivation for an offense (Shively, 2005).

Despite these limitations, existing hate crime data reveal certain patterns regarding the nature of hate crime in this country. Most hate crime is motivated by racial bias, particularly bias against black Americans. Other important types of bias are religious bias, primarily against Jews; ethnic bias, primarily against Hispanics; and bias based on sexual orientation, primarily against male homosexuals. These patterns help to explain why bias crime legislation has taken the form that it has in the United States.

HATE CRIME LEGISLATION

In 1998, James Byrd, Jr., an African-American man, was murdered by three white men, in Jasper, Texas. Byrd was kidnapped, beaten, tied to the back of a truck and dragged for three miles, before he was decapitated. His body was left in front of an African-American church. The three men were convicted of Byrd's murder; two were sentenced to death, and the third was sentenced to life in prison (Temple-Raston, 2002). A few months later, Matthew Shepard, a university student, was tortured and murdered by two men in Laramie, Wyoming, because he was gay. The two assailants were convicted of Shepard's murder, and received life sentences (Kaufman, 2001). None of the defendants were charged with hate crime because, at that time, neither Texas nor Wyoming had enacted hate crime legislation. Both cases impacted greatly the development of federal and state hate crime legislation.

Federal Law

In 2009, Congress found (1) that "the incidence of violence motivated by the actual or perceived race, color, national origin, gender, sexual orientation, gender identity, or disability of the victim poses a serious national problem;" (2) that "such violence disrupts the tranquility and safety of communities and is deeply divisive;" and (3) that "a prominent characteristic of a violent crime motivated by bias is that it devastates not just the actual victim and the friends of the victim, but frequently savages the community sharing the traits that caused the victim to be selected" (18 U.S. Code § 249).

Based, in part, on these findings, The Matthew Shepard and James Byrd, Jr., Hate Crimes Prevention Act of 2009 was passed by Congress, and signed into law by President Barack Obama. The Act provides funding and technical assistance to state, local and tribal jurisdictions to assist in the investigation and prosecution of hate crimes. The Act also makes it a federal crime to cause willful bodily injury, or to attempt, with the use of a firearm or other dangerous weapon, to cause willful bodily injury to any person, because of the actual or perceived religion, national origin, gender, sexual orientation, gender identity, or disability of any person (18 U.S. Code §249).

State Laws

Because states have jurisdiction over most criminal matters, the vast majority of criminal offenses that are prosecuted as hate crimes are prosecuted under state law. Today, nearly every state has some form of legislation that targets bias-motivated criminal conduct. Forty-five states have enacted statutes that enhance penalties for bias-motivated crimes (Meli, 2014). States still vary substantially in terms of which groups are protected by hate crime statutes. All state laws protect victims selected on the basis of race, ethnicity, national origin, and religion. Some protect victims selected on the basis of sexual orientation, gender, disability, and gender identity. Although the general trend is towards the expansion of groups protected under state laws (Meli, 2014), some groups, for instance the transgendered community, remain largely outside the protection of hate crime laws.

CONSTITUTIONALITY OF HATE CRIME LEGISLATION

A conviction in a hate crime case requires that the prosecution prove beyond a reasonable doubt that the defendant committed the underlying criminal offense, *and* that the defendant was motivated to commit the crime and/or selected his victim(s), based on his bias against a protected group. Proving a defendant's bias motivation is typically more difficult than proving that she committed the underlying crime. Often the best evidence of bias motivation is the defendant's own *expression* of prejudice or hate toward the target group. And, it is well-settled that the First Amendment protects hateful and offensive speech *Cohen v. California*, 403 U.S. 15 (1971). Thus, legal challenges to the constitutionality of hate crime laws are often grounded primarily in First Amendment principles governing freedom of expression.

In *Wisconsin v. Mitchell*, 509 U.S. 476 (1993), a nineteen-year-old black man directed several other young black men to attack a fourteen-year-old white boy, stating, "There goes a white boy, go get him." The victim suffered serious bodily injuries. Mitchell was convicted of aggravated assault, with a maximum penalty of two years. Wisconsin's bias crime statute, however, provided for a maximum penalty of seven years for aggravated battery, if the perpetrator intentionally selected his victim based on race, religion, color, disability, sexual orientation, national origin or ancestry. Because the jury found that Mitchell had intentionally selected his victim based on the boy's race, the court enhanced Mitchell's sentence to four years imprisonment.

Mitchell challenged the statute, contending that the law violated his First Amendment rights, by punishing bigoted and offensive thought. The Court upheld the bias crime law, reasoning that the statute targets for enhancement bias-inspired *conduct*, i.e., intentional selection of a victim. The Court also noted that such conduct has the potential to "provoke retaliatory crimes, inflict distinct emotional harm on victims, and incite community unrest"; and that "[t]he State's desire to redress these perceived harms provides an adequate explanation for its penalty-enhancement provision over and above mere disagreement with offenders' beliefs or biases" *Wisconsin v. Mitchell* at 487.

In *Virginia v. Black*, 538 U.S. 343 (2003), the Court considered the constitutionality of a state statute making it unlawful "for any person . . . , with the intent of intimidating any person or group . . . , to burn . . . a cross on the property of another, a highway or other public place." The law bans *all* cross burnings that are intended to intimidate, regardless of the race, ethnicity or religion of the victim. The law was challenged by defendants from two separate cases. One defendant, a Ku Klux Klan leader, had been found guilty of burning a cross at a Klan rally in a privately-owned open field; two other defendants had been found guilty of attempting to burn a cross on the yard of an African-American neighbor.

The Court upheld the law, reasoning that the state prohibition on cross burning targets, not hateful speech, but "a particularly virulent form of intimidation," that is unprotected by the First Amendment. Indeed, without the intent to intimidate, cross burning, arguably a racist, hateful, offensive undertaking, is constitutionally protected expression. The mere act of cross burning does not satisfy the intent requirement; and the jury may not infer the intent to intimidate from the mere act cross burning. To satisfy the First Amendment, the state has the burden of proving the intent to intimidate beyond a reasonable doubt.

These cases establish the importance of drafting legislation that avoids criminalizing even hateful, offensive beliefs and speech; and instead targets bias-motivated conduct, or expressive conduct that is intended to intimidate.

Emerging Issues in Hate Crime Legislation

Sexual Orientation and Gender Identity

Recently released hate crime statistics for 2014 reflect an overall decrease in reported hate crimes. That same report, however, reveals a threefold increase in bias-motivated violence and threats against transgender and non-gender conforming persons, with thirty-one such incidents reported in 2013, and ninety-eight incidents reported in 2014 (FBI, 2014; FBI, 2015b). Many trans-right activists suspect that the real numbers may be much higher.

Yet despite the disturbing increase in crime against members of the transgendered community, only fifteen (15) states, along with the District of Columbia and the federal government, have enacted hate crime laws that encompass crimes motivated by bias based on gender identity. The expansion of hate crime legislation to encompass protection for transgendered and non-gender conforming individuals is likely to be at the forefront of future discussions on hate crime legislation (National Gay and Lesbian Task Force, 2013).

Anti-Muslim Hate Crime

Bias motivated incidents against Muslims represent another category of hate crime that has increased notably in recent years. Before September 11, 2001, the UCR typically reported twenty to thirty anti-Muslim hate crimes annually. In 2002, that number spiked dramatically to over four hundred eighty incidents. Since that time, the numbers have levelled to between one hundred sixty and one hundred eighty per year — still approximately five to six times greater than pre-9/11 rates. (FBI, 2015b).

UCR statistics are not yet available for 2015. There is anecdotal evidence, however, of a sharp increase in crimes against Muslims, mosques and Muslim-owned businesses, most notably following the terrorist attack by ISIS in November in Paris, and the attack by a radicalized Muslim couple in December in San Bernardino, California. Anti-Muslim hate crime appears likely to be of significant concern for the foreseeable future.

Conclusion

Bias crimes are unique both in terms of the perpetrator's motivation, and the nature and extent of harm caused by such crimes. The perpetrator of a bias crime is motivated by bias toward her victim, based on that victim's real or perceived membership in a group identifiable by certain immutable traits, such as race, religion, national origin, disability, sexual orientation, or gender identity. Hate crime inflicts unique harm on its direct victims, on the group targeted by the bias-motivated perpetrator, and indeed on society as a whole.

Statistics indicate that hate crime is a significant problem in this country. Legislation has been enacted at the federal and state levels to address the problem of hate crime. This legislation has withstood challenges, with the Court concluding that the Constitution permits the criminalization and punishment of bias-motivated criminal conduct; and that such laws are justified due to the nature and extent of harm created by bias-motivated crimes.

Much work remains to be done to combat hate crime in this country. Legislation must expand to encompass still unprotected groups; and an environment must be created that encourages victims to report instances of hate crime, police to investigate those reports, states to prosecute those charged with hate crimes, and courts to punish those convicted of hate crimes.

References

Bureau of Justice Assistance. (2000). Addressing hate crimes: Six initiatives that are enhancing the efforts of criminal justice practitioners. Washington, DC: U.S. Government Printing Office.

Bureau of Justice Statistics. (2014). Hate crime victimization, 2004–2012 statistical tables. Washington, DC. Retrieved January 2, 2016 from http://www.bjs.gov/index.cfm?ty=pbdetail&iid=4883.FBI (2015a). Crime in the United States, 2014. Washington, DC: U.S. Government Printing Office. Retrieved January 2, 2016 from https://www.fbi.gov/stats-services/crime stats.

FBI (2015a). About the Uniform Crime Report (UCR) Program. Washington, DC: U.S. Government Printing Office. Retrieved January 12, 2016 from https://www.fbi.gov/about-us/cjis/ucr/crime-in-the-u.s./2014

FBI (2015b). Hate crime statistics, 2014. Washington, DC: U.S. Government Printing Office. Retrieved January 2, 2016 from https://www.fbi.gov/stats -services/crimestats.

FBI (2014). Hate crime statistics, 2013. Washington, DC: U.S. Government Printing Office. Retrieved January 12, 2016 from https://www.fbi.gov/stats -services/crimestats.

FBI (1999). Hate crime data collection guidelines. Washington, DC: U.S. Government Printing Office.

Kaufman, M. (2001). The Laramie Project, New York: Vintage Books.

Lawrence, F.M. (1999). Punishing hate: Bias crime laws under American law, Cambridge: Harvard University Press.

Meli, L. (2014). Hate Crime and Punishment: Why Typical Punishment Does Not Fit The Crime. 2014 U. Ill. L. Rev. 921.

National Gay and Lesbian Task Force. (2013). Hate Crime Laws in the United States.

Temple-Raston, D. (2002). A Death in Texas: A Story of Race, Murder, and a Small Town's Struggle for Redemption. New York, Henry Holt.

Statutes

18 U.S. Code §249 — The Matthew Shepard and James Byrd, Jr. Hate Crimes Prevention Act of 2009

Cases

Virginia v. Black, 538 U.S. 343 (2003)

Wisconsin v. Mitchell, 508 U.S. 476 (1993)

Cohen v. California, 403 U.S. 15 (1971)

CHAPTER 8

CHILD FATALITY: AN OVERVIEW OF ESSENTIAL FACTS AND INVESTIGATIVE TECHNIQUES FOR UNDERSTANDING UNDERREPORTED VICTIMIZATION

Robyn McDougle and Carolyn J. Zeppa
VIRGINIA COMMONWEALTH UNIVERSITY

INTRODUCTION

Of all aspects of personal crime, victimization of children is one of the least documented concentrations (USDOJ, 1998). Researchers, physicians, mental health workers and law enforcement personnel know much less about the extent, nature and ramifications of child victimization than those regarding adults (Bower, 1996). There is a lack of comprehensive statistical data regarding child victimization and fatality, which narrows the scope of research to include limited types of victimization such as sudden infant death syndrome and accidental death (Bower, 1996). One of the few sources of nationwide data is specifically about child maltreatment and is compiled by the U.S. Department of Health and Human Services (DHHS) Children's Bureau, currently in its 24th edition. The economic burden of child maltreatment is significant, estimated at a total lifetime economic burden of $124 billion resulting from new cases of fatal and nonfatal child maltreatment in the United States (Fang, Brown, Florence, and Mercy, 2012). Both the economic and the emotional costs of child victimization should be cause for concern. Until the last decade, child victimization data were all but ignored within the research community, which grossly underestimates the burden of victimizations that children experience as well as the interpersonal relationships within differing types of victimizations (Finkelhor, Ormrod, Turner, and Hamby, 2005).

UNDERSTANDING CHILD VICTIMIZATION

In recent years, overall rates of child victimizations have declined from over a million victims to 679,000, although many cases still go unreported. While victimization rates have decreased from 9.3 to 9.1 per 1,000 children from 2009 to 2013, the rates of children visited by child protective services (CPS) agencies has increased from 3 million to 3.18 million (DHHS, 2015). Child victimizations are a major societal problem nationwide. Over 12,000 children in the United States, ages 0–19, die as a result of unintentional injuries (Borse, Gilchrist, Dellinger, Rudd, Ballesteros, and Sleet, 2008) while 1,740 children ages 0–19 were victims of violent crime homicides in 2014 (Federal Bureau of Investigation (FBI), 2015). In the last two decades, homicide rates of victims ages 0–19 have fallen by almost half, from 3,165 reported in 1996 to 1,740 in 2014 (FBI, 1996, 2015). In a national study, Finkelhor and colleagues found that one half of children and youth experienced a physical assault in the span of a year, one in eight suffered some form of maltreatment, one in twelve were sexually assaulted, and over a third witnessed or experienced another form of indirect victimization (Finkelhor et al, 2005). Further determination state that only 29 percent of children had not experienced a direct or indirect victimization (Finkelhor et al, 2005).

As a result, a considerable proportion of infant and child fatalities are preventable. An estimated 1,520 children died from abuse or neglect in 2013. Of these deaths, 79.5 percent of the children had experienced neglect and 18 percent experienced physical abuse (DHHS, 2015). However, these numbers may not reflect the actual numbers since many child fatalities are misreported. The misreporting that occurs makes understanding true levels of childhood victimization difficult for both academics and practitioners alike. As a result, effective coordination of data collection within the individual departments and jurisdictions associated with handling child deaths, as well as other agencies providing family, community-based service to children, and their families, must occur if one hopes to acquire a greater understanding of the size of the victimization phenomenon.

Child Fatality Victims: An Overview

Over twenty-six percent of children that die as a result of a homicide are 4 years old or younger, 8 percent are between the ages of five and twelve, 15.6 percent are between the ages of thirteen and sixteen, and almost 50 percent of child homicide victims are adolescents between the ages of seventeen and nineteen (FBI, 2015). While it is evident that older adolescents make up the majority of homicide victims, a staggering 26 percent of victims are 4 years old or younger and these rates only include homicide victims of violent crimes included in the Federal Bureau of Investigation's Uniform Crime Report (FBI UCR). According to DHHS, 1,520 children are estimated to die from abuse or neglect with 73.9 percent of this number occurring in children under the age of three (DHHS, 2015). Maltreatment fatality rates for boys are higher than those of girls, at 2.36 per 100,000 children versus 1.77 per 100,000 children comparatively. Additionally, fatality rates generally decrease in both males and females as the children increase in age.

Violent crime victimization rates do not differ by race in a simple pattern and are not consistent over time. Race and ethnicity maintain an inconsistent association within varying forms of victimization. Victimizations such as aggravated physical assault, sexual assault, and child maltreatment do not vary considerably across racial and ethnic lines (Finkelhor et al, 2005). However, most recent statistics indicate that rates are highest for non-Hispanic American Indian/Alaska Native and non-Hispanic Black children with rates of 47.6 per 100,000 and 37.3 per 100,000 respectively (DHHS, 2014). Additionally, African-American children have slightly higher rates of property-related victimizations and experiencing indirect victimization through witnessing violent events. Similarly, White and Hispanic children have higher rates of assaults without injury and assaults by a sibling. Hispanic children are also more likely to suffer from sexual assault, sexual harassment and family abduction (Finkelhor et al, 2005).

Child Fatality Perpetrators: An Overview

One or more parents consistently cause about 80 percent of child fatalities while the mother alone perpetrates 31 percent of those fatalities (DHHS, 2015). Mothers are more likely to be perpetrators of neglect fatalities while fathers are more likely to perpetrate physical abuse (Klevens and Leeb, 2010). Non-parental perpetrators, almost always known to the victim/family, such as family members, foster parents, or legal guardians, are responsible for 17 percent of fatalities. Also important to consider is the fact that investigative procedures determined that the non-parental perpetrators were the male partner of the child's parent in 2.9 percent of the occurrences (DHHS, 2015). The remaining 4.2 percent is attributed to "unknown."

CATEGORIES OF CHILD FATALITIES

Based on the examination of both victims and perpetrators of child fatalities, such events are usually classified in one of the following five categories: Sudden Infant Death Syndrome (SIDS), child abuse, accidental, suicide or homicide. Each of the five fatality categories is unique in their definition, criteria and investigative techniques.

Sudden Infant Death Syndrome

Four thousand infants die of Sudden Infant Death Syndrome (SIDS) each year (Goldstein, Trachtenberg, Sens, Harty, and Kinney, 2016). A baby is considered a neonate from birth to twenty-eight days; thereafter it is an infant from twenty-eight days to one year old. Currently, SIDS is defined as the sudden, unexpected death of an infant less than one year of age, which remains unexplained after the complete post-mortem investigation, including autopsy, examination of the death scene, and a review of case history. SIDS deaths are diagnoses of exclusion. SUDI (sudden unexpected death in infancy) is a slightly different classification that occurs when the forensic autopsy shows a finding in which something in the vicinity of the dead infant could have contributed to the death, but the medical examiner is unable to associate it directly with the death. The typical SIDS case is that of a well-cared-for infant between one and six months of age that is placed in bed with no known health conditions and found unresponsive several hours later. Occasionally, the parent or caregiver may state that the infant exhibited mild cold symptoms, yet the autopsy is likely to reveal no adequate cause of death. In most SIDS cases, the autopsy will reveal petechial hemorrhaging and/or pulmonary congestion. SIDS deaths are often misinterpreted with those of children that have been abused. In the last three decades there has been a 71.3 percent decline in SIDS-related deaths, most notably linked to Back-to-Sleep programs promoted by the Academy of Pediatrics and the National Institute of Child Health and Development in the mid 1990s (Goldstein et al, 2016).

Abused Children

This year alone over one million children will suffer some form of abuse in the United States, and of those, 1,000 children will die as of a result. Investigations of abused children are challenging for police personnel due to the difficulty in determining differences between battered children and children that are simply injured and/or killed due to household accidents. In most cases, signs of abuse are documented from birth. This abuse is physical, emotional, neglect or sexual assault. In 2013, there were an estimated 1,520 child fatalities due to abuse and/or neglect (DHHS, 2015), although these numbers are still believed to be underreported. Child abuse and neglect fatalities have decreased slightly according to recent data, showing an estimated 23,000 fewer victims in 2013 (679,000) compared with 2009 (702,000) (DHHS, 2015). Natural parents commit and average of 80 percent of all sexual assaults on children, and make up 80 percent of perpetrators of child fatalities due to abuse and/or neglect (DHHS, 2015). While previous data has shown an increase in child deaths (Child Welfare Information Gateway, 2004), this was most likely due to the advancement in reporting procedures rather than an increase in fatal victimizations.

In case of child battering, common circumstances include unexplained illness or injury, repeated physical abuse, abuse of a parent or caretaker, delay or failure to report injuries, and misleading statements by the abuser to medical attendants. Investigators are likely to notice a variety of external and internal injuries on children that have died from abuse. The external injuries noted by the police investigator may include burns, abrasions, bruises of differing ages, and lacerations of the frenulum (forehead) and bite marks. Internal injuries noted by the medical examiner include head injuries (which are the most common cause of death), abdominal injuries, and skeletal injuries including multiple rib fractures, long bone injuries and avulsion of the metaphyses (soft tissue torn from the bone). In a recent study by Klevens and Leeb of 600 child maltreatment fatality cases, two-thirds of the 600 cases were the result of Abusive Head trauma (AHT). AHT fatalities are most often perpetrated by fathers, leading the researchers to suggest AHT interventions that target fathers in particular (Klevens and Leeb, 2010).

Accidental Death

Among children ages 1–4, accidental deaths (unintentional injuries) are the leading cause of death at 8 deaths per 100,000 children (Forum on Child and Family Statistics, 2015). The most common type of accidental death among children results from motor vehicle accidents. In many case, children are un-restrained while riding inside a motor vehicle. With the increased number of sport utility vehicles on the roadways, there are an increasing number of deaths due to backing over a child. These larger vehicles increase blind spots and limit areas of vision that attribute to these heightened rates. Out of 496 vehicle incidents with 589 children involved, there were 194 fatalities resulting from vehicle accidents, 49 percent of which were from backing over a child (Fennell, 2005). Overall, motor vehicle traffic death rates declined between 1980 and 2013 by more than 70 percent (Forum on Child and Family Statistics, 2015).

Suicide

The rate of suicide among children ranging between 10 and 14 years old has dramatically increased in the past two decades. Suicide is currently the second leading cause of death for adolescents ages 10 to 14, as well as for high school and college-aged youth (Center for Disease Control and Prevention, 2014). Research shows that in across 26 industrialized countries, over 50 percent of child suicides occurred among U.S. children. According to the Center for Disease Control and Prevention (CDC), the suicide rate for children in the United States was two times higher than that in the other 25 countries combined (0.55 compared with 0.27). The CDC also reports that suicide rates differ among boys and girls, with boys being more likely to die from suicide and girls being more likely to report a suicide attempt. As of 2015, reported suicides in the 10 to 24 age group were comprised of 81% of the deaths were males and 19% were females. Native American/Alaskan Native youth were reported as having the highest rates of suicide-related fatalities. Since 1990, there has been a small decline in global teenage suicide rates with an average of 8.4 suicides per 100,000 teenagers were observed in 1990, a rate of 6.2 suicides per 100,000 teenagers was observed in 2008 (Organization for Economic Co-operation and Development, 2011). In most cases of child suicide, the event occurs in the home. In many cases, the child told a friend, parent, counselor, or school employee of his/her intent to commit suicide. In concluding that a death is actually attributed to suicide, a precipitating event had occurred within days prior to the child's suicide. These may include relationship breakups, arguments with parents or friend or interactions with the juvenile justice system.

Children that commit suicides are more likely to utilize a firearm or to forcefully overdose on drugs or other poisonous substances. It is important for police personnel to work closely with the medical examiner in investigating child suicides. Medical examiners should conduct a full toxicology screening of all child deaths in an attempt to assess the impact that the substance abuse or prescription drugs might have had on the suicide victim. In a case where firearms were used, the medical examiners and police must work closely to determine if the gunshot wound was self-inflicted. If a firearm was utilized in the child suicide, the police must also remember to investigate child access to firearms issues that might come forth by the prosecutor's office. Rates for firearm-related injuries and deaths in ages 15–19 dropped from 27.8 per 100,000 in 1994 to 11.4 per 100,000 in 2009, driven mainly by a decline in firearm-related homicides (American Academy of Pediatrics, 2012). The American Academy of Pediatrics found that safe gun storage was most effective in preventing firearm-related injuries and deaths, keeping guns unloaded and locked away separately from ammunition.

Homicide

The rate of homicide among children in the past decade has decreased in comparison to prior years. According to the Crimes against Children Research Center (CACRC) (2001), "There was an 84% increase in the number of juvenile homicide victims between 1985 and 1993, however the number of juvenile homicide victims declined 48% between 1993 and 2002 to the lowest level in over 20 years" (CACRC, 2006, pg.3). Homicide rates for children were at their highest in 1993 at 2.2 per 100,000, and declined to their lowest level in 2004 at 1.4 homicides per 100,000, remaining stable through 2008 (Cooper and Smith, 2011). Different age ranges show different variation in the rates of child homicide. The homicide of preadolescent children is relatively low in relationship to the rates of young children or teenagers. With children ages five years and below, homicides are mainly enacted by family members utilizing suffocation and beating as the means of murder. Females tend to kill children more frequently than men, and there is no appearance of a large variation in the gender of the victims (CACRC, 2006; Kim, Pears, Fisher, Connelly, and Landsverk, 2010).

INVESTIGATING CHILD FATALITIES

Child fatalities almost certainly present an investigative challenge independent of manner and cause. No system of uniformity currently exists regarding investigations specific to child fatalities, although every state but Idaho now has a Child Fatality Review Team (CFRT). CFRTs vary in personnel size, training, and funding, all of which contribute to the inconsistencies of child fatality investigations. Recently, there has been research on the use of web-based technology to improve CFRT data collection and personnel training to address such inconsistencies (Douglas and McCarthy, 2011; Zonfrillo, Kumar, Fortes, and Winston, 2012). In the event of a premature death, investigative personnel enlist the consultation of medical examiners, public health officials, physicians, and representatives from state agencies such as child welfare, education, social services, law enforcement, and mental health to assist in a timely determination of death.

Research in the last decade has highlighted the importance of victimization review teams or CFRTs; groups of individuals representing such agencies to form a collaborative effort in the investigation of the circumstances surrounding the fatality (Douglas and McCarthy, 2011, Finkelhor et al, 2005, Bower, 1996, American Academy of Pediatrics, 1999). The alliance between these agencies through the use of CFRTs will help to ensure the retrospective investigation of the circumstances surrounding the child's premature death while providing data that may lead to improved preventative measures. Interagency cooperation provides many benefits to the investigation such as enhanced quality assurance at local levels, improved allocation of limited resources, increased epidemiological data regarding cause of death, and improved accuracy of death certificates (American Academy of Pediatrics, 1999). CFRTs have been required since the 1996 Child Abuse Prevention and Treatment Act, although most state laws place a heavier focus on prevention rather than investigation (Douglas and McCarthy, 2011). Research has shown that there has been a correlation between the passing of state-level legislation on child maltreatment fatalities and the volume of media coverage such cases receive, with those states that have a higher volume of media coverage passing substantive legislation (Gainsborough, 2009; Douglas, 2009).

Federal Legislation, through the amendment of the Child Abuse Prevention and Treatment Act (1996), states that several provision are required when the death of a child is uncertain. All reports and/or records concerning the deceased become part of the investigation and are given to the investigative team. These records, such as medical records, social services reports, child protective services statements, emergency and paramedic records, law enforcement reports, childcare and/or school reports assist in the interagency collaboration. Similarly, legislation permits the publication of findings from any child abuse or neglect case, which resulted in a fatality or near fatality. State government maintains the right to terminate parental rights of any surviving children when a parent receives a conviction for killing or assisting in the murder of a child. This legislation further requires each state to report the number of children that were on record with child protective services prior to their death (Child Abuse Prevention and Treatment Act, 1996). Amendments were made to the Child Abuse Prevention and Treatment Act by the Keeping Children and Families Safe Act of 2003, and most recently amended by CAPTA Reauthorization Act of 2010 (Child Welfare Information Gateway, 2011).

Legislation regarding CFRTs and their purpose for functioning is overwhelmingly oriented towards prevention (Douglas and McCarthy, 2011), placing the burden of investigations and prosecutions of perpetrators on police and the court systems. In the case of any child fatality, the police investigator must interview all potential witnesses, suspects, and family members. Family members and neighbors may serve as the key investigative tool for most child fatality cases, specifically those that involve child maltreatment. In the case of child maltreatment, family members living outside the home, neighbors, and friends may provide important information about the previous treatment of the child, the activities of the family, and the overall well-being of the child's daily environment.

In the examination of the scene and evidence collection from a child fatality the police investigator must be aware of all potential evidence that encompasses the child's life. This is crucial in the investigation of potential SIDS and accidental deaths of children. In potential SIDS cases the investigator should collect and preserve the following: 1) infant's bedding including sheets, blanket, and mattress; 2) objects in the crib including toys and bottles; 3) unusual or dangerous items found near the death scene such as plastic bags, sharp objects, and paint chips and 4) all medications, even those belonging to the adults. Similar attention is required regarding the evidence within accidental child death cases. Instances in which a child accidentally chokes on an ingested toy, all toys in the vicinity should be collected for later analysis.

Law enforcement personnel will always maintain the lead in child fatality investigations due to overt legal issues such as interviewing witnesses, interrogating suspects, dealing with confessions and evidence collection (Walsh, 2005). However, whenever a death investigation of a child occurs, a collaborative partnership between all associated agencies must take place. While the scope of each agency is slightly different, the varying degrees of expertise within each unit, enhances the probability of utilizing the most appropriate evaluative measures.

Conclusion

Child victimization is a major societal problem nationwide. With causes of death including sudden death syndrome, sudden unexpected death in infancy, abuse, neglect, and homicides, it is evident that the topic of child fatality cannot be ignored. Additionally, training and education on the reporting of child victimization must be implemented across criminal justice agencies. People must be made aware of the importance in reporting such incidents, in order to more accurately collect statistics on child fatalities to create effective prevention programs as well as to make the public aware of this very serious and sensitive issue.

References

American Academy of Pediatrics. (1999). Investigation and Review of Unexpected Infant and Child Deaths. *Pediatrics. 104(5).* 1158–1160.

American Academy of Pediatrics. (2012). Firearm-related injuries affecting the pediatric population. *Pediatrics, 130*(5), e1416–23.

Borse, N.N., Gilchrist, J., Dellinger, A.M., Rudd, R.A., Ballesteros, M.F., and Sleet, D.A. (2008). *CDC Childhood Injury Report: Patterns of Unintentional Injuries among 0 -19 Year Olds in the United States, 2000–2006.* Atlanta, GA: Centers for Disease Control and Prevention, National Center for Injury Prevention and Control.

Bower, B. (1996). Growing Up in Harm's Way: Child Victimization Develops into a Scientific Challenge. *Science News.* 149(21). 332(2).

Center for Disease Control and Prevention. (2013). *Ten Leading Causes of Death by Age Group, United States — 2013.* Retrieved on January 1, 2016 from http://www.cdc.gov/injury/wisqars/pdf/leading_causes_of_death_by_age_group2013-a.pdf

Center for Disease Control and Prevention. (2015). *Suicide Prevention: Youth Suicide.* Retrieved on January 1, 2016 from http://www.cdc.gov/violenceprevention /suicide/youth_suicide.html

Child Abuse Prevention and Treatment Act 5101, 42 U.S.C. 5116 (1996).

Child Welfare Information Gateway. (2004). Child Abuse and Neglect Fatalities: Statistics and Intervention. Retrieved December 4, 2006 from http://www.childwelfare.gov/pubs/factsheets/fatality.cfm.

Child Welfare Information Gateway. (2011). About CAPTA: A legislative history. Washington, DC: U.S. Department of Health and Human Services, Children's Bureau.

Cooper, A., and Smith, E. L. (2011). Homicide trends in the United States, 1980–2008. *Washington (District of Columbia): Bureau of Justice Statistics.*

Crimes Against Children Research Center (CACRC). (2006). Child Homicide Fact Sheet. Retrieved December 4, 2006 from http://www.unh.edu/ccrc/factsheet/pdf/homicide.pdf

Douglas, E. M. (2009). Media coverage of agency-related child maltreatment fatalities: Does it result in state legislative change intended to prevent future fatalities? *Journal of Policy Practice*, *8*(3), 224–239.

Douglas, E. M., and McCarthy, S. C. (2011). Child fatality review teams: A content analysis of social policy. *Child welfare*, *90*(3), 91.

Fang, X., Brown, D. S., Florence, C. S., and Mercy, J. A. (2012). The economic burden of child maltreatment in the United States and implications for prevention. *Child abuse & neglect*, *36*(2), 156–165.

Federal Bureau of Investigation. (1996). Crime in the United States—1996. *Uniform Crime Report*. Retrieved on January 1, 2016 from https://www.fbi.gov/aboutus/cjis/ucr/crime-in-the-u.s/1996/96sec2.pdf

Federal Bureau of Investigation. (2015). 2014 Crime in the United States. *Uniform Crime Report*. Retrieved on January 1, 2016 from https://www.fbi.gov/aboutus/cjis/ucr/crime-in-the-u.s e-2014/tables/expandedhomicidedata/expanded_homicide_data_table_2_murder_victims_by_age_sex_ad_race_2014.xls

Fennel, J.E. (2005). Reauthorization of the National Highway Traffic Safety Administration. Retrieved on December 4, 2006 from http://energycommerce.house.gov/108/hHearings/06232005hearing1559/Fennellpdf.

Finkelhor, D., Ormrod, R., Turner, H., and Hamby, S. (2005). The Victimizarion of Children and Youth: A National Survey. *Child Maltreatment*. 11(4). 5–25.

Forum on Child and Family Statistics. (2015). Child and Injury Mortality. Retrieved on January 1, 2016 from http://www.childstats.gov/americaschildren/phys7.asp

Gainsborough, J. F. (2009). Scandals, lawsuits, and politics: Child welfare policy in the US States. *State Politics & Policy Quarterly*, *9*(3), 325–355

Goldstein, R. D., Trachtenberg, F. L., Sens, M. A., Harty, B. J., and Kinney, H. C. (2016). Overall Postneonatal Mortality and Rates of SIDS. *Pediatrics*, peds-2015.

Kim, H. K., Pears, K. C., Fisher, P. A., Connelly, C. D., and Landsverk, J. A. (2010). Trajectories of maternal harsh parenting in the first 3 years of life. *Child abuse & neglect*, *34*(12), 897–906.

Klevens, J., and Leeb, R. T. (2010). Child maltreatment fatalities in children under 5: Findings from the National Violence Death Reporting System. *Child Abuse & Neglect, 34*(4), 262–266.

Organization for Economic Co-operation and Development. (2011). http://www.oecd.org/els/family/48968307.pdf

U.S. Department of Health and Human Services, Health Resources and Services Administration, Maternal and Child Health Bureau. (2015). *Child Health USA 2014*. Rockville, Maryland: U.S. Department of Health and Human Services. Online at http://mchb.hrsa.gov/chusa14/

U.S. Department of Health and Human Services, Administration for Children and Families, Administration on Children, Youth and Families, Children's Bureau. (2015). *Child maltreatment 2013*. Available from http://www.acf.hhs.gov/programs/cb/research-data-technology/statisticsresearch/child-maltreatment

United States Department of Justice. (1998). Child Victimization. Retrieved October 11, 2006 from http://www.ojp.usdoj.gov/ovc/assist/nvaa/supp/n-ch15.htm.

Walsh, B. (2005). *Investigating Child Fatalities*. U.S. Department of Justice, Office of Justice Programs, Office of Juvenile Justice and Delinquency Prevention, Washington, DC.

Zonfrillo, M. R., Kumar, M., Fortes, J. A., and Winston, F. K. (2012). Telecenter for secure, remote, collaborative child fatality review. *Injury prevention, 18*(6), 399–404.

CHAPTER 9

Children's Advocacy Centers: Improving the Child Maltreatment Response

Tammy Bracewell
Texas A&M University — Central Texas

The nature of child maltreatment investigations has changed considerably since professionals first acknowledged the problem of child maltreatment. Although the first organization for the protection of children was created over a century ago, the nature of investigating and prosecuting child maltreatment continues to evolve today (APSAC, 2012). This evolution includes the development of Children's Advocacy Centers (CACs) across the United States. Child maltreatment is a general term that includes child sexual abuse and child physical abuse and neglect.

A CAC provides a child-friendly, non-partisan location for children to be interviewed in reference to alleged child maltreatment, specifically child sexual abuse, severe child physical abuse and neglect, and child witnesses to violent crime (Faller & Palusci, 2007; Jensen, Jacobson, Unrau & Robinson, 1996). Additionally, CACs provide forensic interviewers who receive specialized training in how to solicit accurate and reliable information from children (Newman, Dannenfesler & Pendleton, 2005). In 2013, over 700 CACs served more than 290,000 children across the country who were the focus of child maltreatment investigations (NCA, 2014). In addition to conducting interviews with alleged child maltreatment victims, CACs also coordinate multidisciplinary teams (MDTs) in an attempt to facilitate communication between professionals from multiple agencies involved in child maltreatment allegations with the goal of fostering better case outcomes (Lalayants & Epstein, 2005). Services provided by CACs, in addition to forensic interviews and MDTs, include child and family-friendly facilities, victim advocacy and support, specialized medical evaluation and treatment, specialized mental health services, and training, education and support for child maltreatment professionals (NCA, 2013).

History of Child Maltreatment Investigations

Public and professional opinions about child maltreatment have evolved considerably over the last 150 years. It was not until 1875 that the first organization devoted to child protection, The New York Society for the Prevention of Cruelty to Children, was created (Myers, 2011; Watkins, 1990). The creation of this society was in response to the case of Mary Ellen Wilson. Wilson was severely physically abused and animal protection laws were used to remove her from the abusive home because no legal response existed for abused children. This case is frequently referred to as the beginning of the child protection movement in the United States (Myers, 2011; Watkins, 1990).

Prior to 1960s

Prior to 1960, there was little interest in the field of child maltreatment (Ceci & Bruck, 1993). Children's disclosures of abuse were discounted as unreliable. According to Ceci and Bruck (1993) the beliefs of the unreliability of child witnesses during this time were shaped by the works of psychologists who became convinced that young children are highly suggestible and their statements unreliable. In 1935 Congress passed the Social Security Act. Within the Social Security Act the Children's Bureau was given the power to cooperate with states to establish child welfare services. However, nongovernmental agencies were the only agencies available that provided any services to child maltreatment victims. By the 1950s virtually all nongovernmental agencies had dissolved. Additionally, any protective services available prior to the 1960s were not available to most of the population (Myers, 2011).

1960s–1970s

According to Faller (1996) child maltreatment was rediscovered as a social problem during the 1960s. This rediscovery began with recognition and concern over physical abuse and proceeded to include sexual abuse. During this time, physicians began to study child physical abuse and publish literature on their findings (Myers, 2011). Although the process was slow, this did begin the trend towards scholarly research on child maltreatment. The article "The Battered-Child Syndrome" by Kempe, Silverman, Steele, Droegemueller, and Silver (1962) was seen as revolutionary and is often cited as bringing widespread attention to the problem of child maltreatment, specifically child physical abuse. This article was a response to the frustration of physicians with no training who treated child physical abuse victims (Myers, 2011; Myers, Diedrich, Lee, Fincher & Stern, 2002). While child sexual abuse was not a topic in Kempe et al.'s seminal article, their contribution did pave the way for future research in child maltreatment (Whittier, 2009). By the late 1970s, Henry Kempe described child sexual abuse as a hidden and neglected area (Kellogg, 2005; Lamb, Hershkowitz, Orbach & Esplin, 2008; Myers, et al., 2002).

Prior to the mid-1970s, the limited information published on child sexual abuse featured four common themes (Myers, et al., 2002; Whittier, 2009). First, there were often claims that children were responsible for their own sexual abuse. This was explained by the belief that children played an active role in their victimization; moreover, children could have prevented the victimization by avoiding or getting out of the abusive situation. The second common theme was that mothers of the victims were to blame. Mothers were considered blameworthy because of the perception that they caused their husbands to participate in an incestuous relationship with the victims. Third, child sexual abuse was considered a rare event. Psychological textbooks provided exaggerated underreports of child sexual abuse. Lastly, the belief that sexual abuse does no harm was purported in the limited research that existed. These themes were also present in legal opinions of the time. The first federal legislation on child maltreatment, Child Abuse Prevention and Treatment Act (CAPTA) of 1974, set a minimum definition of child maltreatment. The definition included any act or omission by a caretaker that results in death, serious physical or emotional harm, sexual abuse or exploitation. Additionally, CAPTA provided states with funding for the development of prevention programs and research (Myers, 2011; Whittier, 2009).

Myers, et al. (2002), asserts that the literature regarding child maltreatment began to change when the number of female lawyers and professors began to increase, indicating females published both court documents and academic manuscripts regarding child maltreatment that differed substantially from previous works written by the predominantly male professionals. Studies began to report the child sexual abuse of college students, leading the way to more professional interest in child maltreatment, specifically child sexual abuse. In 1979, Finkelhor published his seminal work on child sexual abuse. Specifically, he was able to bridge the gap between academia and social work (Whittier, 2009). He surveyed college students and found that 19.2% of college women and 8.6% of college men reported sexual victimization as children (Finkelhor, 1979). Additionally, he clearly defined child sexual abuse as a different social problem than rape and child physical abuse. Finkelhor's original work challenged traditional thinking on child maltreatment, specifically child sexual abuse.

Prior to the 1980s, physical abuse and neglect cases represented the majority of investigations conducted by child protection services; sexual abuse cases were the exception (Chandler, 2006). Physical abuse cases investigated by law enforcement during this time were typically only the most severe cases with substantial physical evidence. During the investigation of neglect and physical abuse cases children were frequently observed and not questioned (Faller, 1996). While child maltreatment investigations received more attention during this time, specialized investigations were still in their infancy.

1980s

In the early 1980s, the United States experienced a surge of child maltreatment reports. Perhaps most notable was the increase in reports of child sexual abuse (Jacobson, 2001; Myers, 2011; Whittier, 2009). The dramatic shift from child sexual abuse being excluded from the literature to nationwide attention led to an increase in reports of suspected child maltreatment cases in the 1980s (Bruck & Ceci, 1999; Lamb, Hershkowitz, Orbach & Esplin, 2008). Adult women began to publically recount sexual abuse during their childhoods. This, coupled with several high profile sexual abuse cases, is thought to have contributed to the dramatic increase in reporting experienced in the 1980s. The increased reporting led to an increase in professional interest. According to Jacobson (2001), the increase in child sexual abuse reports was symbolic of an increase in public awareness and interest, as opposed to a general increase in child sexual abuse.

Asking children about maltreatment did not become a common practice until the 1980s. Professionals began interviewing children with very little training and experience (Faller, 1996). During this time the slogan "believe the child" was coined (Bruck & Ceci, 1999; Faller, 1996). The early 1980s were marked by the belief that children do not make up sexual abuse allegations. Children's accounts of sexual abuse were taken at face value. No standard existed on how to interview suspected victims of child maltreatment. Child protection workers and law enforcement officials were left to interview children based upon what they thought was best. By 1983, the interviews used when investigating child sexual abuse claims came under scrutiny from academics and professionals (Faller, 1996). By the mid-1980s, cases involving extraordinary claims of child sexual abuse created a heightened scrutiny of interviewing practices and the slogan "believe the child" was replaced with disbelief (Bazelon, 2014; Faller, 2004).

Because of the increased reliance on children's statements, professionals in the child maltreatment field felt a need for an interdisciplinary organization that focused on child maltreatment. This led to the creation of the American Professional Society on the Abuse of Children (APSAC) in 1986 (Faller, 1996). APSAC was the first organization to provide guidelines for interviewing children. Unfortunately, before APSAC began coordinating and providing professional training on how to interview suspected victims of child maltreatment, several high profile child sexual abuse cases emerged that highlighted the need for standardized protocols and training for interviewing alleged child victims. Assertions that bad interviews led to false accusations began to appear in courtrooms (Faller, 1996). Two cases have consistently been cited as examples of false allegations in response to suggestive interviewing of children: the McMartin Preschool and Kelly Michael's cases. According to Bellah, Martinez, Mclaurin, Strok, Garven, and Wood (2006), these daycare cases were not genuine instances of mass sexual abuse, however, the national attention that they both received led to a national panic about satanic sexual abuse occurring in daycare settings (Ceci & Bruck, 1993; Myers, 2011). Others argue that these cases are not examples of false allegations, rather they exemplify the need for evidence based practices and interviewing in child maltreatment cases (Berry, 2014; Cheit, 2014). Cheit (2014) argued that the suggestive questioning of the children in the Kelly Michaels and McMartin Preschool cases does not negate the fact that evidence suggested that sexual abuse of at least some of the children, in both cases, did occur. Regardless of what evidence existed, improper interviewing techniques in both cases led to children being victimized through the criminal justice and social services systems. Ceci and Bruck (1993) alleged that these cases exemplify how children's testimonies can become so tainted that they are of no probative value.

1990s–2000s

Because of the skepticism created in the 1980s and more children testifying in criminal trials, additional attention has been directed to research involving best practices for interviewing children (Bruck & Ceci, 1999; Ceci &

Bruck, 1993; Faller, 1996). Ceci and Bruck (1993) acknowledge that research conducted on child suggestibility was relatively new, stating that more research was conducted during the early 1980s and 1990s than in any other time in history. During this time, one interview of the child was preferred and it was assumed that a victimized child was willing to disclose maltreatment and was able to provide details on alleged incidents (Lamb, et al., 2008; Pipe, Lamb, Orbach & Cederborg, 2007). More than one interview of a child was viewed as problematic and suggestive. Considerable stress, therefore, was placed on both the child and the interviewer to get all information about alleged maltreatment at one point in time.

In the early 1990s the False Memory Syndrome Foundation (FMSF) was created in response to adult children accusing their parents of child sexual abuse based on recovered memories (Whittier, 2009). Whittier (2009) described what followed as the "memory wars." FMSF was successful in changing conventional belief about sexual abuse allegations. By the mid-1990s suspicion and doubt were common regarding child sexual abuse allegations. The ability of children to serve as competent witnesses was questioned, as were allegations made by adults. By the late 1990s research in reference to false memories coexisted with research and books encouraging adults to trust their memories of child sexual abuse (Whittier, 2009). The "memory wars" were successful in encouraging research on memory and suggestibility regarding child sexual abuse allegations.

In the early 2000s research from both activists and critics continued to emerge and coexist in an ever divergent body of literature. Investigation and interviewing techniques in child maltreatment are still evolving. Today, there is a shift towards allowing more than one session for forensic interviews, recognizing that disclosure of child sexual abuse is a process, not an event (CACTX, 2014; Lamb, et al., 2008). This evolution will likely continue as more research is conducted and the utility of child maltreatment investigation techniques continues to be critiqued. Regardless of the future direction in child maltreatment investigations, the need will remain for effective interviews and investigations.

Children's Advocacy Centers

In 1984, the first CAC, the National Children's Advocacy Center (NCAC), was founded in Huntsville, Alabama, and in 1985 opened its doors to children (Faller & Palusci, 2007; Jenson, et al., 1996). The idea of a CAC originated from professional knowledge that children were re-victimized by well-meaning professionals in the investigation process through repeated questioning and court proceedings that were designed for adults. Moreover, the investigation process was decentralized and uncoordinated. The vision of the NCAC was that a child maltreatment investigation should be brought to the victim in a child-friendly atmosphere (Faller & Palusci, 2007; Jensen, et al., 1996). This vision expanded into a national movement. According to Chandler (2006), there are three core principles that every CAC must embrace: (1) a multidisciplinary team (MDT) approach is the most effective response to child maltreatment, (2) ongoing cross-training of all MDT members is necessary to ensure proper investigations, and (3) the needs of the child must be at the center of the investigatory activities.

In 1984, the primary goal of the NCAC was increasing the number of successful prosecutions of serious child maltreatment cases coupled with conducting more child-friendly investigations (Faller & Palusci, 2007; Jenson, et al., 1996). This goal has since expanded to include providing a child friendly environment, limiting the number of times a child is interviewed, conducting the interviews of children by trained child forensic interviewers, offering medical and therapeutic services, and providing victim advocacy and court education programs (Bonach, Mabry & Potts-Henry, 2010; Jones, Cross, Walsh & Simone, 2005).

Multidisciplinary Teams

Historically, child maltreatment allegations involve a variety of different professional entities, all with their own, sometimes competing, interests and separate investigations (Kienberger & Martone, 1992). The recognition of this has led, in part, to the development of CACs and accompanying Multidisciplinary Teams (Sheppard & Zangrillo, 1996). The CAC model has a unifying philosophy that child sexual abuse is a community problem that requires a multidisciplinary response (Jackson, 2004). However, the specifics of each CAC are tailored to individual community needs (Walsh, Jones & Cross, 2003). CACs offer communities a way to provide services to child maltreatment victims while bringing together different entities with varying goals involved in child maltreatment. The multidisciplinary team (MDT) approach seeks to fulfill the different professional needs while putting the welfare of the child first (Walsh, et al., 2003).

An MDT is built upon the premise that in order to respond to the individual needs of a child victim and the family, the most effective response builds upon the expertise of multiple agencies (Chandler, 2000; Cross, Finkelhor & Ormrod, 2005; Jenson, et al., 1996; Jones, et al., 2005; Lalyants & Epstein,

2005). No single agency has the ability to respond adequately to child maltreatment (Lalayants & Epstein, 2005). With this more effective approach comes improved protection, treatment, and legal services provided to child maltreatment victims and their families (Bonach et al., 2010; Chandler, 2000; Cross, Jones, Walsh, Simone & Kolbo, 2007). Because an MDT is a core component, a CAC cannot exist in its true form without one. The MDT not only coordinates investigative strategies, it also facilitates services for victims such as medical evaluations, therapy, victim advocacy, family support, and case review (Bonach et al., 2010; Simone, Cross, Jones & Walsh, 2005; Walsh, Cross, Jones & Simone, 2007).

The MDT approach is embedded in the CAC philosophy. No CAC can be effective without the cooperation of the different entities involved in child protection: law enforcement, child protection services, prosecution, mental and medical health, victim advocacy, and CAC staff (Chandler, 2006; Jackson, 2004; Smith, Witte & Fricker-Elhai, 2006; Walsh et al., 2007). These entities comprise the core of the MDT model. Other organizations such as probation and court appointed special advocates may be MDT members, depending on the individual needs of the community. The CAC model is designed to improve the community response to child maltreatment through a collaborative response (Jackson, 2004).

A majority of states now require law enforcement and child protective services to work together as part of an MDT when investigating criminal cases of child maltreatment (Newman, et al., 2005). The Children's Justice Act provides grants to states in an effort to improve child maltreatment investigations and judicial proceedings to reduce trauma to the child involved. The Children's Justice Act requires states receiving grants to establish a multidisciplinary task force (Lalayants & Epstein, 2005). In communities without formal MDT protocols, there may be little to no communication between investigative agencies (Cross, et al., 2005). Prior to the CAC movement most decision making involving child maltreatment was not coordinated and involved multiple agencies performing redundant, sometimes competing tasks (Cross, et al., 2007).

Investigation benefits

Tjaden and Anhalt (1994) evaluated five communities that varied in the degree that law enforcement and child protective service investigations were conducted jointly. They found that those with joint investigations, defined as both law enforcement and child protective services working together, had shorter response times than those without joint investigations. Furthermore, an increase in alleged perpetrator confessions and alleged perpetrators removed from the home of the child was found in cases with joint investigations. The investigations in which both law enforcement and child protective services worked together were lengthier than those conducted by only one agency. One explanation regarding this finding is that the investigations were more thorough, requiring more time, however, later research by Walsh, Lippert, Cross, Maurice, and Davidson (2008) found that MDTs resulted in quicker charging decisions by prosecutors. Additionally, Pence and Wilson (1994) found that MDTs resulted in an increase in accuracy regarding assessment of risk, indicating that CPS investigators were better able to determine if any safety concerns existed.

MDTs lead to decreased fragmentation, less role confusion, reduced duplication of services, and enhanced quality of evidence for lawsuits or criminal prosecution (Kolbo & Strong, 1997; Pence & Wilson, 1994). Kolbo and Strong (1997) conducted a survey of respondents from all 50 states in reference to their MDT usage. They found an increase in joint decisions after the MDT approach was implemented. Also, there was a greater range of viewpoints considered in the decision making process, a greater number of resources being identified, and an overall better quality of assessment and treatment services provided to the child (Cross, et al., 2005; Kolbo & Strong, 1997). Additionally, Cross et al. (2007) conducted comparison research on four Children's Advocacy Centers with comparison jurisdictions without Children's Advocacy Centers. They found that team interviews and joint child protection and law enforcement investigations were more common in jurisdictions with Children's Advocacy Centers. They argue for the importance of a team approach to child maltreatment by alleging that uncoordinated investigations can lead to undiscovered evidence and misinformation provided to the families.

Forensic Interviews

A forensic interview of a child is designed to "obtain a statement from a child, in a developmentally and culturally sensitive, unbiased and fact-finding manner that will support accurate and fair decision making by the involved multidisciplinary team in the criminal justice and child protection systems" (NCA, 2011, p11). Forensic interviews have become an integral part of child maltreatment investigations. Skillful forensic interviews of suspected child maltreatment victims are important, not only to protect children, but also to protect innocent individuals from wrongful convictions (Cronch, et al., 2006). Interviewers have the ability to determine the probability of disclosure and likelihood of prosecution, therefore, it is paramount that interviews be standardized and evidence based (Cronch, et al., 2006). Forensic interviews are conducted, at the request of investigators, after a preliminary investigation has provided some information about what may have occurred (Lamb, et al., 2008). Forensic interviews are used in cases regarding allegations of child sexual abuse, serious child physical abuse and neglect, and child witnesses to violent crime.

A forensic interview is conducted in a child friendly environment with a trained forensic interviewer, with the use of a one way mirror and/or closed circuit television. This allows MDT members to observe the interview in real time (Bonach, et al., 2010). Moreover, it allows for a variety of professional experts to collaborate on the specific needs of an individual child (Kolbo & Strong, 1997). Because alleged victims are the primary, and often only, source of evidence, the quality of the child's interview is critical (Pipe, Orbach, Lamb, Abbott & Steward, 2013; Walsh, Jones, Cross & Lippert, 2010). It is vital that forensic interviewers have formal training and participate in a peer review process (Lamb, et al., 2008). Faller (1996) asserted that the need for an impartial, educated, and trained interviewer ultimately led to the field of forensic interviewing, arguing that there was a virtual absence of other alternatives to reliably collect information regarding child maltreatment allegations.

There is a consensus in the academic literature regarding the ways in which investigative interviews of children should be conducted regarding the use of non-leading questions and the use of free narrative, a practice that allows the child to explain an event with little prompting (Lamb, et al., 2008; Pool & Lamb, 1998). While Poole and Lamb (1998) assert that this consensus is in response to a review of the experimental and empirical literature, it is noteworthy that not one protocol exists for interviewing children. On the contrary, there are several nationally recognized protocols, all developed using the same literature, but all different (Anderson, 2014; Toth, 2011). Experts agree that as much information as possible should be solicited in the form of open-ended free-recall questions (Lamb, et al., 2008; Pipe, et al., 2007; Toth, 2011). These questions force the respondent to recall information from memory, increasing the response reliability. According to Bruck and Ceci (1999) poor interviewing conditions can negatively affect a child's memory. Lamb, et al. (1995) argue that errors of omission are more common than errors of commission, meaning that children are more likely to leave details out than to fabricate details when children are interviewed correctly. The interviewer's ability to elicit information from the child and the child's willingness and ability to express it are more important than the child's ability to remember (Lamb, et al., 2007). Studies have consistently shown that children can remember salient events such as sexual abuse. Although children can remember, they may not readily disclose information. Additionally, interview skill and perceived bias plays an important role in child disclosures.

Lamb, Esplin, and Sternberg (1995) found that the interviewer's skills can greatly influence the outcomes of forensic interviews. Everything the interviewer does, verbal and nonverbal, has the potential to influence a child's testimony. Interviewers must avoid pressuring children to simply agree with the interviewer's suggestions while encouraging them to dispel false allegations. Because preschoolers are more suggestible it is important for trained interviewers to elicit the information from young children. High variability exists in children between ages 3 and 5 in their competency. However, children can remember with accuracy detailed events, especially when interviewed properly (Lamb, et al., 1995).

Medical exams

Medical exams are an important aspect of child maltreatment investigations. While medical exams of sexually abused children frequently lack any findings indicative of sexual abuse, experts in the medical aspects of child sexual abuse can testify during trial to explain a lack of medical evidence (Walsh, et al., 2007). Additionally, there are hearsay rules that allow medical professionals to testify to what the child stated, known as the "history" during the exam (Kellogg, 2005). According to Kellogg (2005), medical personnel should obtain a history statement from the child prior to examination. The medical history can help determine what tests should be administered, assist in interpreting medical findings, and provide helpful information regarding what services the child may need. The medical statement can also be used during the investigation to show consistencies or inconsistencies in the child's statement.

Walsh, et al. (2007) examined a sample of cases from four large, urban CACs and compared them with samples from similar demographics not served by a CAC. The authors found that CACs are not uniform in how medical examinations are carried out. However, they did find that 48% of child sexual abuse victims seen at a CAC received a medical exam while only 21% of the children at the comparison sites received medical exams. They argue that CACs are an effective response to ensuring medical exams when sexual abuse allegations are made. This study supported Smith, et al. (2006) who found that 57.1% of sexual abuse cases serviced by a CAC received a medical exam compared to only 12.7% of cases served by standard procedures. According to Finkel (2011) all children who indicate sexual abuse should have a medical examination, regardless of whether penetration is indicated. The

MDT approach facilitated by CACs allows for collaboration to ensure that all victims of child sexual abuse receive the medical exams needed. Additionally, it ensures that needed evidence, in the form of physical evidence or statements, is preserved for the investigation and any subsequent legal proceedings.

Case Outcomes

The research that has been conducted on caregiver satisfaction has reported overall satisfaction with services received at CACs; however, the individual satisfaction with different MDT members has not been established. Cross et al. (2007) compared four jurisdictions with well-established CACs with like jurisdictions without CACs. They found that families reported, on average, a more positive experience when their cases were handled through a CAC. Their positive experiences were linked to case coordination. Their findings indicate that cases processed through a CAC are more likely to have police involvement (41% vs. 15%). Additionally, they were much more likely to have case reviews (56% vs. 7%). Case reviews are formal meetings where information is shared between MDT members. Information shared includes case status, investigative needs, and needs of the involved families (NCA, 2011). This study suggests that CACs offer a more thorough and child-oriented response to child sexual abuse cases.

Wolfteich and Loggins (2007) compared the CAC model with traditional investigations on several outcome measures including arrest, prosecution, and efficacy of CACs. Included in this study were Florida Child Protection Teams. These teams exist as part of the multidisciplinary team approach but do not offer services found at CACs. CACs, Child Protection Teams, and traditional investigations with no official coordination were compared. Both CACs and Child Protection Teams were correlated with higher rates of substantiated child maltreatment than the traditional model. This finding supports other studies on the utility of coordinated investigations. Traditional investigations were omitted from arrest and prosecution analyses due to missing data. However, when compared to Child Protection Teams, CAC arrest and prosecution rates did not significantly differ. These findings support CAC efforts to coordinate multidisciplinary teams. Bonach, et al. (2010) evaluated one CAC in reference to caregiver satisfaction. They found that when the CAC model worked well, indicating that the multidisciplinary team was engaged, the stress of the child and family throughout the investigative process was less than families who experienced traditional forms of investigations. According to Bonach, et al. CACs have greatly improved nonoffending caregiver satisfaction with the way child maltreatment cases are investigated. Overall care-givers and child victims provide good ratings for CAC services.

PROSECUTION OF CHILD SEXUAL ABUSE

Because of the legal status of children as minors and the high incidence of intra-familial child sexual abuse, criminal prosecution is not a straight forward process (Stroud, Martens & Barker 2000). Prosecutors face many challenges in prosecuting child maltreatment, most notably child sexual abuse (Hagborg, Strömwall & Tidefors, 2012). There are a number of reasons that prosecutors decide not to file charges against alleged perpetrators of child maltreatment. The four most common being: no corroborating evidence, in-consistencies in the child's narratives of the maltreatment, the family is not supportive of prosecution, and the victim is considered too young to testify (Cross, et al., 2003; Cross, Whitcomb & De Vos, 1995; Hagborg, et al., 2012; Pipe, et al., 2013).

Prosecuting child sexual abuse poses unique challenges for prosecutors. The decision to prosecute child sexual abuse can be controversial for a number of reasons (Cross, et al., 2003; Walsh, et al., 2010). The crime of child sexual abuse most often occurs in private with the only witnesses being the child victim and offender (Walsh et al., 2008). While other crimes may also rely on victim testimony, it is the child victim's testimony that is highly scrutinized because of interviewing techniques and developmental abilities. The perception may be that a young child has been coerced into fabricating a story; or an older child may have fabricated a story as a means to an end (Cheit, 2014). This creates a unique problem when the only evidence is a child's statement or testimony. Although experts can testify that a young child is not developmentally capable of inventing a complex, consistent story about child sexual abuse, convincing the public that the word of a child is enough evidence to prosecute is an uphill battle.

There is rarely any evidence in child sexual abuse other than the victim and alleged perpetrator statements (Cross, et al., 2003; Faller, 1996; Staller & Faller, 2010). Additionally, in cases where the alleged perpetrator does not provide a statement, the only evidence may be the child's statement which begs the question: is the statement of a young child sufficient to successfully prosecute an adult? According to Cross, et al. (2003) prosecution relies heavily on the child victim's testimony. Therefore, it is imperative that a trained forensic interviewer conduct the interview of the child victim.

Effects of Child Advocacy Centers on the Decision to Prosecute

Walsh and colleagues (2008) examined three communities served by the Dallas County District Attorney's Office. They found that cases serviced through the CAC had significantly quicker charging decisions than those not serviced through the Children's Advocacy Center. Walsh et al. (2008) theorize that the quicker resolution time was because the prosecutors are involved with the case from the beginning when it is routed through the Children's Advocacy Center. Wolfteich and Loggins (2007) found that organizations with MDTs were associated with higher frequency of substantiated child maltreatment than the traditional child protection model that does not facilitate an MDT. The authors assert that the MDT approach leads to improved outcomes. These findings support the earlier research of Tjaden and Anhalt (1994) who found that those cases with joint investigations involving both law enforcement and child protective services had more criminal prosecutions and more guilty pleas than those without joint investigations and Smith, et al. (2006) who found that 80% of cases substantiated though a MDT at a CAC were referred for prosecution. However, only 42.8% of substantiated cases not served through an MDT had prosecution referrals.

In one of the largest studies on the effects of CACs and the first to thoroughly examine the link between CACs and prosecution rates of child sexual abuse, Miller and Rubin (2009) compared prosecution rates in two districts of a large urban city between 1992 and 2002. Because these two districts were in the same city, they were comparable across many variables with the exception of their use of the local Child Advocacy Center. Both cities had CACs that met all of the National Children's Alliance standards. In one district, the use of the Child Advocacy Center tripled while use in the other district remained constant. The district that tripled use, doubled the prosecution rates of child sexual abuse while experiencing a 59% decrease in reports. The second district experienced a 49% decrease in reports of sexual abuse while their prosecution rates remained constant with their use of the Child Advocacy Center. During this time the number of cases substantiated by Child Protective Services dropped similarly in both cities, consistent with the national trend. Miller and Rubin caution that there were many limitations to this study. While inferring causality is problematic, the results show a clear association that cannot be discounted.

CONCLUSION

Understanding and investigating child maltreatment has changed dramatically in recent history. Central to these changes is the CAC movement. CACs have effectively redefined how child maltreatment investigations should occur. Paramount to these changes is how children are viewed and treated during the investigative process. Child maltreatment investigations now proceed with the welfare of the child at the forefront. Since the case of Mary Ellen Wilson every aspect of investigating child maltreatment has changed significantly. Prior to 1974, the federal government only played a minor role in child protection. In 1974, the Child Abuse Prevention and Treatment Act of 1974 (CAPTA) was passed. This was the first time the federal government allocated funds to improve the response to child maltreatment. Within two years of the passage of CAPTA, all states had statutes requiring professionals to report child maltreatment (Myers, 2011). Additionally, until the 1980s the investigation of child maltreatment was an uncoordinated process with little cooperation between agencies. This type of investigation frequently resulted in the revictimization of child victims and duplicative efforts from different agencies.

The creation of the first CAC paved the way for a complete overhaul of child maltreatment investigations. Although the first CAC was established in 1984, the practices are still evolving today. Children are now routinely interviewed by trained forensic interviewers in response to child maltreatment allegations. Additionally, investigators are now able to conduct more thorough investigations through case coordination. CACs now provide investigators, prosecutors, victims, and families with much needed services while assisting in uncovering the truth.

REFERENCES

American Professional Society on the Abuse of Children. (2012). Practice guidelines: Forensic interviewing in cases of suspected child abuse. Elmhurst, IL: Author.

Anderson, J. (2014). Recent changes to the CornerHouse Forensic Interview Protocol. *National Center for Prosecution of Child Abuse, 24(1)*, 1–7.

Bazelon, E. (2014, June 9). Abuse cases, and a legacy of skepticism: 'The witch-hunt narrative': Are we dismissing real victims? *The New York Times*. Retrieved from: http://www.nytimes.com/2014/06/10/science/the-witch -hunt-narrative-are-we-dismissing-real-victims.html?_r=0.

Bellah, L., Martinez, Y., Mclaurin, K., Strok, R., Garven, S. & Wood, J. (2006). Suggestive interviewing in the McMartin Preschool and Kelly Michaels daycare abuse cases: A case study, *Social Influence, 1(1)*, 16–47.

Berry, J. (2014, June 12). How the 'Witch Hunt' myth undermined American justice. *The Daily Beast*. Retrieved from: http://www.thedailybeast .com/articles/2014/07/12/how-the-witch-hunt-myth-undermined -american-justice.html.

Bonach, K., Mabry, J. & Potts-Henry, C. (2010). Child advocacy centers and credentialing: Issues for practitioners. Exploring nonoffending caregiver satisfaction with a children's advocacy center. *Journal of Child Sexual Abuse, 19(6)*, 687–708.

Bruck, M. & Ceci, S. (1999). The suggestibility of children's memory. *Annual Review of Psychology. 50(1)*, 419–439.

Ceci, S. & Bruck, M. (1993). Suggestibility of the child witness: A historical review and synthesis. *Psychological Bulletin, 113(3)*, 403–439.

Chandler, N. (2000). *Best practices for establishing a children's advocacy center (3ʳᵈ ed.)*. Washington, DC: National Children's Alliance.

Chandler, N. (2006). Children's Advocacy Centers: Making a difference one child at a time. *Hamline Journal of Public Law & Policy, 28(1)*, 315–337.

Cheit, R. (2014). *The Witch-Hunt Narrative: Politics, Psychology, and the Sexual Abuse of Children*. New York: Oxford University Press.

Children's Advocacy Centers of Texas. (2014). *Child Abuse in Texas*. Retrieved from: http://www.cactx.org/child-abuse-in-texas.

Cross, T., Finkelhor & Ormrod, R. (2005). Police involvement in child protective services investigations: Literature review and secondary data analysis. *Child Maltreatment, 10(3)*, 224–242.

Cross, T., Jones, L., Walsh, W., Simone, M. & Kolko, D. (2007). Child forensic interviewing in Children's Advocacy Centers: Empirical data on a practice model. *Child Abuse & Neglect, 31(10)*, 1031–1052.

Cross, T., Walsh, W., Simone, M. & Jones, L. (2003). Prosecution of child abuse: A meta-analysis of rates of criminal justice decisions. *Trauma, Violence & Abuse, 4(4)*, 323–340.

Cross, T., Whitcomb, D. & De Vos, E. (1995). *Criminal justice outcomes of prosecution of child sexual abuse: A case flow analysis. Child Abuse & Neglect, 19(12)*, 1421–1442.

Faller, K. (1996). Interviewing children who may have been abused: A historical perspective and overview of controversies. *Child Maltreatment, 1(2)*, 83–95.

Faller, K. (2004). Sexual abuse of children: Contested issues and competing interests. *Criminal Justice Review. 29(2)*, 358–376.

Faller, K. & Palusci, V. (2007). Children's advocacy centers: Do they lead to positive case outcomes? *Child Abuse & Neglect, 31(10)*, 1021–1029.

Finkel, M. (2011). Medical issues in child sexual abuse. In J. Myers (Ed.), *The APSAC Handbook on Child Maltreatment, 3rd ed* (pp. 233–266). Thousand Oaks, CA: Sage Publications, Inc.

Finkelhor, D. (1979). *Sexually victimized children*. New York: Free Press.

Hagborg, J., Strömwall, L. & Tidefors, I. (2012). Prosecution rate and quality of the investigative interview in child sexual abuse cases. *Journal of Investigative Psychology and Offender Profiling, 9(2)*, 161–173.

Jackson, S. (2004). A USA national survey of program services provided by child advocacy centers. *Child Abuse & Neglect, 28(4)*, 411–421.

Jacobson, M. (2001). Child sexual abuse and the multidisciplinary team approach: Contradictions in practice. *Childhood, 8(2)*, 231–250.

Jensen, J., Jacobson, M., Unrau, Y. & Robinson, R. (1996). Interventions for victims of child sexual abuse: An evaluation of the children's advocacy model. *Child and Adolescent Social Work Journal, 13(2)*, 139–156.

Jones, L., Cross, T., Walsh, W. & Simone, M. (2005). Criminal investigations of child abuse: The research behind "best practices." *Trauma, Violence & Abuse, 6(3)*, 254–268.

Kellogg, N. & American Academy of Pediatrics Committee on Child Abuse and Neglect. (2005). The evaluation of sexual abuse in children. *Pediatrics, 116(2)*, 506–512.

Kempe, C. H., Silverman, F. N., Steele, B. F., Droegemueller, W. & Silver, H. K. (1962). The battered child syndrome. *Journal of the American Medical Association, 181*, 17–24.

Kienberger, P. & Martone, M. (1992). Interdisciplinary evaluations of alleged sexual abuse cases. *Pediatrics, 89(6)*, 1164–1168.

Kolbo, J. & Strong E. (1997). Multidisciplinary team approaches to the investigation and resolution of child abuse and neglect: A national survey. *Child Maltreatment, 2(1)*, 61–72.

Lamb, M., Esplin, P. & Sternberg, K. (1995). Making children into competent witnesses: Reactions to the Amicus Brief *In re Michaels*. *Psychology, Public Policy, and Law, 1(2)*, 438–449.

Lamb, M., Hershkowitz, I., Orbach, Y. & Esplin, P. (2008). *Tell Me What Happened: Structured Interviews of Child Victims and Witnesses*. England: Wiley.

Lamb, M., Orbach, Y., Hershkowitz, I., Esplin, P. & Horowitz, D. (2007). A structured forensic interview protocol improves the quality and informativeness of investigative interviews with children: A review of research using the NICHD Investigative Interview Protocol. *Child Abuse & Neglect, 31(11)*, 1201–1231.

Lalayants, M. & Epstein, I. (2005). Evaluating multidisciplinary child abuse and neglect teams: A research agenda. *Child Welfare, 84(4)*, 433–458.

Miller, A. & Rubin, D. (2009). The contribution of children's advocacy centers to felony prosecutions of child sexual abuse. *Child Abuse & Neglect, 33(1)*, 12–18.

Myers, J. (2011). *The APSAC Handbook on Child Maltreatment.* Thousand Oaks, CA: SAGE Publications, Inc.

Myers, J., Diedrich, S., Lee, D., Fincher, K. & Stern, R. (2002). Prosecution of child sexual abuse in the United States. In J. Conte (Ed.), *Critical Issues in Child Sexual Abuse: Historical, Legal, and Psychological Perspectives.* (pp.27–69). Thousand Oaks, CA: SAGE Publications, Inc.

National Children's Alliance. (2011). *Standards for Accredited Members.* Retrieved from http://www.nationalchildrensalliance.org.

National Children's Alliance. (2013). *Child and Family Friendly Facilities.* Retrieved from: http://www.nationalchildrensalliance.org/index.php?s=36.

National Children's Alliance. (2014). *CAC statistics.* Retrieved from: http://www .nationalchildrensalliance.org/cac-statistics.

Newman, B., Dannenfelser, P. & Pendleton, D. (2005). Child abuse investigation: Reasons for using child advocacy centers and suggestions for improvement. *Child and Adolescent Social Work Journal, 22(2)*, 165–181.

Pence, D. & Wilson, C. (1994). *Team investigation of child sexual abuse: The uneasy alliance.* Thousand Oaks, CA: Sage.

Pipe, M., Lamb, M., Orbach, Y. & Cederborg, A. (2007). *Child Sexual Abuse: Disclosure, Delay, and Denial.* New York: Routledge.

Pipe, M., Orbach, Y., Lamb, M., Abbott, C. & Steward, H. (2013). Do case outcomes change when investigative interviewing practices change? *Psychology, Public Policy, and Law, 19(2)*, 179–190.

Poole, D. & Lamb, M. (1998). Investigative interviews of children: A guide for helping professionals. Washington, DC: American Psychological Association.

Sheppard, D. & Zangrillo, P. (1996). Coordinating investigations of child abuse. *Public Welfare, 54(1)*, 21–31.

Simone, M., Cross, T., Jones, L. & Walsh, W. (2005). Children's advocacy centers: Understanding the impact of a phenomenon. In K. Kendall-Tackett & S. Giacomoni (Eds.), *Victimization of children and youth: Patterns of abuse, response strategies* (pp. 22–24). Kingston, NJ: Civic Research Institute, Inc.

Smith, D., Witte, T. & Fricker-Elhai, A. (2006). Service outcomes in physical and sexual abuse cases: A comparison of child advocacy center-based and standard services. *Child Maltreatment, 11(4)*, 354–360.

Staller, K. & Faller, K. (2010). *Seeking justice in child sexual abuse: Shifting burdens & sharing responsibilities.* New York: Columbia University Press.

Stroud, D., Martens, S. & Barker, J. (2000). Criminal investigation of child sexual abuse: A comparison of cases referred to the prosecutor and those not referred. *Child Abuse & Neglect, 24(5)*, 689–700.

Tjaden, P. & Anhalt, J. (1994). The impact of joint law enforcement-child protective services investigations in child maltreatment cases. Denver, CO: Center of Policy Research.

Toth, P. (2011). Comparing NICHD and RATAC child forensic interview approaches: Do differences matter? *The Link, 20(1)*, 1–6.

Walsh, W., Cross, T., Jones, L. & Simone, M. (2007). Which sexual abuse victims receive a forensic medical examination? The impact of children's advocacy centers. *Child Abuse & Neglect, 31(10)*, 1053–1068.

Walsh, W., Jones, L. & Cross, T. (2003). Children's advocacy centers: One philosophy many models. *APSAC Advisor, 15(3)*, 3–7.

Walsh, W., Jones, L., Cross, T. & Lippert, T. (2010). Prosecuting child sexual abuse: The importance of evidence type. *Crime & Delinquency, 56(3)*, 3–13.

Walsh, W., Lippert, T., Cross, T., Maurice, D. & Davison, K. (2008). How long to prosecute child sexual abuse for a community using a children's advocacy center and two comparison communities? *Child Maltreatment, 13(1)*, 3–13.

Watkins, S. (1990). The double victim: The sexually abused child and the judicial system. *Child and Adolescent Social Work, 7(1)*, 29–43.

Whittier, N. (2009). *The Politics of Child Sexual Abuse: Emotion, Social Movements, and the State.* New York: Oxford.

Wolfteich, P. & Loggins, B. (2007). Evaluation of the children's advocacy center model: Efficiency, legal and revictimization outcomes. *Child and Adolescent Social Work Journal, 24(4)*, 333–352.

CHAPTER 10

Understanding Elder Maltreatment and Identifying Social Responses

Christopher M. Bellas
Youngstown State University

Mary G. Wilson
Kent State University at Trumbull

Michelle L. Foster
Kent State University

According to 2013 data from the Administration on Aging (see Figure 1 on pg. 152), those persons age 65 and older living in the United States composed roughly 14.1% of the U.S. population (44.7 million people), and that percentage is expected to increase to 21.7% by 2040 (U.S. Department of Health and Human Services, Administration for Community Living, n.d.). This number will continue to rise to a projected 98 million elderly citizens by 2060, primarily as a result of the baby boom generation reaching retirement age (Colby & Ortman, 2015). The increase in this growing population will present unique challenges to criminal justice personnel in both identifying and responding to elder maltreatment.

This chapter should be an important topic of concern to criminal justice scholars and practitioners and is meant to define and categorize the types of elder maltreatment that exist, highlight the policies currently in place to address the issue, and demonstrate ways in which one can respond to this serious problem.

Figure 1: America's Growing Elderly Population

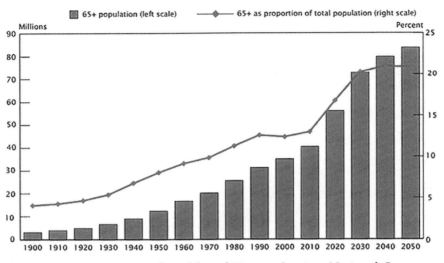

Source: U.S. Department of Health and Human Services National Center on Elder Abuse, n.d.-a

ELDER MALTREATMENT EXPLAINED

What Is Elder Maltreatment?

In studying Victimology, one would be remiss if elder maltreatment was excluded from the discussion. As surprising as this may be to some, elder maltreatment does exist, and like many other types of abuse, it is often difficult to detect or to get an accurate number of those who suffer from such victimization. The American Medical Association defines elder maltreatment as, "an act or omission that results in harm or threatened harm to the health or welfare of an elderly person" (Collins, 2006, p. 1290). Adult Protective Services (APS) provides aid to the elderly by investigating reports of abuse. Unfortunately, even if abuse has taken place, the finding(s) by APS may yield an unsubstantiated claim due to lack of evidence. As elder maltreatment is explored throughout this chapter, a clearer picture as to why these victims are overlooked and/or misidentified will hopefully come to light so that we can protect this growing population.

Issues in Identifying Elder Maltreatment

Historically, the occurrence of elder maltreatment had not been commonly explored or researched in the medical field due to the difficulty with detection. Medical professionals utilize a "gold standard test" to assess patients for abuse and neglect (McNamee & Murphy, n.d.). The standard procedure includes looking for forensic markers on the individual to determine if abuse or neglect has taken place. Forensic markers include patterns and coloring of bruises along with location of injury. What makes detection so difficult with the elderly is that medications, accidental injury, and simple aging of the body can mask the existence of abuse. Even bruise coloring can be misleading in older individuals for these very same reasons. Following the literature on pediatric child abuse, a report by Mosqueda, Burnight, and Liao (2006) found that nearly 90 percent of all bruises identified on elders were on the extremities. What we know from their research is that location matters. When bruises were identified on the neck, ears, genitals, buttocks or feet of the elderly participants in their study, none were caused by accidental means (Mosqueda, et al., 2006). Subjects were less inclined to know how the injury happened in those areas as well. Size and color patterns of bruises were not predictable. The authors did not discover a color pattern (yellow versus red for example) which could identify the date of injury as commonly thought.

Given these issues, medical professionals need to be properly trained to screen patients who may be in danger (McNamee & Murphy, n.d.). A sample scenario created by the authors demonstrates how forensic markers can be misinterpreted as abuse or attributed to a medication side-effect.

> Ruth Ann is 80 years old and lives with her son, John, and sister-in-law, Margaret. Ruth Ann takes Coumadin, a blood thinner. A side effect of Coumadin is bruising that can appear on the skin even with the slightest bump. Ruth Ann has several bruises on her arms; one that looks rather new and a few that have yellowed and seem to be fading. During the visit, Ruth Ann jokes that she is quite clumsy since she fumbles around in the dark a lot. She hates her electricity bill to be too high after all. With further prodding from her doctor he discovers that John is her primary caregiver and is currently unemployed. Ruth Ann reveals that John is a great help but sometimes squeezes her arms and hands too hard when he is "helping."

> *Is this a sign of abuse? Should the doctor continue to assess the patient for abuse or conclude the bruises are related to the medication or accidental injury?*

In the scenario above, Ruth Ann's bruising can be important; however, without proper screening by the doctor, it may go undetected and even continue to worsen. To reduce incidents of harm to patients, medical professionals need to find a way to more clearly determine abuse or neglect in the home. Just following forensic markers alone can yield inaccurate information. These issues demonstrate a need for more effective and consistent screening measures in the entire medical field. Of course, today, practitioners have basic questions that are asked of their patients such as, "Are there any safety concerns at home?" and, "Have you fallen since you were last seen by a doctor?" These questions, while important, can still be problematic as the abuser may be in the room with the patient during questioning. Fear of disclosure may result if safety questions are not asked of the patient in a fully private setting; even then the patient may be unable to disclose the abuse out of fear or confusion.

Elder maltreatment is also problematic due to the isolation that exists as a result of aging. Often older individuals who are less active spend more time in isolation and can suffer from neglect or abuse by caregivers. Consider the following example, again created by the authors:

> Diana, an 85-year-old mother of 7, often lives alone, but recently her daughter, Joselyn, has been living with her. Diana needs help with everyday self-care activities such as bathing and dressing. She also needs help with preparing meals. Diana's other children believe that Joselyn has been caring for their mother, but several weeks pass and the other children realize that no one has heard from Diana or Joselyn. One of Diana's other children, Danielle, stops by the home for a visit. Diana answers the door in her robe and looks happy for the company. Diana quietly inquires if she can get help changing because she has been in her robe for almost two weeks. Diana also reveals that she could use some groceries like milk and fresh bread. It is with this visit that Danielle discovers Joselyn has not been home in weeks, and their mother has been alone all this time. The refrigerator is also empty.
>
> *Is this a sign of neglect? If so, who should be held accountable? What could the family do differently to ensure their mother is cared for?*

Situations such as these highlight the difficulty with detection. There are recommendations to combat these barriers to obtaining information and identifying abuse. Specifically, the authors recommend that medical professionals spend more time with the patient in order to address universal screening questions that are asked by both a nurse and then another health care professional. These two persons can share their opinions about the responses given. If there are any red flags, then the markings should be documented in the patient file. A follow up visit should occur rather quickly (within three to four weeks) whereby the patient is screened again. If this is a standardized process for all elderly patients, the patient may become more comfortable with disclosing any safety concerns. The perpetrator may not suspect he/she is being reported, which could itself pose additional risks to the patient.

THEORIES REGARDING ELDER MALTREATMENT

Understanding why elder maltreatment happens is complex and is no easier than attempting to understand why other forms of violence exist. Most of the studies that seek to understand elder maltreatment center on sociological explanations (National Institute of Justice, 2014). However, biological accounts of elder maltreatment, specifically explaining elderly self-neglect, has been explored through studies conducted on elderly cognition. Cognitive impairment is "one of the most robustly studied co-factors of self-neglect in elderly populations" (Hildebrand, Taylor & Bradway, 2014, p. 456). Elder self-neglect is theorized to stem from neurological shortcomings given the advanced age of the person. Thus, because the elderly can often suffer from a type of brain dysfunction, i.e., Alzheimer's or dementia, we cannot therefore blame the elder for not being aware of his/her own destructive behavior (Hildebrand, et al., 2014). Furthermore, what is important in attempting to understand a link between an elderly person's current cognitive state and self-neglect can also be an issue of temporal order. For example, does cognitive dysfunction lead to self-neglect, or does the persistent state of self-neglect eventually lead to cognitive dysfunction? Before making a diagnosis, it is important to understand causation and correlation and not speculate on definitive causes.

Although biological explanations for elder maltreatment are important for explaining possible self-neglect situations, most attention focuses on sociological justifications. Many of the same theories identified in other forms of violence have been used to explain elder maltreatment. The Intergenerational Transmission Theory, states that violence is a learned behavior that is taught to us when we are young (National Institute of Justice, 2014). In domestic settings one witnesses others being abused and then learns that this behavior is an acceptable means for handling disputes. When applied to cases of elder maltreatment, it suggests that adults who abuse their elderly parents learned, perhaps from those very parents they are now abusing, that this is appropriate and acceptable behavior. However, as critics point out, there are several adults who have witnessed violence in the home that do not go on to abuse the elderly and thus there tends to be inconsistent support for this theory when applied to elder maltreatment (National Institute of Justice, 2014).

One criminological theory that has been employed to explain stress as it relates to perpetrator violence is Strain Theory. Agnew's (1992) General Strain Theory states that sources of individualized strain can lead to inadequate coping mechanisms and the ways in which the offender deals with strain in their life. In cases of elder maltreatment, "caregiver burden" cannot be ignored as a significant cause of victimization (Gainey & Payne, 2006). Many adults, who have to suddenly learn to take over the financial, emotional and physical daily responsibilities of managing an elderly adult, can be overwhelmed. Even for those who are trained in caregiving, the job can be monumental. Research suggests the burnout rate for those employed in the caregiver field such as nursing assistants is tremendously high. These caregivers are under an incredible amount of stress both from elderly patients, the bureaucratic culture of the facility, as well as the lack of interpersonal and medical training, which creates a level of stress coupled with a lack of coping skills that give rise to abusive situations (Goodridge, Johnston & Thomson, 1996; Reader & Gillespie, 2013). This situational stress has been used to explain both institutional and domestic forms of elder maltreatment. Critics of strain theory with respect to explaining elder maltreatment, suggest that such explanations amount to victim blaming, somehow faulting the elderly person for causing the stress and minimizing the perpetrators' actions by sidestepping the seriousness of the abusive situation (Brandl, 2002).

Social Exchange Theory serves as another possible motive for abuse and its unique application specifically to elder maltreatment makes applying the theory of particular interest to elder maltreatment scholars. The theory postulates that relationships require mutual benefit for successful positive outcomes. There is a value to both parties in the relationship. As advanced age sets in and an older person's contribution to the relationship diminishes, the other party feels threatened or abandoned. More importantly, the other person in the relationship, (daughter, son, spouse, and/or grandchild) sees the relationship as one-sided, where the younger person receives little benefit, while the elderly person has become increasingly vulnerable and reliant on the other party. Consequently, the perpetrator becomes resentful and overwhelmed with this unequal balance and the anger spills out in abusive situations (Gordon & Brill, 2001).

Another theory that can help explain elderly maltreatment is Routine Activity Theory (Payne & Gainey, 2006; Byers & Crider, 2002). Routine Activities Theory discusses the convergence in time and space of three situational factors for victimization to occur. First, there must be a motivated offender (someone who wants to commit the crime). Second, there must be a suitable target in order for the crime to be carried out (the target is either something or someone). Third, there must be a lack of guardianship or a watchful eye on the person or item (Cohen & Felson, 1979). In the previous discussion of institutional elder maltreatment, not only does stress serve as a person's primary motivation for why violent and neglectful acts against the elderly occur, but the other two situational factors also shed light on factors for elder maltreatment, lack of guardianship and the obvious defenseless suitable target. In such cases low level staffing within an institutional setting and absent family members, suggest that in many instances where abuse takes place, there is absent the presence of a guardian watching out for the elderly person (Harris & Benson, 2006; Payne & Gainey, 2006). This of course increases the odds that an abusive situation will arise.

Types of Elder Maltreatment

Self-Neglect and Care-Giver Neglect

Self-neglect is the most common form of maltreatment of the elderly and can occur when the elder individual purposefully or unknowingly does not provide self-care (self-neglect can present itself in many forms, including, but not limited to, improper nutrition, cleanliness, and shelter (U.S. Department of Health and Human Services, n.d.-b)). Data provided by social service agencies suggest that elderly self-neglect accounts for more cases of elder maltreatment than all other abuse categories (physical, sexual, emotional and financial), and is the number one indicator that subsequent elder maltreatment, particularly financial exploitation, will occur in the future (Dong, Simon & Evans, 2013). "In 2005, the National Association of Protective Services Administrators reported a 34% increase in 34 states in cases of elderly self-neglect" (Hildebrand, et.al., 2014, p. 452). As the elderly population continues to rise in the U.S. over the next several years, self-neglect issues will continue to be a leading cause of elderly maltreatment.

Self-neglect commonly comes to the attention of APS by reports from family, friends, community members or professionals in the medical or criminal justice fields. The elderly may become depressed as a result of declining health, an ailing body, or social isolation. Apathy by the victim, a common response to these issues, can result. Thus, it is important to ensure "welfare checks" or health checks on our aging family members and friends because social isolation is not only a hazard, but it is especially dangerous for the aging population (Rathbone-McCuan, 2014). Key indicators of self-neglect and self-care includes the following:

- Hoarding of objects, newspapers/magazines, mail/paperwork, etc., and/ or animal hoarding to the extent that the safety of the individual (and/or other household or community members) is threatened or compromised
- Failure to provide adequate food and nutrition for oneself
- Failure to take essential medications or refusal to seek medical treatment for serious illness
- Leaving a burning stove unattended
- Poor hygiene
- Not wearing suitable clothing for the weather
- Confusion
- Inability to attend to housekeeping
- Dehydration

Source: U.S. Department of Health and Human Services, n.d. — c para 3

To say that an elderly person self neglects, does not necessarily mean that the person suffers from any particular mental disease or defect. According to Naik, Lai, Kunik & Dyer, (2008), "Among adults who are vulnerable to self-neglect, the capacity to make some decisions may remain intact. However, the capacity to identify and extract oneself from harmful situations, circumstances, or relationships may be diminished" (p. 26). One must look at the decisional capacity of the elderly person in several categories to determine whether they have the cognitive ability to not only make choices, but also to implement those choices for their own benefit. Naik, et al. (2008) identify five domains of self-care and protection in order to assess cognitive capacity: personal care, conditions of the home; independent living; medical self-care and awareness and financial matters. Not only must the elderly person be able to appreciate their limitations, but they must also have a system in place for addressing such limitations if they are to avoid self-neglect situations. It is important that clinicians identify the signs of self-neglect through assessment tools that measure depression, dementia, and other disorders. Furthermore, an integrative approach between primary care personnel and mental health workers can assist with the ability to gain an individual's assessment of self-worth or self-awareness (Rathbone-McCuan, 2014). When clinicians, as well as criminal justice personnel, examine cases of self-neglect, one must keep in mind that older adults still have the freedom to make bad decisions and these potentially bad choices alone do not necessarily lead to a classification of self-neglect (Connolly, 2008).

According to Connolly (2008), identifying cases of self-neglect for criminal justice investigative purposes pose several potential problems. First, these cases are difficult to discern owing to the inability to readily distinguish between intentional abuse by others and neglect of one's own care. Next, forensics may only tell us so much (that bruises exist, for example, but the person who inflicted them may not be so easily identifiable). Furthermore, it is important for prosecutors who are investigating such cases to seek outside information from caretakers, primary care physicians, and gerontologists if possible, in order to get a clearer picture of the elderly persons living conditions.

There is also evidence that mental factors alone cannot fully explain self-neglect, but rather environmental influences within the home can instigate self-neglect situations. For example, as pointed out by Burnett, Dyer, Halphen, Achenbaum, Green, Booker & Diamond (2014), clutter within the home may create physical barriers to restrict movement or a depletion of financial resources could mean there is no money for electricity and walking in the dark is especially dangerous for an elderly person. These circumstances contribute to risky environments for the elderly and signal potential hazardous situations.

Emotional/Psychological/Mental Abuse

Emotional or psychological abuse is defined as, "the infliction of anguish, pain, or distress through verbal or nonverbal acts" (U.S. Department of Health and Human Services, n.d-b para 3). Emotional/psychological abuse includes but is not limited to verbal assaults, insults, threats, intimidation, humiliation, and harassment. The signs and symptoms of emotional/psychological abuse include:

> Being emotionally upset or agitated; being extremely withdrawn and non-communicative or non-responsive; unusual behavior usually attributed to dementia (e.g., sucking, biting, rocking); and an elder's report of being verbally or emotionally mistreated.
> Source: U.S. Department of Health and Human Services, n.d.-b para 3

The elderly person may be threatened with the destruction of important property; i.e., damage to cherished heirlooms or pets (Wilson, 2015). The person may become fearful of his/her relatives, often the caregivers. He or she may be called names and spoken to in a degrading manner. Examples of emotional abuse are verbal taunts and "threats to put the person in a nursing home" or on the "street" or in a "homeless shelter" (Wilson, 2015). In addition, treating an older person like an infant demoralizes the victim. Many elderly persons are intentionally isolated from his/her family and friends and are prevented from engaging in regular activities. Also, a caretaker may intentionally refrain from speaking with the elderly person thus denying basic communication also known as giving an older person the "silent treatment," an example of emotional neglect.

Physical and Sexual Abuse

According to the National Research Council (2003), one to five million older adults, 65 and older, are physically or sexually injured or mistreated by their caregivers in family settings. The National Institute of Justice (NIJ) found that eleven percent of elders reported experiencing at least one form of mistreatment in the past year (Acierno et al., 2008). These staggering numbers include only those persons known to have been abused, and given that about half of crimes (and thus victimizations) go unreported, one can assume that doubling this estimate would yield a more accurate number. Furthermore, an overwhelming majority of victims suffer at the hands of his/her own family members (children, grandchildren, and spouses) (Heydrich, Schiamberg & Chee, 2012). Elder adults' inability to control their own environment and have input into their care leads to situations where there is not only the potential for physical abuse, but social isolation and alienation. There are important social constructs that can cause social isolation and alienation for elderly people; the former resulting from fewer friendships and the latter because the elder does not feel as though they fit in their community.

All non-accidental injuries by another constitute physical abuse. In an effort to identify risk factors, Heydrich, et al. (2012) examined the family dynamics and contextual situations where elderly adults were living with their adult children and receiving care. Often stress is comingled with alcohol and substance abuse by the perpetrator leading to elder harm. The research suggests that if greater effort is put into building the relationship between the caregiver and the elder individual, the less likely there is to be physical harm. Social stress within the family is a source of family violence, and elder maltreatment is no exception. Therefore, learning ways to communicate effectively may lead to less volatile situations. Specifically, identifying the risk and protective factors in both the elder and his/her child, can highlight possible therapeutic measures that can be identified and put into place (Heydrich et. al, 2012, p. 88–90).

Sexual abuse of the elderly is understood to constitute, "a sexual relationship with an elderly person . . . [who does not provide] consent" (Benbow & Haddad, 1993, p. 803). Sexual abuse of the elderly has not been extensively covered in the literature like other populations who often suffer from sexual assault. Research in this area began in the early 1980s, nearly 20 years after the topic of child abuse was more thoroughly analyzed (Benbow & Haddad, 1993). The distinction between the two populations has a lot to do with how society views the issue of sexuality. For example, young attractive females as victims of sexual assault are more readily understood because in our society they are seen as "wanted," whereas we often associate the elderly population as a "sexless" and less desirable people (Benbow & Haddad, 1993). Of course, it does not matter which gender you are, as anyone can be sexually assaulted, but it is significantly more common for elderly females to experience this threat. Actually, females are six times more likely to be sexually assaulted over their male counterparts (Pennsylvania Coalition Against Rape, 2013).

There is conflicting literature as to the identification of the perpetrators of sexual assault against the elderly. Older studies indicate that sexual assault is often committed by an outside assailant, unknown to the victim, and who has committed the act in tandem with another violent act, such as robbery, (i.e., the elderly person just happened to be in the wrong place at the wrong time) (see Safarik, Jarvis & Nussbaum, 2002; Muram, Miller & Cutler, 1992). Other studies cite caregivers and family members known to the victim as perpetrators. Sexual assault by caregivers can include nursing home facilities or long-term care facilities where a member of the staff engages in inappropriate touching or sexual activity with the elderly resident. Statistics indicate this is the most common location for sexual abuse, where as many as 70% of the sexually assaulted have been in a care facility at the time of the incident (Nursing Home Abuse Guide, n.d.). Family members (brothers, sisters, children, nephews) have been known to abuse an older family member as well. One poignant demographic factor seems to remain constant — that the perpetrators of sexual assault against the elderly appear to be much younger than the victim, usually not over the age of 40 (Roberto & Teaster, 2005; Muram, et al., 1992). Other sexual abuse situations arise when one spouse is significantly older than the other. While it may be unintentional on the part of the younger spouse to abuse his/her spouse sexually, the key concern remains whether the elderly spouse gives consent, knowingly and willingly.

The type of injuries suffered during sexual assault of an elderly person range from direct penile penetration causing genital injury, to other forms of sexual touching and kissing. Sex abuse can also occur by someone who is engaging in other acts of abuse during the same period of time, usually psychological and/

or financial abuse; the latter becoming increasingly more common (Roberto & Teaster, 2005; Safarik, Jarvis & Nussbaum, 2002; Muram, et al., 1992).

Financial Abuse

Financial exploitation of the elderly can occur when one or more person(s) has complete control over the fiscal decisions of another and there is no accountability for how money may be spent. Gibson and Qualls (2012) indicate this area is the "fastest growing" form of abuse and consists of: theft from bank accounts, retirement checks, and siphoning of funds from investments. Persons who have any type of cognitive impairment are especially prone to this type of victimization as the individual may not recall handing over funds or signing checks to an entrusted person.

To protect oneself from possible financial abuse, proper estate planning for the elderly reduces the likelihood of harm. For example, elderly parents may be influenced by one of their adult offspring to sign a very broad Power of Attorney, a document granting decision-making authority to another, that is effective immediately (not upon the parents' incapacity) (B. Fink, Personal Interview, November 21, 2015). Generally, the intent is for the adult child to have an easier time doing banking, etc., for the elderly parent, but these powers may be very broad and can lead to the children actually transferring the title from the elder, with regard to vehicles, bank accounts, etc., to themselves. As Brian Fink, an estate planning attorney indicates, these areas create the potential for financial abuse. Fink states that another area of concern is whether the perpetrators' siblings are either unaware of these arrangements or are coaxed into believing the parent gave him/her permission to execute the Power of Attorney before they became incapacitated. Likewise, in each of these cases, the situation could have been avoided by a thoughtful estate plan that is reviewed with each of the children so the parents' wishes are very clear to all parties (B. Fink, Personal Interview, November 21, 2015).

Institutional Abuse

The exact number of elderly persons who suffer maltreatment in the institutional setting is not known. A 2001 report suggests that nearly one third of all certified facilities had been cited for some type of abuse violation causing harm to an elderly resident (National Center on Elder Abuse Research Brief, 1). In a study of 2,000 interviews of nursing home residents, 44% said they had been abused and 95% said they had been neglected or had seen another resident neglected (Broyles, 2000). Perpetrators within the institutional setting are normally caregivers; specifically nurses, certified nursing assistants (CNA) or other direct personnel (Hodge, 1998). Patients tend to suffer the same types of abuse discussed previously (physical, sexual, psychological, and financial), only here it is within an organization designed to maintain care, custody and control of the patient. The elderly are supposed to be safe in health care facilities but sometimes they are in fact exposed to more dangerous conditions. Too often one thinks of the physical and sexual abuse that can occur in nursing homes but there is also financial abuse in the form of bureaucratic fraud, specifically with Medicare/ Medicaid billing. Although prosecutions are rare, such occurrences can be investigated at the federal level, especially if the nursing home is receiving federal funds through Medicare/Medicaid. When prosecutions do arise, the acts tend to focus on the failure to provide adequate medication, to supervise, and failure to properly assess the residents' condition (Hodge, 1998). Not only have individual caregivers been prosecuted in several states for neglecting patients (victims had bed sores, suffered from dehydration etc.), but nursing home administrators and owners have also been held criminally liable.

Although long-term care facilities have policies in place to address these issues with staff, employment practices need to change to make sure potential employees meet background check requirements for the safety of residents. There needs to be additional accountability measures enabling more transparency of the daily care provided to those in institutional settings. As one example, the Florida Attorney General's Office has initiated a "Spot Check" program in order to carefully examine the living condition in nursing homes. In other states across the U.S. Adult Protective Services now operate in a working group fashion to share information among ombudsmen, state regulators and county protective personnel in monitoring nursing home operations (Hodge, 1998).

Legal and Policy Responses to Elderly Maltreatment

Legal Responses at the National Level

Medicare, Medicaid and the Older Americans Act have been in existence for 50 years, while Social Security has existed for 80 years. Collectively they represent significant legislative enactments designed to protect elderly Americans (White House Conference on Aging, 2015). Legislation to protect the elderly began with *The Older Americans Act of 1965* (42 U.S.C. Ch 35 sec 3001 et seq.). The Act has provided an important broad range of services to assist the elderly with sustenance, transportation, and legal services among other provisions. One of the key features of the Act continues to be the prevention of elder maltreatment and support for caregivers. More recently the Act was amended in 2006 under President Bush. As a result, the role of the Administration on Aging was expanded. The amended Act increased the funding formula for state-sponsored nutrition programs for the elderly and expanded the types of programs receiving funding at the state level.

In another effort to protect the elderly, President Obama declared *Older Americans Month* for the first time in April of 2013 (Dorner and Lab, 2015). Similarly, President Obama announced June 15, 2015 as World Elder Maltreatment Awareness Day (White House Proclamation on World Elder Abuse Awareness Day, June 12, 2015). These federal-level declarations underscore the importance of protecting the elderly. More importantly, they are a powerful signal to the states to follow a similar approach in addressing elder maltreatment. In an effort to reinforce the federal commitment to elder abuse prevention, the White House held a forum on Elder Justice. The forum, the sixth since 1961, is held every decade (White House Conference on Aging, press release, July 13, 2015). The forum participants discussed how best to address and prevent elder maltreatment and financial exploitation. As a follow-up, the White House held a conference on aging in July of 2015. The final report on the conference was issued at the end of 2015. The report highlighted the new rules for Medicare and Medicaid, the first in 25 years. New rules will be applied to the S.N.A.P. (Senior Nutrition Assistance Program). Furthermore, the U.S. Department of Housing and Urban Development (H.U.D) will apply the Equal Access rule to housing for the elderly (White House Conference on Aging, 2015). These executive actions suggest that the issue of elder maltreatment is clearly a priority at the highest elected office in the nation and conveys the importance of addressing elder maltreatment.

Another important piece of legislation is *The Elder Justice Act* (EJA) (2010). The Act was ratified as part of the Patient Protection and Affordable Care Act (PPACA) on March 23, 2010. The Elder Justice Act (EJA) was the first federal legislation passed to authorize a specific source of federal funds dedicated to addressing elder maltreatment, neglect, and exploitation. The Act mandates cooperation between APS and law enforcement (Wilson, 2007; Dubble, 2006). Unfortunately as of 2015, funding for the legislation has not been authorized by Congress (Wilson, 2015). Outside of the legislation an advisory board has been created in the federal Department of Health & Human Services (HHS) to work on issues related to funding. In addition, a webcast held in November of 2010 specifically addressed the lack of funding and full implementation of the Act.

State

With the exception of New York, all states maintain Mandated Reporter Laws (U.S. Department of Justice, n.d.-a). New York has resisted implementing mandatory reporting laws for reasons ranging from costs, training of professionals, and unintended negative consequences for the elderly (NYC Elder Abuse Center, 2015). Furthermore, state officials are not convinced that such laws will produce increased awareness of, prevention of, or improve responses to elder maltreatment. In contrast to New York, the other 49 states maintain Mandated or Universal Reporter laws requiring the reporting of elder maltreatment by certain professions. In instances of suspected elder maltreatment, the designated professional must have reasonable cause to believe that an adult is being abused, neglected, or exploited, or is in a condition which is the result of abuse, neglect, or exploitation (RAINN, 2009). A host of professions: legal, medical and mental health, education, and clergy are required to report suspected elder maltreatment. All 50 states and the U.S. territories have initiated services and programs to protect the elderly (U.S. Department of Justice, n.d.-b).

Adult Protective Services (APS) is present in all states (U.S. Department of Justice, n.d.-c). APS is mandated to report and investigate elder maltreatment (Ohio Department on Aging, 2007; Ohio Attorney General, 2005). Reporting of elder abuse can be anonymous and seniors may decline services from APS. In order for there to be APS involvement, an elderly person must be in danger of physical harm, mental pain, or illness. APS is an elder maltreatment advocate. They offer a host of services including: 24/7 hotline counseling, Medicare, financial management assistance, legal services, adult day care and basic needs (clothing, shelter, food) (Ohio Department on Aging, 2007).

The Area Agency on Aging was created by the Older Americans Act of 1965. The local Area Agencies on Aging respond to the needs of the elderly in the communities they serve. They advocate on behalf of the elderly, work with local funders and educators along with public and private partners to respond to the unique needs of older citizens and their families. The local agencies are designated to develop and implement plans for the elderly based on the population and the available community resources. Concurrently, the National Association of Area Agencies on Aging, or n4a, has been in existence since 1975 and represents 623 Area Agencies on Aging throughout the United States. The n4a serves as an advocate for policies concerning the elderly along with providing basic services including meals, transportation and caregiver support.

Legal Responses Internationally

"The World Health Organization has declared that elder maltreatment is a violation of one of the most basic and fundamental human rights: to be safe and free of violence" (Elder Rights and the Older Americans Act, 2011). The International Network for the Prevention of Elder Maltreatment (INPEA) was formed in 1997. The INPEA is dedicated to the global dissemination of information as part of its commitment to the world-wide prevention of elder abuse. INPEA engages in educational activities, victim advocacy and promotes research on causes and prevention of elder maltreatment.

The United Nations has developed a Plan of Action to address the aging world population. The first conference was held in Vienna in 1982 and called for specific action on issues such as health and nutrition, protecting elderly consumers, and housing. The conference focused on the role of the family, social welfare, income security and employment, and education (United Nations, 1982). During an international conference held in 2010, the United Nations recognized the 20th International Day of Older Persons. The event was designed to further support the significant UN milestones acknowledging older persons as an increasingly major segment of society. These efforts will continue the dialog on the implementation of the Madrid International Plan of Action on Ageing and the United Nations UN Principles for Older Persons. Specifically, the Madrid Plan outlined a series of actions and objectives including: full and active participation of the elderly in society in terms of economic, social, and technological endeavors; participation in decision-making at all political levels; and providing employment opportunities for those who are able and want to work (Madrid Plan, 2002). Another area of focus is on rural areas in developing countries, including immigration and urban areas. The Plan identified how the elderly are often left behind when families in developing countries move to more urban areas. The living conditions in these areas are often fraught with infrastructure problems including access to clean water, medical treatment, nutritional support, and lack of educational and social interaction opportunities.

Advocacy Response to Elder Maltreatment

Criminal Justice Initiatives: Triad Programs

Triad is a national community policing initiative where law enforcement professionals, seniors and community groups partner to meet the crime-safety needs of the seniors. The program has existed for 26 years (Ohio Triad Program, 1989). It represents a shared commitment by these groups to keep senior citizens safe. Triad strives to reduce crime against the elderly and reduce unwarranted fear of crime often experienced by the elderly. Triad is committed to reducing criminal victimization of older persons; improving the quality of life for older adults; educating and involving the community in implementing solutions; and enhancing delivery of law enforcement services to the elderly.

The U.S. Department of Justice (n.d.-d) maintains a website dedicated to assisting the elderly and their families. It is a resource for victims of elder maltreatment and financial exploitation. The website provides information to the families, health care practitioners and advocates, law enforcement agencies as well as researchers. Through the process of self-education by way of access to helpful resources, reporting cases of abuse can increase. It was announced that the U.S. Department of Justice, National Institute of Justice and its Elder Justice Initiative will fund a multi-year pilot project to evaluate potential means to avoid and respond to elder mistreatment (White House Conference on Aging, 2015). In addition, the National Institute of Health (NIH) convened a state of the science workshop in 2015. The workshop focused on elder maltreatment with researchers, and clinicians to review the current science on understanding and preventing abuse. In addition, topics covered developing screening tools to identify abuse victims and implement effective intervention. NIH will continue to direct areas of research in related fields such as child abuse and domestic violence. The belief is that such efforts might inform better practices on elder maltreatment as well as highlight opportunities for future research.

The National Adult Protective Services Association (NAPSA) is a national non-profit 501(c) (3) organization with membership in all 50 states (National Adult Protective Services Association, n.d.). Formed in 1989, the goal of NAPSA is to provide APS programs a forum for sharing information, solving problems, and improving the quality of services for victims of elder and vulnerable adult mistreatment. Its mission is to strengthen the capacity of APS at the national, state, and local levels. Within that mission, APS is poised to effectively and efficiently recognize, report, and respond to the needs of elders and adults with disabilities. APS is focused on elders who are the victims of abuse, neglect, and/or exploitation. The agency seeks to prevent, where possible, incidents of abuse.

Formerly known as the American Association of Retired Persons, AARP, Inc., is a national, interest-group founded in 1958. AARP advocates on behalf of their membership of persons aged 50 and older. The AARP Foundation Litigation (AFL) is an advocate in courts nationwide for the rights of people

50 and older, addressing diverse legal issues that affect their daily lives and assuring that they have a voice in the judicial system.

In an effort to better coordinate responses to elder maltreatment, MDTs (Multidisciplinary Teams) have been developed. Over the past decade, the use of MDTs is quite common in crimes of child sexual abuse, domestic and familial violence and sexual assault. The same model is now being implemented to address elder maltreatment (U.S. Department of Health and Human Services, n.d. -d). Starting in the early 1980s, the original elder maltreatment multidisciplinary teams (MDTs) included professionals from different disciplines who came together, usually monthly, to review cases and address system problems. The teams reviewed cases of abuse, neglect, and self-neglect, and provided resources, advice, and new perspectives to the agency. Traditional multidisciplinary teams focus on complex cases of all types of abuse, neglect, exploitation, self-neglect, and possibly adults with disabilities, depending on the state. Teams typically are comprised of representatives from public agencies that investigate elder maltreatment including: Adult Protective Services, LTC Ombudsman, law enforcement, city or county counsel, and non-profit (and occasionally for-profit) agencies that provide services to seniors. In a White House Forum on Elder Justice in 2015, the panel members renewed the call for a multidisciplinary approach to address the treatment of older Americans.

Summary

Physical, sexual, emotional and financial abuse and neglect of the elderly happens throughout the United States every day. Even though there are more available resources today for victims, many, including law enforcement, may still have the perception that elder maltreatment is a private matter that needs to be addressed within the family unit (Band-Winterstein, 2015). It is important to recognize that if we are to make progress in combating the elder maltreatment problem across the United States, we need to know what it is, the types that exist, its root causes and the policies and programs needed to address it. This chapter has discussed these important considerations in the hope of becoming better people by protecting those who cannot protect themselves.

Web Activity: Visit the National Center on Elder maltreatment for further details on the EJA (2010):

http://ncea.aoa.gov/Resources/Publication/docs/Elder_Justice_Act_Q_and_A.pdf

Web Activity: View the conference on World Elder maltreatment Awareness Day held on May 22, 2015.

https://www.youtube.com/watch?v=stwqKXXPQP8&feature=youtube

REFERENCES

AARP Inc. (n.d.). Retrieved from http://www.aarp.org/aarp-foundation/our -work/legal- advocacy.html

Acierno, R., Hernandez-Tejada, M., Muzzy, W., & Steve, K. (2008). National Elder Mistreatment Study: Final report to the National Institute of Justice. Granted number 2007-WC-BX-0009, March 2008, NCJ 226456.

Agnew, R. (1992). Foundation for a general strain theory of crime and delinquency. *Criminology, 30,* 47–87.

Area Agency on Aging. Retrieved from https://aging.ohio.gov/resources/area agenciesonaging/

Band-Winterstein, T. (2015). Whose suffering is this? Narratives of adult children and parents in long-term abusive relationships. *Journal of Family Violence, 30,* 123–133. Doi 10.1007/s/10896-014-9660-z.

Benbow, S., & Haddad, P. (1993, April). Sexual abuse of the elderly mentally ill. *The Fellowship of Postgraduate Medicine, 69,* 803–809.

Brandl, B. (2002). Power and control: Understanding domestic abuse in later life. *Generations, 24*(2), 39–45.

Broyles, K. (2000). The silenced voice speaks out: A study of abuse and neglect of nursing home residents. Atlanta, GA: A report from the Atlanta Long Term Care Ombudsman Program and Atlanta Legal Aid Society to the National Citizens Coalition for Nursing Home Reform. Retrieved from www .atlantalegalaid.org/abuse.htm

Burnett, J., Dyer, C., Halphen, J., Achenbaum, A., Green, C., Booker, J., & Diamond, P. (2014). Four subtypes of self-neglect in older adults: Results of a latent class analysis. *The American Geriatrics Society, 62,* 1127–1132.

Byers, B. D., & Crider, B. W. (2002). Hate crimes against the Amish: A Qualitative analysis of bias motivation using routine activities theory. *Deviant Behavior, 23*(2), 115–148.

Cohen, L. E., & Felson, M. (1979). Social Change and crime rate trends-routine activity approach. *American Sociological Review, 44*(4), 588–608.

Colby, S. L., & Ortman, J. M. (2015, March). Projections of the size and composition of the U.S. population: 2014 to 2060 population estimates and projections current population reports. Retrieved from: (https://www.census.gov/content/dam/Census/library/publications/2015/demo/p25-1143.pdf).

Collins, K.A. (2006). Elder Maltreatment: A Review. *Archives of Pathology & Laboratory Medicine, 130*(9), 1290–1296.

Connolly, M. (2008). Elder self-neglect and the justice system: An essay from an interdisciplinary perspective. *The American Geriatrics Society, 56*(S2), pg. 244–252

Doerner, W.G., & Lab, S.P. (2015). *Victimology* (7ᵗʰ ed.). Massachusetts: Anderson Publishing.

Dong, X., Simon, M., & Evans, D. (2013). Elder self-neglect is associated with increased risk for elder maltreatment in a community-dwelling population: Findings from the Chicago Health and Aging Project. *Journal of Aging and Health, 25*(1), 80–96.

Dubble, C. (2006). A Policy Perspective on elder justice through APS and law enforcement collaboration. *Journal of Gerontological Social Work, 46*(3–4), 5–55.

Elder Justice Act. (2010). Subtitle H in Title VI of Public Act 111–148 PPACA.

Elder Rights and the Older Americans Act: Hearing before the Special Committee on Aging, Senate. (2011) (Testimony of Kathy Greenlee, Assistant Secretary, Administration on Aging). Retrieved http://www.hhs.gov/asl/testify/2011/08/t20110823a.html.

Fink, B. L. (2015, November 21). Personal Interview.

Gainey, R.R., & Payne, B.K. (2006). Caregiver burden, elder abuse, and Alzheimer 's Disease: testing the relationship. *Journal of Health and Human Services Administration, 29*(2), 245–259.

Gibson, S. C., & Qualls, S. H. (2012, fall). A family systems perspective of elder financial abuse. *Generations: Journal of American Society on Aging, 36*(3), 26–29.

Goodridge, D., Johnston, P., & Thomson, M. (1996). Conflict and aggression as stressors in the work environment of nursing assistants: Implications for institutional elder maltreatment. *Journal of Elder Maltreatment & Neglect, 8*(1), 49–67.

Gordon, R.M., & Brill, D. (2001). The abuse and neglect of the elderly. *International Journal Law & Psychiatry, 24,* 183–197.

Harris, D. K., & Benson, B. M. L. (2006). Maltreatment of patients in nursing homes: There is no safeplace. Binghamton: Haworth Pastoral Press.

Heydrich, L., Schiamberg, L.B., & Chee, G. (2012). Social-relational risk factors for predicting elder physical abuse: An ecological bifocal model. *International Journal on Aging and Human Development, 75*(1) 71–94.

Hildebrand, C., Taylor, M., & Bradway, C. (2014). Elder self-neglect: The failure of coping because of cognitive and functional impairments. *Journal of the American Association of Nurse Practitioners, 26*, 452–462.

Hodge, P. (1998). National law enforcement programs to prevent, detect, investigate and prosecute elder maltreatment and neglect in health care facilities. *Journal of Elder maltreatment & Neglect, 9*(4), 23–41.

The International Network for the Prevention of Elder maltreatment (INPEA). (n.d.). Retrieved from http://www.inpea.net/about.html

Madrid Plan. (2002). 2nd *Assembly on Ageing*. Madrid, Spain, April 8–12.

McNamee, C. C., & Murphy, M. B. (n.d.). Elder maltreatment in the United States. *National Institute of Justice, 255*. Retrieved from http://www.nij.gov/journals/255/pages/elder_abuse.aspx

Mosqueda, L., Burnight, K., & Liao, S. (2006, June). *Bruising in the Geriatric Population*. National Institute of Justice, Washington, DC: (NCJ 214649). Available at www.ncjrs.gov/pdffiles1/nij/grants/214649.pdf

Muram, D., Miller, K., & Cutler, A. (1992, March). Sexual Assault of the Elderly Victim. *Journal of Interpersonal Violence, 7*(1), 70–76.

Naik, A., Lai, J., Kunik, M., & Dyer, C. (2008, February). Assessing capacity in suspected cases of self-neglect. *Geriatrics, 63*(2), 24–31.

National Association of Area Agencies on Aging. (n.d.). Retrieved from http://www.n4a.org/

National Center on Elder Abuse. (n.d.). *Abuse of residents of long term care facilities. research brief*. Retrieved from http://www.ncea.aoa.gov/resources/publication/docs/ncea_ltcf_researchbrief_2013.pdf

National Adult Protective Services Association (NAPSA). (n.d.). Retrieved from http://www.napsa-now.org/

National Institute of Justice. (2014, June) Elderly mistreatment: Using theory in research. Retrieved from http://www.nij.gov/topics/crime/elder-abuse/Documents/elder-mistreatment-theory-meeting-summary.pdf

National Institute of Justice. Elder maltreatment in the United States. (Issue No. 255). Retrieved from http://www.nij.gov/journals/255/pages/elder_abuse.aspx.

National Research Council. (2003) Elder mistreatment: Abuse, neglect and exploitation in an aging America. Washington, D.C.: The National Academies Press.

NYC Elder Abuse Center. (8 January 2015). New York state doesn't have manda-tory reporting: good or something to change? Retrieved from http://nyceac.com/elder-justice-dispatch-new-york-state-doesnt-have-mandatory-reporting-good-or-something-to-change/

Nursing Home Abuse Guide. (n.d.). *Where does elder abuse happen?* Retrieved from http://nursinghomeabuseguide.com/elder-abuse/sexual-abuse/.

Ohio Attorney General's Office. (2005). Adult Protective Services. Retrieved from http://www.ohioattorneygeneral.gov

Ohio Department on Aging. (2007). Retrieved from http://aging.ohio.gov/home/

Ohio Triad Program. (1989). Retrieved from http://www.sheriffs.org/content/national-triad

Older Americans Act. (1965). 42 U.S.C. Chapter 35 Section 3001, Pub.L.89-73.

Payne, B. K., & Gainey, R. R. (2006). The criminal justice response to elder maltreatment in nursing homes: A routine activities perspective. *Western Criminology Review, 7(3),* 67–81.

Rathbone-McCuan, E. (2014). An improved approach to treating elder self-neglect: The self-care framework. *Journal of American Society on Aging, 38*(3), 80–85.

Rape, Abuse and Incest National Network (RAINN). (2009). Retrieved from www.rainn.org

Reader, T.W., & Gillespie, A. (2013). Patient neglect in healthcare institutions: a systematic review and conceptual model. *BMC Health Services Research, 13*(1), 1–15.

Pennsylvania Coalition Against Rape. (2013). *Elderly sexual abuse.* Web. 18 May 2013. Retrieved from http://www.pcar.org/elder-sexual-abuse

Roberto, K., & Teaster, P. (2005, April). Sexual abuse of vulnerable young and old women. *Violence Against Women, 11*(4), 473–504.

Safarik, M., Jarvis, J., & Nussbaum, K. (2002, May). Sexual homicide of elderly females. *Journal of Interpersonal Violence, 17*(5), 500–525.

United Nations. (1982). *Global issues: ageing.* Retrieved from http://www.un.org/en/globalissues/ageing

U.S. Department of Justice. (n.d.-a). Elder Justice. *What is mandatory report-ing?* Retrieved from https://www.justice.gov/elderjustice/support/faq.html#what-is-mandatory-reporting

U.S. Department of Justice. (n.d.-b). Elder Justice. *Who is responsible?* Re-trieved from https://www.justice.gov/elderjustice/support/faq.html#who

-is-responsible-for-responding-to-reports-of-elder-abuse-in-the -community

U.S. Department of Justice. (n.d.-c). *Elder justice resources by state.* Retrieved from https://www.justice.gov/elderjustice/support/resources.html

U.S. Department of Justice. (n.d.-d). *Elder justice initiative.* Retrieved from http://www.justice.gov/elderjustice/

U.S. Department of Health and Human Services/Administration for Community Living. Administration on Aging (n.d.). *Aging Statistics.* Retrieved from http://www.aoa.acl.gov/aging_statistics/index.aspx

U.S. Department of Health and Human Services/National Center on Elder Abuse. Administration on Aging. (n.d.-a). *America's growing elderly population.* Retrieved From http://www.ncea.aoa.gov/Library/Data/index.aspx

U.S. Department of Health and Human Services/National Center on Elder Abuse. Administration on Aging. (n.d.-b). *Types of Abuse.* Retrieved from http://www.ncea.aoa.gov/FAQ/Type_Abuse/index.aspx

U.S. Department of Health and Human Services/National Center on Elder Abuse. Administration on Aging. (n.d.-c). *What is self-neglect and what are the signs?* Retrieved from http://www.ncea.aoa.gov/faq/index.aspx

U.S. Department of Health and Human Services/National Center on Elder Abuse. Administration on Aging. (n.d.-d). *Multidisciplinary Teams.* Retrieved from http://www.ncea.aoa.gov/Stop_Abuse/Teams/index.aspx

White House Conference on Aging (2015). Retrieved from http://www .whitehouseconferenceonaging.gov/2015-WHCOA-Final-Report.pdf

White House Conference on Aging Press Release. (13 July 2015). Retrieved from https://www.whitehouse.gov/the-press-office/2015/07/13/fact-sheet -white-house-conference-aging

White House Proclamation on World Elder Abuse Awareness Day, Press Release (12 June 2015). Retrieved from https://www.whitehouse.gov/the -press-office/2015/06/12/presidential-proclamation-world-elder-abuse -awareness-day-2015

White House Forum on Elder Justice. (2015). Retrieved from http://www .justice.gov/elderjustice/blog/

Wilson, M. G. (2007). Responding to elder maltreatment: The role of law enforcement. Paper presented at the Academy of Criminal Justice Sciences March 14, 2008, Cincinnati, Ohio.

Wilson, M. G. (2015). Lecture. Elder abuse and maltreatment. Warren, Ohio, Kent State Trumbull Campus

CHAPTER 11

ELDER NEGLECT AND STRAIN: CAN'T GET NO SATISFACTION IN THE CAREGIVER ROLE[*]

Christina Policastro
University of Tennessee at Chattanooga
Randy R. Gainey
Old Dominion University
Brian K. Payne
Old Dominion University

INTRODUCTION

Borrowing from the child abuse literature, a recent study on elder neglect concluded that criminologists "neglect elder neglect" (Payne, Blowers & Jarvis, 2012). The authors highlighted a glaring absence of research on elder neglect, noting that a search of the phrase "elder neglect" in criminal justice abstracts and other databases yielded virtually no empirical studies by criminologists or other social scientists for that matter. The lack of research on the topic is problematic given that most prevalence studies on elder mistreatment find that elder neglect is among the more common varieties of elder mistreatment (Acierno, Hernandez, Amstadter, Resnick, Steve, Muzzy & Kilpatrick, 2010; Teaster, Dugar, Mendiondo, Abner, Cecil & Otto, 2007). Failing to study neglect among the elderly population limits our understanding of the problem and fosters emotionally-based responses to the problem as opposed to empirically-driven strategies.

[*] This research was supported in part by Award No. 04-4 from the Commonwealth of Virginia's Alzheimer's and Related Diseases Research Award Fund, administered by the Virginia Center on Aging, Virginia Commonwealth University Medical Center.

Criminologists have ignored elder neglect for at least four reasons (see Payne, 2011). First, many erroneously believe that the behavior is so infrequent that it is not worthy of criminological attention. Second, difficulties defining elder abuse have made it challenging to study any of the elder mistreatment types. Third, politically speaking, most of the legislative attention given to elder mistreatment has focused specifically on physical abuse. Finally, until recently, virtually no federal funding was available for research on crimes against older persons. Although new funding opportunities have become available through the National Institute of Justice and National Institutes of Health, researchers continue to focus on active offenses, such as physical abuse, at the expense of crimes of omission, such as elder neglect. Thus, it is important that scholars consider how the characteristics and potential causes of neglect vary from other forms of elder maltreatment. In order to address this gap in the literature, the current study utilizes data from adult protective services files to explore the differences between neglect and non-neglect cases, as well as examine the utility of criminological theory, specifically general strain theory, for understanding the underlying causes of elder neglect. Distinguishing elder neglect from other elder abuse cases and identifying the role of burden in these cases is useful for informing policy and practice, as well as can help foster further theoretical development across multiple disciplines including criminology and gerontology.

Review of Literature

At the most general level, one can define elder neglect as failing to provide care to an older person when one has a duty to provide that person care. Experts differentiate between active neglect and passive neglect (Lacher, Wettstein, Senn, Roseman & Hasler, 2016; Jirik & Sanders, 2014). Active neglect occurs when caregivers intentionally decide not to provide care to an older person, while passive neglect refers to situations where the failure to provide care is unintended and rooted in a lack of knowledge about caregiving. Beyond these general characterizations of elder neglect, a great deal of debate exists surrounding specific definitions of elder neglect.

Indeed, one of the primary reasons that elder neglect has been studied so infrequently by criminologists is that a clear definition of the concept does not exist. The conceptual ambiguity stems from vague definitions of elder mistreatment. While much debate remains on different elder maltreatment topics, there is one topic that most experts seem to agree on: there is no universally accepted definition of elder maltreatment (Wolf, 1996). The fact that experts cannot agree on definitions of the broader category of elder maltreatment should make it obvious that experts also do not agree on definitions of specific forms of maltreatment such as neglect. In fact, one expert team noted more than three decades ago that "little consensus" exists surrounding definitions of neglect (Fulmer & Ashley, 1986). As evidence of the ambiguity surrounding the conceptualization of elder neglect, one can point to five different ways that elder neglect is defined. These definitions include (1) elder neglect as harmful behavior, (2) elder neglect as a type of elder abuse, (3) elder neglect as behavior prohibited by statute, (4) elder neglect as socially constructed behaviors, and (5) elder neglect as occupational crime, white-collar crime, or corporate deviance.

In considering *elder neglect as harmful behavior*, one can draw attention to definitions that focus attention more on the outcome of the behavior rather than the actual behavior itself. In particular, the focus is given to the harm that older victims receive (or could receive) from not receiving appropriate care. From this perspective, the failure to provide care would not be problematic unless actual negative outcomes were experienced by the older person. Those defining elder neglect based on the harm experienced by the victim often dichotomize neglect as active (e.g., intentional) and passive (e.g., unintentional) neglect. In this regard it is important to note that some researchers collapse the two types of neglect into one category. After all, the consequences of neglect are not tied to degree of intent formed by offender.

Some experts also define *elder neglect as a type of elder abuse* (see Bullock, 2007; Buri, Daly, Hartz & Jogerst, 2006). Generally speaking, elder abuse is categorized as either domestic or institutional abuse with the following definitions:

> Domestic elder abuse generally refers to any . . . types of mistreatment that are committed by someone with whom the elder has a special relationship (for example, a spouse, sibling, child, friend, or caregiver). Institutional abuse generally refers to any . . . types of mistreatment occurring in residential facilities (such as a nursing home, assisted living facility, group home, board and care facility, foster home, etc.) and is usually perpetrated by someone with a legal or contractual obligation to provide some element of care or protection. (National Center on Elder Abuse, 2016a, para. 3–4).

The National Center on Elder Abuse (NCEA) defines elder neglect from this perspective. In particular, the NCEA (2016b) defines elder neglect as:

> The refusal or failure to fulfill any part of a person's obligations or duties to an elder. Neglect may also include failure of a person who has

fiduciary responsibilities to provide care for an elder (e.g., pay for necessary home care services) or the failure on the part of an in-home service provider to provide necessary care. Neglect typically means the refusal or failure to provide an elderly person with such life necessities as food, water, clothing, shelter, personal hygiene, medicine, comfort, personal safety, and other essentials included in an implied or agreed-upon responsibility to an elder.

Focusing on elder neglect as a type of elder abuse/mistreatment is useful in that such an approach helps to distinguish the behavior from other forms of elder maltreatment. These other forms of elder abuse include physical abuse, sexual abuse, financial abuse, emotional abuse, and self-neglect. The problem is that few researchers have actually empirically distinguished neglect from other forms of abuse in their research efforts.

Those who define *elder neglect as behavior prohibited by statute* focus on the way criminal and civil laws prohibit or regulate behavior. In Illinois, for example, the Adult Protective Services Act (2013) defines elder neglect in the following way:

'Neglect' means another individual's failure to provide an eligible adult with or willful withholding from an eligible adult the necessities of life including, but not limited to, food, clothing, shelter or health care. This subsection does not create any new affirmative duty to provide support to eligible adults. Nothing in this Act shall be construed to mean that an eligible adult is a victim of neglect because of health care services provided or not provided by licensed health care professionals (320 ILCS 20/2(g)).

Note that individuals can only be found guilty of neglect if they have a legal duty to provide care and choose not to (e.g., someone with no legal duty to provide care would not be criminally or civilly liable for failing to provide care). Also note that criminal penalties are prescribed by statute. Perhaps not surprisingly, legal definitions of neglect vary across the states (Kapp, 2002). In comparison to the "harmful behavior" perspective, those who define neglect from a statutory perspective focus attention on the actions of the offender and are less concerned with the actual harm experienced by the victim. Indeed, some people can be found criminally guilty of neglect even if the older victim experienced no harm whatsoever from the offender's behavior (or lack of behavior).

It is also possible to define *elder neglect as socially constructed behavior.* Defining elder neglect from this perspective calls to attention the fact that various cultures have different norms and rules guiding the way that younger individuals interact with older persons. In some cultures, for example, it is expected that the younger generation will provide for their older relatives' needs. Failing to provide for an aging parent's needs in those cultures would constitute neglect. In other cultures, younger generations are not necessarily expected to provide for their older relatives. In these cultures, in fact, the failure to provide such care would potentially be seen as normal, rather than deviant, behavior. In effect, cultures socially construct definitions of elder neglect through the development of norms, rules, values, and customs. Put another way, cultural factors shape how societies and specific subcultures define neglect (Mercurio & Nyborn, 2006).

Some scholars and researchers conceptualize *elder neglect as occupational crime, white-collar crime, or corporate deviance.* The basis for such a conceptualization has to do with the employment relationship that neglect offenders have with victims. Neglect can be viewed as an occupational crime if the offender is in a lower status job (like a nurse's aide) and fails to perform his or her duties in a way that brings harm to the victim (see Green, 1990). Neglect can be viewed as a white-collar crime if the neglecting offender is in a white-collar profession (like physicians, nursing home administrators, etc.). Alternatively, neglect can be seen as corporate deviance if the institution itself is promoting neglectful activities (Hirschel, 1996; Jenkins & Braithwaite, 1993). In cases of occupational, white-collar, and corporate crimes involving elder neglect, a different response system is followed to address the wrongdoing than would be used in responding to cases where a family member neglects his/her aging relative. Regulatory, administrative, civil, and criminal justice systems become involved depending on the nature of the offense. Some prosecutors have used RICO laws to respond to institutional neglect on the grounds that understaffing of nursing homes fits within the domain of the organized crime statutes (Vron, 2003). In terms of the civil justice system's response, one study of three states found that the success of lawsuits filed between 1990 and 2004 against nursing homes for neglect and other torts ranged from 38% in California to 68% in Florida (Rustad, 2006). In terms of cost, the same study found the average awards/settlements in these cases ranged from $146,340 in California, to $1.47 and $34.85 million in Florida and Texas, respectively.

It is clear that no simple and concrete definition of neglect exists. Just as it is difficult to define elder neglect, it is also difficult to explain the behavior. From a criminological perspective, general strain theory offers a useful framework to understand this phenomenon. While we argue that general strain theory provides insight into why elder neglect occurs, it is important to note that caregiver burden has been frequently cited as a cause of elder mistreatment, so much so that experts have called the explanation "an oversimplification" (Korbin, Antezberger & Eckert, 1989, p. 7). Some researchers have even suggested that the reliance on caregiver burden as an explanation of elder abuse are possibly overstated (Gainey & Payne, 2006).

Two facets of this past research warrant clarification and point to the need to examine the link between burden and elder neglect. First, it is important to note that few elder abuse researchers have used criminological theories to explain the ties between burden and elder abuse. From our perspective, Agnew's (1992) general strain theory provides a framework from which we can begin to explore not whether burden leads to elder mistreatment, but how individuals who experience caregiver burden might adapt in ways that either foster or inhibit abuse and particularly neglect. Agnew's theory cites three sources of strain: (1) the removal of positive stimuli, (2) confronting negative stimuli, and (3) failure to achieve positively valued goals. The way individuals adapt to strain could either minimize the likelihood of mistreatment, or exacerbate its likelihood. Hence, it is important to examine the link between burden and elder neglect to determine whether potential support for strain theory exists.

A second rationale for exploring the link between neglect and burden builds directly on past research that suggests the role of burden may be overstated in elder abuse cases. In particular, researchers have recognized that criminologists must distinguish among the various types of abuse in order to accurately portray and understand the risk factors of those abuse types (Payne, Gainey & Jarvis, 2012). In effect, it could be that the causes of elder mistreatment vary across different types of elder mistreatment. Consider, for example, that some research has found some support for stress explanations when examining elder abuse and theft in nursing homes (Payne & Gainey, 2006; Van Wyk, Benson & Harris, 2000). Taking this a step further, it is plausible that burden manifests itself differently in elder neglect cases than it does in elder physical abuse cases.

The Current Study

The current work builds on Payne and colleagues' (2012) research, which focused on cases of neglect by formal caregivers prosecuted by fraud control units. This study extends past research by examining reported cases of elder neglect committed by any type of caregiver in an effort to distinguish neglect cases from non-neglect cases and identify the role of caregiver burden in neglect cases. More specifically, we examine three research questions: (1) What individual-level factors are related to the presence of caregiver burden in elder maltreatment cases? (2) How are reported cases of elder neglect different from other forms of elder maltreatment?, and (3) Does burden apply differently to elder neglect than it does to other forms of elder maltreatment?

METHODS

To examine the similarities and differences between reported elder neglect cases and other elder maltreatment cases, the researchers used data gathered from adult protective services files from three cities located in southeastern Virginia. As part of a broader study, we collected data from 750 reported cases of elder maltreatment (see for example: Gainey & Payne, 2006; Gainey, Payne & Kropf, 2010; Payne & Gainey, 2009). More specifically, the most recent 250 cases of elder maltreatment reports were reviewed in the three cities. Data gathered from the files included demographic characteristics, abuse type, health problems of the victim, and indicators of caregiver burden. These measures typically were included in the Uniform Assessment Instrument completed by the caseworker when the report was investigated. If the assessment instrument was not completed in the case file, the coder reviewed the rest of the file to collect information about the case. For this study, we excluded cases of self-neglect that were collected in the broader study and restricted the sample to adults ages 60 and above. This resulted in a total sample size of 335 cases involving elder neglect, elder physical abuse, and/or financial exploitation. Finally, missing data on certain variables resulted in a slightly lower sample size (n=313).

Measures

Dependent Variables

Caseworkers coded each case for signs of *neglect*. Cases were coded as "1" if the caseworker indicated neglect was present and as "0" if neglect was not present. Similarly, an item on the Uniform Assessment Instrument asked if *caregiver burden* was present. If the caseworker checked yes, this case was reported in our sample as including caregiver burden. If the caseworker did not complete the instrument, the coder read the narrative in the case file to determine if caregiver burden was present in the case.

Independent Variables

Nineteen items were included in the Uniform Assessment Instrument to ascertain victim's state of health. These 19 items assessed whether a victim suffered from a wide array of medical conditions such as heart, respiratory, and neurological problems. For the current analysis, the 19 measures were used to create a dichotomous variable measuring the presence of victim *medical problems*. Victims were then coded as a "1" if they reported that they currently suffered from at least one of the 19 medical conditions included in the instrument and "0" if they reported that they did not suffer from any of the 19 medical conditions.

Eight items were included in the instrument that asked victims whether they were experiencing "any stressful events that currently" affect their lives. Victims were asked about the following stressful life events: 1) change in work/environment, 2) death of someone close, 3) family conflict, 4) financial problems, 5) a family or friend diagnosed with a major illness, 6) a recent move/relocation, 7) criminal victimization, and 8) failing health. Responses were originally coded "0" for no and "1" for yes for each individual item. A single dichotomous *victim stressor* variable was created for the current analysis. As with the medical problem measure, victims were coded as "1" if they reported experiencing at least one of the stressful life events included in the instrument and "0" if they reported that they had not experienced any of the stressful events.

Type of caregiver was coded as (1) for formal caregiver and (0) for others. Other caregivers were mostly family members (sons, daughters, a spouse, and other relatives) or friends. While it would be interesting to break this down further, the cell sizes were too small for such analyses.

A number of control variables were also included. Victim's age was coded in years and victim sex was coded as male (0) or female (1). A measure indicating type of residence was also included in analyses and indicated whether the victim resided in the community (0) or in a long-term care setting (1).

FINDINGS

Descriptive Statistics

The majority of the cases involved female elders (69%) and victims ranged in age from 60 to 100 years old (mean = 77.5 years, s.d. = 8.95). The majority of the sample were living in the community with only 24% living in long-term care facilities and the majority were receiving care from informal sources (68%). The vast majority of cases (95%) involved individuals with some sort of medical problem, though only a minority reported experiencing at least one stressful life event (18%). Additionally, a sizable minority of cases demonstrated evidence of caregiver burden (23%) and over half (55%) of the cases involved neglect.

Bivariate Analyses Results

Cross tabulations were first conducted in order to examine correlates of caregiver burden and neglect cases (as opposed to non-neglect cases). The results are outlined in Table 1. As indicated in the table, there are several significant correlates of caregiver burden but, we need to be cautious in over-interpreting two of them. First, type of residence is relatively strongly related to caregiver burden but, there are only two cases of caregiver burden in long-term care settings. This is not a statistical problem as the expected cell counts are high (17.7) and the Fishers exact is also statistically significant (p<001). Further, it also makes theoretical sense that, although, professionals can and often do experience caregiver burden, there is likely greater supervision, support, and resources for these workers. Slightly more problematic, with 95% of the cases experiencing medical problems only one of the 17 cases without medical problems involved caregiver burden. The expected value for that cell is less than five and Fischer's exact test is only marginally significant (p=.062). Perhaps a larger sample with more cases without medical problems might confirm this correlation, however, at this point we are cautious.

The bivariate findings associated with type of maltreatment (neglect vs. non-neglect cases) indicate that residency, informal care status, and caregiver burden are associated with neglect cases. Individuals who resided in the community represented a greater percentage of neglect victims compared to those residing in long-term care settings. Further, individuals who relied on informal caregivers comprised a significantly larger percentage of elder neglect victims compared to those relying on formal care. Finally, caregiver burden was significantly associated with neglect cases with a larger percentage of neglect cases involving evidence of caregiver burden compared to non-neglect cases.

Multivariate Analyses Results

Table 2 reports the findings of the multivariate logistic regression analysis. The first model predicts caregiver burden and only two variables remain statistically significant. Consistent with the bivariate analysis, residency status, that is, living in long-term care facility has a negative effect on caregiver burden and stressful live events are positively associated with caregiver burden. Residency status reduce the odds by over 90% while stressful events increase

Table 1. Bivariate Analyses (n=333)

	% Burden	% Neglect
Sex		
Male	22.9	56.2
Female	23.1	54.6
Residence		
Community	30.0**	59.1*
Long-Term	2.6	42.1
Medical Problems		
No	5.9!	35.3!
Yes	24.3	56.1
Stressful Event		
No	19.4**	52.7!
Yes	41.8	65.5
Informal Care		
No	10.1**	45.6*
Yes	29.4	59.3
Caregiver Burden		
No	49.2**	
Yes	74.0	
Age	Mean (s.e.)	
No Burden	77.59 (9.02)	
Burden	77.29 (8.89)	
No Neglect	76.85 (9.00)	
Neglect	78.07 (8.98)	

! p<.10
* p<.05
**p<.01

the odds three fold. These are robust coefficients. In the second model focusing on neglect, we find that age emerges as a significant predictor (albeit at only the .10 level). More interesting is that the only strong and statistically significant predictor of neglect is caregiver burden. That is, caregiver burden diminishes the effects of residency status, stressful life events, and informal care found at the bivariate level.

**Table 2. Logistic Regressions Predicting Caregiver Burden
and Neglect (n=313)**

Variables	b	(s.e.)	Exp b	b	(s.e.)	Exp
Sex (female)	−.004	(3.15)	.996	−.095	(.260)	.910
Age	.015	(.017)	1.015	.0251	(.014)	1.025
Residence (LTC)	−2.601	(.802)**	.074	−.278	(.389)	.758
Medical Problems	1.562	(1.052)	4.769	.755	(.536)	2.175
Stress Events	1.228	(.352)**	3.415	.375	(.331)	1.455
Informal Caregiver	.407	(.452)	1.503	.371	(.363)	1.449
Caregiver Burden				.889**	(.320)	2.432
Nagelkerek r2		.103			.077	

! p<.10
*p<.05
**p<.01

Discussion

This study compared elder neglect cases with elder non-neglect cases with
an eye towards identifying the role that caregiver burden plays in elder neglect
versus other types of APS cases. A number of important findings were uncovered. First, the best predictors of caregiver burden were residency status
(long-term care providers) and stressful life events. Formal care was important at the bivariate level as well but was reduced to nonsignificance with the
inclusion of residency status. The two are highly correlated (phi=.70) and residence status takes precedence in the multivariate model, presumably because
of the added resources available to those in nursing homes. At the bivariate
level, neglect was related to residence status with long-term care facilities seeing fewer cases of neglect, formal caregivers seeing less neglect, and caregiver
burden being a strong predictor of neglect. In fact, in the multivariate model,
only caregiver burden was a significant predictor of neglect. Collectively, these
findings have implications for theory, practice, and future research.

Indeed the most important findings from this study have to do with the
importance of stress in predicting caregiver burden, and the importance of
caregiver burden in predicting neglect. Recent elder abuse researchers have
tacitly implied that burden should no longer be viewed as a primary cause of

elder maltreatment (Gainey & Payne, 2006; Whitcomb, 2012). What the current findings suggest is the burden may not cause caregivers to hit the person they are caring for or steal from them, but it may cause individuals to neglect their loved ones either intentionally or unintentionally. This suggests that responses to elder neglect should perhaps be at least somewhat distinct from responses to other forms of elder mistreatment. In terms of practical reasons, it is important to note that responses to elder mistreatment tend to be couched within an "abuse framework" as opposed to a "neglect framework." In other words, it is assumed, perhaps wrongfully, that the most appropriate way to address elder mistreatment cases is to view the case through an "abuse lens" rather than a "neglect lens." In doing so, offenders are generally seen as intentional actors who commit great harms by physically assaulting victims. Such a perspective does not seemingly fit with typical elder neglect cases (Payne et al., 2012).

With regard to implications for theory, criminologists have devoted minimal attention to crimes against older persons. To be sure, a handful of criminologists have conducted important studies on the topic (Blakely & Dolon, 1989; Fisher & Regan, 2006; Harris, 1999; Harris & Benson, 1998; Johnson, Sigler & Morgan, 2006). Despite these efforts, criminologists have a long way to go towards increasing understanding about elder mistreatment and the current study provides an essential step in the direction towards testing the viability of criminological theory for understanding the abuse and neglect of older adults. The current findings show at least some support for Agnew's general strain theory, particularly his premise that adaptations to strain could result in offending. Most tests of his theory have focused on active types of offenses. Indeed, researchers have examined the ties between strain and delinquency (Agnew & Brezina, 1997; Agnew & White, 1992; Hoffman & Su, 1997; Mazerolle, 1998; Mazerolle & Maahs, 2000; Paternoster & Mazerolle, 1994), child abuse (Margolin & Gordis, 2003), adolescent violence towards parents (Brezina, 1998; Brezina, 1999), partner abuse (Anderson & Lo, 2011; Gibson, Swatt & Jolicoeur, 2001; Mason & Smithey, 2011), white-collar crime (Langton & Piquero, 2007) and homicide (Defronzo, 1997; Pratt & Godsey, 2003). The distinction in the current study is that strain was not used to predict active offending; rather, it was used to study neglect — a crime of omission — and the findings show that strain was a strong predictor of neglect. Given the current findings, further research is needed to examine how criminological theory can be applied to various forms of elder neglect (i.e., physical, psychological, financial, as well as passive versus active neglect).

These findings can be further understood through an integration of the life course perspective with Agnew's strain theory. It is important to recognize that caregiving and strain vary over the life course (Agnew, 1997). Young adults might experience caregiving strain as new parents. While being a new parent is stressful, the new parent has "seen other parents in action" and may learn to cope from what they have learned from other parents (Payne & Gainey, 2009). Later in the life course, when adults are called upon to provide care for their aging relatives, it is likely that they have had little preparation for such a caregiving scenario. Rather than turning to their learned experiences to cope with strain, some may ignore the strain and subsequently ignore the caregiving situation. Such a process would explain the high prevalence of passive neglect.

The life course perspective also helps to distinguish elder neglect from other forms of neglect occurring earlier in the life course. For example, one can see how power dynamics vary among the types of neglect across the life course. In child neglect cases, the older person has more power. In elder neglect cases, the younger person typically has more power. Somewhat similarly, different relationships exist among those experiencing neglect at different stages of the life course. For child neglect victims, the relationship centers around familial dependence that the child has for the parent. For elder neglect victims, the relationship is either familial in nature (e.g., when a caregiver fails to provide care) or employment-based (when a paid caregiver fails to provide care).

Also in line with the life course perspective, one can see different sources of neglect. For child neglect victims, poverty is often identified as a source of neglect (Payne & Gainey, 2009). For elder neglect victims, earlier research suggests that ignorance (in domestic elder neglect) and profit (in institutional elder neglect cases) are the sources of neglect for elder neglect victims (see Payne, 2012), while the current study suggests that burden is a key source of neglect. Additional research is needed that incorporates measures of caregiving knowledge, profit motivations, and caregiving burden to determine how these factors may differentially influence the type of neglect experienced, as well as how these factors may affect neglect occurring across different settings and the life course.

Given that strain and the life course perspective can be used to understand and to a certain degree predict elder neglect, it seems fruitful to suggest that future efforts integrate the two theoretical perspectives to explain elder maltreatment. In particular, strain and adaptations to strain vary over the life course. Adaptations that serve to prevent crime in one stage of the life course might actually increase certain types of crime in other stages of the life course. A simple example comes to mind. If parents need time away from their young children, they might put them to bed early and seek some much needed respite. If caregivers need time away from their aging relatives, ignoring the pressing needs of the older adult might result in a form of passive neglect. The simple point is that elder caregivers are often ill-prepared for the caregiving situation. When they confront that situation later in their life course, traditional adaptations that worked earlier in the life course might actually be criminogenic. Paradoxically, the adaptation does not necessarily lead to crime; instead, the adaption (e.g., ignoring the problem) might actually be the crime in elder neglect cases.

These results have at least three implications for responding to elder abuse. First, it is important that caregivers be adequately trained how to provide care for their aging relatives. The U.S. Census Bureau projects that the number and proportion of elderly persons in our society will substantially increase within the next 20 years (Bulman, 2010). With individuals living longer, the simple fact is that there will be more elderly persons in the future, meaning that there will be more older persons in need of caregiving. As it is, individuals may be thrust into these situations with little preparation and guidance. It is this sort of scenario that is a recipe for neglect. Given the aging nature of our society, many of us will be called upon to provide care to an older person at some point in our life course. Thought should be given to promoting practices that encourage individuals to become more prepared for these situations.

Second, while elder neglect was found to be somewhat similar to elder non-neglect cases, those responding to these cases must resist the temptation to treat all types of elder maltreatment cases alike. It is far too early to call for a "one-size-fits-all" response to elder maltreatment cases. Indeed, the very finding that burden is predictive of one type of elder maltreatment, but not others, suggests that practitioners must respond to these cases cautiously and with a more individualized approach.

Third, practitioners should recognize that their reactions, in many cases, foster distinctions between abuse types. In essence, the portrayal or social construction of elder maltreatment may often reflect what criminal justice officials do more so than the actual dynamics of the maltreatment. With expected increases in the number of older persons criminal justice officials will be serving in the future, it is important that these officials are adequately prepared for working with older persons.

This research is not without limitations. Relying on reported cases, we have excluded a significant number of elder maltreatment cases. As noted above, our findings may reflect reporting behavior as much as "neglectful behavior." Indeed, one adaptation to burden in neglect situations might entail a call to social services for help. As well, our findings are limited to one geographical region. It is plausible that neglect and other forms of maltreatment vary across the country. In addition, our findings did not capture the type of neglect (active or passive) or the severity of the neglect. These factors are potentially relevant, but were not included in the dataset. Finally, due to our reliance on case files, we were only able to consider a limited number of factors that may influence caregiver burden, as well as neglect.

Despite these limitations, a number of questions surface for future research. For instance, researchers should explore how strain varies across the life course with an aim towards integrating general strain theory and the life course perspective when studying the causes of elder maltreatment, including neglect. As well, researchers should explore whether regional and neighborhood differences exist in terms of the degree of strain, adaptations to strain, and subsequent elder neglect. In addition, researchers should compare reported elder neglect cases with prosecuted elder neglect cases to shed some light on the way that enforcement patterns shape our understanding of elder neglect and other crimes against older persons. Existing research shows that neglect has extremely serious consequences (Payne et al., 2012). In fact, in some ways, the consequences of neglect are more serious than the consequences of elder physical abuse. Such a comment is not made to diminish the seriousness of physical abuse; instead, the purpose is to highlight the dire consequences that neglect victims can experience. If criminologists and other social scientists "neglect elder neglect," they are inadvertently engaging in a form of passive institutional elder neglect. By building understanding about the topic, criminologists can play a role in explaining, preventing, and responding to future cases of elder neglect. Through such research, criminologists and criminal justice officials will be better prepared for serving the aging society that awaits us in the future.

REFERENCES

Acierno, R., Hernandez, M. A., Amstadter, A. B., Resnick, H. S., Steve, K., Muzzy, W. & Kilpatrick, D. G. (2010). Prevalence and correlates of emotional, physical, sexual, and financial abuse and potential neglect in the United States: The National Elder Mistreatment Study. *American Journal of Public Health*, 100(2), 292–297.

Adult Protective Services Act, 320 ILCS 20/2(g) (2013).

Agnew, R. (1992). Foundation for a general strain theory of crime and delinquency. *Criminology, 30(1),* 47–88.

Agnew, R. (1997). Stability and change in the crime over the live course: A strain theory explanation. In Thornberry (ed) Developmental Theories of Crime and Delinquency. Transaction Publishers, New Brunswick, NJ.

Agnew, R. & Brezina, T. (1997). Relational problems with peers, gender, and delinquency. *Youth & Society, 29(1)*, 84–111.

Agnew, R. & White, H. R. (1992). An empirical test of general strain theory. *Criminology, 30(4)*, 475–500.

Anderson, A. S. & Lo, C. C. (2011). Intimate partner violence within law enforcement families. *Journal of Interpersonal Violence, 26(6)*, 1176–1193.

Blakely, B. & Dolon, R. (1989). Elder abuse and neglect: A study of adult protective service workers in the United States. *Journal of Elder Abuse & Neglect, 1*(3), 31–49.

Brezina, T. (1998). Adolescent maltreatment and delinquency: The question of intervening processes. *Journal of Research in Crime and Delinquency*, 35(1), 71–99.

Brezina, T. (1999). Teenage violence toward parents as an adaptation to family strain: Evidence from a national survey of male adolescents. *Youth & Society, 30(4)*, 416–444.

Bullock, K. (2007). Vulnerability for elder abuse among a sample of custodial grandfathers: An exploratory study. *Journal of Elder Abuse & Neglect, 19(3–4)*, 133–150.

Bulman, P. (2010). Elder abuse emerges from the shadows of public consciousness. NIJ Journal, 265, 4–7.

Buri, H. M., Daly, J. M., Hartz, A. J. & Jogerst, G. J. (2006). Factors associated with self-reported elder mistreatment in Iowa's frailest elders. *Research on Aging, 28(5)*, 562–581.

Defronzo, J. (1997). Welfare and homicide. *Journal of Research in Crime and Delinquency, 34(3)*, 395–406.

Fisher, B. S. & Regan, S. L. (2006). The extent and frequency of abuse in the lives of older women and their relationship with health outcomes. *The Gerontologist, 46*(2), 200–209.

Fulmer, T. & Ashley, J. (1986). Neglect: What part of abuse? *Pride Institute Journal of Long Term Health Care, 5(4)*, 18–24.

Gainey, R. R. & Payne, B. K. (2006). Caregiver burden, elder abuse, and Alzheimer's disease: Testing the relationship. *Journal of Health and Human Services Administration, 29(2)*, 245–260.

Gainey, R.R., Payne, B.K. & Kropf, N. (2010). Neighborhood disadvantage and refusal of formal services among cases reported to adult protective services. *Journal of Evidence-Based Social Work, 7,* 348–360.

Gibson, C. L., Swatt, M. L. & Jolicoeur, J. R. (2001). Assessing the generality of general strain theory: The relationship among occupational stress experienced by male police officers and domestic forms of violence. *Journal of Crime and Justice, 24(2),* 29–57.

Green, G. S. (1990). Occupational Crime. Chicago: Nelson-Hall

Harris, D. K. (1999). Elder abuse in nursing homes: The theft of patients' possessions. *Journal of Elder Abuse & Neglect, 10(3–4),* 141–151.

Harris, D. K. & Benson, M. L. (1998). Nursing home theft: The hidden problem. *Journal of Aging Studies, 12(1),* 57–67.

Hirschel, A. E. (1996). Setting the stage: The advocate's struggle to address gross neglect in Philadelphia nursing homes. *Journal of Elder Abuse & Neglect, 8,* 5–20.

Hoffman, J. P. & Su, S. S. (1997). The conditional effects of stress on delinquency and drug use: A strain theory assessment of sex differences. *Journal of Research in Crime & Delinquency, 34(1),* 46–78.

Jenkins, A. & Braithewaite, J. (1993). Profits, pressures, and corporate lawbreaking. *Crime, Law and Social Change, 20,* 221–232.

Jirik, S. & Sanders, S. (2014). Analysis of elder abuse statutes across the United States, 2011–2012. *Journal of Gerontological Social Work, 57,* 478–497.

Johnson, I., Sigler, R. & Morgan, E. (2006). Public definitions of the criminalization of elder abuse. *Journal of Criminal Justice, 34,* 275–283.

Kapp, M. B. (2002). Criminal and civil liability of physicians for institutional elder abuse and neglect. Journal *of the American Medical Directors Association, 3(2),* S77–S81.

Korbin, J. E., Antzberger, G. J. & Eckert, J. K. (1989). Elder abuse and child abuse. *Journal of Elder Abuse & Neglect, 1,* 1–14.

Lacher, S., Wettstein, A., Senn, O., Roseman, T. & Hasler, S. (2016). Types of abuse and risk factors associated with elder abuse. *Swiss Medical Weekly, 146.*

Langton, L. & Piquero, N. L. (2007). Can general strain theory explain white-collar crime?: An investigation of the relationship between strain and white-collar offenses. *Journal of Criminal Justice, 32,* 1–15.

Margolin, G. & Gordis, E. B. (2003). Co-occurrence between marital aggression and parents' child abuse potential: The impact of cumulative stress. *Violence and Victims, 18(3),* 243–258.

Mason, B. & Smithey, M. (2011). The effects of academic and interpersonal stress on dating violence among college students: A test of classical strain theory. *Journal of Interpersonal Violence, 27(5)*, 974–986.

Mazerolle, P. (1998). Gender, general strain, and delinquency: An empirical examination. *Justice Quarterly, 15(1)*, 65–91.

Mazerolle, P. & Maahs, J. (2000). General strain and delinquency: An alternative examination of conditioning influences. *Justice Quarterly, 17(4)*, 755–778.

Mercurio, A. E. & Nyborn, J. (2006). Cultural definitions of elder maltreatment in Portugal. *Journal of Elder Abuse and Neglect, 18(2–3)*, 51–65.

National Center on Elder Abuse (2016a). Frequently asked questions: What is elder abuse? Retrieved from: http://www.ncea.aoa.gov/faq/index.aspx

National Center on Elder Abuse (2016b). Types of abuse. Retrieved from: http://www.ncea.aoa.gov/FAQ/Type_Abuse/index.aspx#neglect

Paternoster, R. & Mazzerolle, P. (1994). General strain theory and delinquency: A replication and extension. *Journal of Research in Crime & Delinquency, 31(3)*, 235–263.

Payne, B.K. & Gainey, R.R. (2009). Mapping elder mistreatment cases. *Journal of Human Behavior in the Social Environment. 19*, 1025–1041.

Payne, B.K. (2011). Crime and elder abuse: An integrated perspective. Springfield, IL: Charles C. Thomas.

Payne, B. K., Blowers, A. & Jarvis, D. B. (2012). The neglect of elder neglect as a white-collar crime: Distinguishing patient neglect from physical abuse and the criminal justice system's response, *Justice Quarterly, 29(3)*, 448–468.

Payne, B.K. & Gainey, R. R. (2006). The criminal justice response to elder abuse in nursing homes: A routine activities approach. *Western Criminology Review, 7*, 67–81.

Payne, B. K. & Gainey, R. R. (2009). Family violence & criminal justice. (3rd ed.). New Providence, NJ: Lexis Nexis.

Pratt, T. C. & Godsey, T. W. (2003). Social support, inequality, and homicide: A cross-national test of an integrated theoretical model. *Criminology, 41(3)*, 611–643.

Rustad, M. L. (2006). Neglecting the neglected: The impact of noneconomic damage caps on meritorious nursing home lawsuits. *The Elder Law Journal, 14*, 331–391.

Teaster, P. B., Dugar, T. A., Mendiondo, M. S., Abner, E. L., Cecil, K. A. & Otto, J. M. (2007). The 2004 survey of state adult protective services: Abuse of adults 60 years of age and older. Washington, D.C.: Administration on Aging.

Van Wyk, J. A., Benson, M. L. & Harris, D. K. (2000). Test of strain and self-control theories: Occupational crime in nursing homes. *Journal of Crime and Justice*, 23(2), 27–44.

Vron, V. (2003). Using RICO to fight understaffing in nursing homes: How federal prosecution using RICO can reduce abuse and neglect of the elderly. *George Washington Law Review, 71,* 1025–1054.

Whitcomb, D. (2012). Research to practice: Elder abuse. Washington, D.C.: Office for Victims of Crime. Retrieved from: http://ovc.ncjrs.gov/news/pdf/OVC_NPU_Feb_2012.pdf

Wolf, R. (1996). Understanding elder abuse and neglect. *Aging*, 367, 4–9.

CHAPTER 12

EVOLVING APPROACHES IN DEALING WITH COLLEGE CRIME VICTIMIZATION IN THE 21ST CENTURY

Max L. Bromley and Nicholas M. Perez
UNIVERSITY OF SOUTH FLORIDA

INTRODUCTION

This chapter describes campus crime victimization and the various approaches used over the last 40 years to deal with this challenge. It begins with an overview of the victim rights movement in the United States. That discussion is followed by a brief history of campus crime during the 20th Century. Subsequent sections focus on the role of the media in highlighting serious campus crimes and the nature and extent of what is known about campus crime based upon victimization research and crimes reported to the authorities. This section will include findings from the most current national-level research on serious campus crime. A discussion of the various legal responses, civil lawsuits and enactment of new campus crime legislation at both the state and federal levels follows. Next is a discussion of administrative responses to campus victimization. Examples of programs and practices to deal with campus crime and subsequent victimization are detailed from a variety of different universities. The chapter concludes with a brief summary and several questions regarding the challenges presented by campus crime to institutions of higher education.

The Victim Rights Movement: 1970–the Present

Historically, crime victims have been neglected by the Criminal Justice System and its components. For example, victims are not notified regarding the status of their case or kept informed as to what to expect as they go through the system (Territo, Halsted, and Bromley 2004). As a result, they frequently become fearful or anxious and are often less than cooperative during subsequent phases of the criminal justice process. Likewise, victims often feel re-victimized by the police, prosecutors, defense attorneys, and the courts when they are treated with little sensitivity.

Fortunately, changes with regard to the treatment of victims of crime have occurred during the last four decades. These changes have often been initiated by private community organizations such as NOVA and MADD, which have been very active in raising public awareness with respect to the rights of crime victims. In addition, several steps have been taken by various levels of government aimed at addressing the needs of crime victims.

Perhaps the first major action affecting crime victims at the federal level of the criminal justice system was the passage of the Law Enforcement Assistance Administration (LEAA) Act in the early 1970s. LEAA ultimately contributed approximately $50 million to victim assistance programs throughout the country (Tomz and McGillis, 1997). Later, in 1982, the President's Task Force on Victims of Crime proposed numerous changes to the manner victims were then treated and suggested that government and private groups work collectively to address victim needs throughout the country. One such recommendation led to the passage of the Victims of Crime Act (VOCA) in 1984 authorizing millions of dollars for state-level victim assistance programs (Territo, et. al., 2004).

As a result of various federal initiatives, many states have also enacted victim-related statutes. For example, 43 states have established victim compensation programs, 49 have passed a victim's bill of rights, and 22 more states have amended their constitutions to require various services for victims of crime (Tomz and McGillis, 1997).

In the 1990s, Congress recognized that many women who are victims of violence had particular needs not sufficiently addressed by the criminal justice system. This fact is evident in officially documented cases as well as in data derived from victimization surveys. Therefore, in 1994 the United States Congress enacted the Violence Against Women Act (VAWA) that provides funding for efforts on the part of police and prosecutors to improve the delivery of services to women victims.

The last four decades have seen many diverse efforts aimed at heightening the public awareness of the needs of crime victims and improving services to assist them. The efforts described have been at the general community level. Given the tremendous growth in the size and enrollment of institutions of higher education over the last forty years, it is not surprising that many college campuses have experienced some of the same types of crime problems being faced by their nearby communities (Smith, 1995). Given the serious nature of criminal victimizations that have occurred on today's campuses they can no longer be considered safe havens or protected environments (Langford, 2004). It is important to understand the nature and scope of campus crime as well as the evolving approaches that have been developed. The remainder of this chapter will focus specifically on issues relating to crime victims on college campuses.

During the early 1920s, American colleges grew both in size and complexity. Yet, even during this time campus watchmen and college deans were most concerned with minor student code violations and the protection of property as opposed to crimes of violence (Esposito and Stormer, 1989). More serious forms of disturbances involving students, events often related to alcohol consumption, occurred with greater frequency on campuses during the 1940s and early 1950s (Powell, 1981).

Following World War II the face of American higher education changed dramatically as student enrollment increased substantially. As noted by Smith (1989, p.10), "As the sizes of institutions grew, and the students came to more closely represent a cross-section of the social and economic classes of the nation, the incidence of campus crime likewise increased." Campus activities during the 1960s and 1970s reflected many of the significant social changes occurring in America during that time. Civil rights and anti-Vietnam War activists often found a supportive atmosphere on the college campus. While much student dissident activity in this era was peaceful in nature, building take-overs, vandalism, arson, and acts of associated violence were not unusual (Powell, Pander, and Nielson, 1994).

While student dissent and its associated crimes had subsided by the mid-1970s, it was during this time that criminal acts on campus including property and violent crimes increased in frequency and severity (Nichols, 1986; Powell, et. al., 1994; Sloan, 1992a; Smith, 1989). Institutions of higher education have continued to grow in size and in complexity throughout the 1990s and into the 21st century (Bromley, 2007) and the issues regarding crime and victimization remain a focus of concern. Thus, the victims of serious campus crime received an increasing amount of attention from the media, social scientists, litigators, legislators, campus administrators, and the general public.

Campus Victims: The Media View

There is little question that the media have played a significant role in raising public awareness with regard to campus crime victimization. Serious crimes of violence on campus have been dramatically highlighted by the media in Canada and the United States (Brantingham, Brantingham and Seagrave, 1995; Sloan and Fisher, 1995). Stories of coeds being raped or professors being murdered by irate or mentally deranged students usually make sensational headlines or lead story lines on the radio and TV daily news. Following acts of extreme violence, universities have been characterized as unsafe places even if the crimes were not committed on campus. For example, several years ago when a serial murderer took the lives of four women and one man who were university students, the University of Florida was the focus of the national media despite the fact that none of the crimes actually occurred on the campus in Gainesville, Florida.

Within the decade of the '90s, national level media coverage of campus crime had become routine. For example, Castelli (1990) and Mathews (1993) have both written feature articles on the topic for the *New York Times* as did Kalette (1990) for *USA Today*. Ordovensky (1990) wrote a lengthy article on campus crime for *USA Today* entitled "Students Easy Prey On Campus." His article also analyzed the relative safety of over 400 American institutions of higher education.

In more recent years, the media coverage of sexual violence has only become more prolific. One well-publicized example was the 2014 Rolling Stone article, "A Rape on Campus" (Erdely, 2014). This article alleged that multiple fraternity members at the University of Virginia engaged in a gang rape of a female student. This article caused a national controversy in its aftermath, leading to harsh media reactions, suspensions, investigations, and even death threats. Soon after its publication, the article was recanted when it was uncovered that there was not sufficient evidence behind the victim's claim. Although there was "no substantive basis to support the account alleged in the Rolling Stone article," the increased attention on the topic of sexual violence continued to grow (Coronel, Coll, and Kravitz, 2015).

In the following year, a documentary film was released, *The Hunting Ground*, focusing on two University of North Carolina students (as well as students from other universities) who were allegedly raped during their time in college. The documentary alleges that the college administrators largely minimized and ignored their attack or required them to go through a complex process to make their claims (Ziering and Dick, 2015). These two recent examples highlight the mounting media coverage on the topic of sexual violence.

Perhaps the most widely read and quoted publication in the field of higher education is the *Chronicle of Higher Education*. Not surprisingly, in the past two decades major stories on campus crime and victimizations have been featured, from earlier reports (Lederman, 1993, 1994a, 1994b; Lively, 1996, 1997) to more recent discussions (Field, 2015; Mangan, 2015; McIntire, 2015; Thomason, 2015). Data from across the country on campus crime and victimizations are now a regularly featured story in the *Chronicle*.

The Nature and Extent of Campus Crime Victimization

Over the course of the last thirty years social scientists and campus police officials have attempted to describe the nature and extent of the campus crime problem. Questions such as the following have been investigated: What types of crimes are committed most frequently on campus? What is the nature of serious crimes of violence? How does campus crime compare with community crime? Does the level of community crime affect campus victimization?

One of the major difficulties that must be overcome when attempting to answer these questions is the absence of a complete database with respect to campus crime and victimization. At present, there is no requirement that campus crime data be forwarded to the FBI for publication in the annual Uniform Crime Report (UCR). According to Fisher and Sloan (1995) fewer than 25% of this country's colleges report their crime statistics to the FBI.

The Crime Awareness and Campus Security Act of 1990 (which will be discussed more thoroughly later in this chapter) requires post-secondary institutions to collect and publish data on UCR index crimes, but excludes larceny/theft. In addition, there is no central national repository for this information. The Act is also deficient in that only raw crime numbers are used without population data which limits the utility of the data that is collected (Fisher and Sloan, 1995; Seng, 1995).

The Act did require the Secretary of Education to prepare a report on campus crime statistics for 1992, 1993, and 1994. In January 1997 the report published data received from a sample of over 1,000 post-secondary institutions that participate in Federal Title IV Financial Aid Programs (National Center for Educational Statistics, (N.C.E.S.) 1997). The results show that for each of the three years, property crimes far outnumber crimes of violence by a 4 to 1 ratio. Given the fact that larceny, the most frequently reported campus crime (Bromley and Territo, 1990; Sigler and Koehler, 1993; Sloan, 1994, 1992a, 1992b; Smith, 1989; United States Department of Justice, 1997) is not included in the N.C.E.S. data, the true ratio of property to violent victimization is probably even higher.

A second national report of campus crime statistics was published in 1997 by the International Association of Campus Law Enforcement Administrators (IACLEA 1997). *The Campus Crime Report 1994–1995* represented responses from 585 (67%) of IACLEA's members. This report, unlike the Secretary of Education's publication, included larceny/theft in the database. In this report, larcenies accounted for the vast majority of all on-campus crime reported to campus law enforcement officials (IACLEA, 1997). Also, the rates of both reported property crime and violent crime were relatively low (less than 19 per 1,000 and less than 1 per 1,000), respectively.

Reaves (2015) found somewhat similar results in a study of campus law enforcement agencies conducted in 2011–2012. This data set of campus index offenses also included larceny/theft. Campuses responding to this survey reported an average of 5 violent crimes and 180 property crimes per year. Approximately 91% of the property crimes reported to the campus police agencies were larceny/thefts (Reaves, 2015).

CAMPUS CRIME VICTIMIZATION RESEARCH

Other attempts to more adequately describe the extent of campus crime have gone beyond the use of crime data reported to campus police. This would seem to be very important particularly with respect to crimes of violence that are often under reported on college campuses (Cerio, 1989, Roark, 1987). Therefore, it is useful to review some of the findings of campus victimization studies in addition to what is formally reported to the police.

One of the earliest comprehensive victimization studies to date was conducted by the Towson State University Campus Violence Prevention Center. Their survey of over 1,000 institutions revealed among other things, that most campuses had experienced physical and sexual assault; that about one third had seen an increase in acts of violence; and for the majority of victimizations drugs or alcohol were involved (Bausell, Bausell, and Siegel, 1991; Siegel and

Raymond, 1992). The relationship between alcohol or drug use in acts of campus violence has been underscored in other research as well (CASA 1994; Kilpatrick, Resnick, Ruggiero, Conoscenti, and McCauley, 2007; Maloy, 1991; Wechsler, et al., 1994).

Numerous studies have also focused on women as victims of violence on campus. Date rape, acquaintance rape, and courtship violence have all been the subject of ongoing research (Krebs, Lindquist, Warner, Fisher, and Martin, 2007). Koss and colleagues suggested date rape was more widespread than had been previously thought (Koss, Gidycz, and Wisniewski, 1987). These findings have generally been supported by others (Berkowitz, 1992; Cokey, Sherril, Cave, and Chapman, 1988; Ward, Chapman, White and Williams, 1991). Burling (1993) notes that as many as 90% of the perpetrators of campus sexual assaults are acquainted with their victims. Given the prevalence of this form of sexual violence on campus (Gordon and Riger, 1989) and the fact that many crimes of violence against women are not reported (Bachman, 1994), date rape is a very difficult problem for institutions to address.

In addition to date or acquaintance rape, the subject of other forms of courtship violence among students has caught the attention of current researchers (Barrick, Krebs, and Lindquist, 2013; Forke, Myers, Catallozzi, and Schwartz, 2008; Kaukinen, Gover, and Hartman 2012). Belknap and Erez (1995) consider this form of violence to be similar to domestic violence in a marital relationship. Sellers and Bromley (1996) conducted a study of almost 1,000 college students currently involved in dating relationships at a large urban university. Close to 22% of the respondents indicated that they had experienced some form of physical or sexual aggression. While the vast majority of those victimizations were minor forms of violent behavior such as being pushed, grabbed, shoved, or slapped, the findings also show that the use of violence increased with the length of the relationship (Sellers and Bromley, 1996). Belknap and Erez (1995) also reported that students who were cohabitating were most often victimized, a finding that appears to support the assumption that courtship violence is similar to domestic violence. These studies have noted the parallel between what is considered domestic violence in the general community and courtship violence among campus community members. Similar studies have been conducted by Bogal-Allbritten and Allbritten (1991); Baier, Rosonweig and Whipple (1991); Durst (1987); Torrey and Lee (1987); and Makepeace (1981).

Campus violence was also the topic of a white paper published by the American College Health Association (Carr, 2005). This publication not only described campus violence, but also made various recommendations for institutions of higher education to consider in an effort to help prevent acts of campus violence.

One report distributed by the American College Health Association (2015) is the National College Health Assessment. This report covers information on a variety of health experiences for college students. One specific area that is covered is personal victimization. Their data suggests that 7.9% of students (9.8% of females and 3.9% of males) experienced sexual touching without consent. Additionally, 3.2% of students experienced an attempted sexual assault (4.2% of females and 1.1% of males) and 1.9% experienced a sexual assault (2.4% of females and 0.6% of males). Another 5.1% of students reported being stalked (6.2% of females and 2.6% of males). Finally, regarding abusive relationships, 8.2% reported being in an emotionally abusive relationship (9.4% of females and 5.7% of males), 1.8% reported being in a physically abusive relationship (1.8% of females and 1.8% of males), and 1.8% reported being in a sexually abusive relationship (2.2% of females and 0.9% of males).

The Bureau of Justice Statistics Research on Campus Victimization

In 1996 the Violence Against Women Act reviewed the status of campus crime victimization. As a result the Bureau of Justice Statistics (BJS) added new items to the National Crime Victimization Survey (NCVS) in an effort to collect college student victimization data. In the past, the BJS has issued two special reports by Hart (2003), and a second report by Baum and Klaus (2005), entitled Violent Victimization of College Students. Data were gathered on college crime victims between 1995 and 2000 and from 1995 to 2002 respectively.

A recent report was issued by Sinozich and Langton (2014) with data on sexual violence in college-aged females from 1995 through 2013. This report highlighted a number of important findings. For starters, the rate of sexual violence was lower for students than nonstudents (6.1 per 1,000 v. 7.2 per 1,000). Additionally, the student victim most often knew their assailant (80%), and the assault occurred most often while the victim was pursuing leisure activities (51%). Sexual assault victimizations were more likely to go unreported for students than non-students (80% v. 67%). Finally, and most alarmingly, only 16% of student rape and sexual assault victims received any assistance from a victim services agency (Sinozich and Langton, 2014).

LEGAL APPROACHES TO CAMPUS VICTIMIZATION

Legal responses to the problem of campus crime victimization have primarily been in two forms (1) by civil law suits brought against post-secondary institutions for failing to provide adequate security, and (2) by enacting campus crime laws by state legislatures and the Federal government (Bromley, 1993; Fisher and Sloan, 1995). Although the courts have not traditionally involved themselves in policy making or managing the operational functions of post-secondary institutions of higher learning, those days are over (Kaplan, 1990). In general, there has been sufficient evidence to suggest that families of campus crime victims are very willing to bring civil suit against colleges (Bromley, 1993; Bromley and Territo, 1990; Burling, 1991; Fisher and Sloan, 1995; Smith, 1989, 1995).

During the last 25 years, post-secondary institutions have had to defend themselves in civil liability lawsuits brought by the victims of serious crimes. According to Smith (1995) student victims may claim that the institution has failed in one or more duties owed them. Specifically, he notes four types of claimed duties: "A duty to warn about known risks; a duty to provide adequate security protection; a duty to screen other students and employees for dangers; and a duty to control student conduct" (p. 26). In Smith's view, both the courts and the legislatures have been more willing to hold colleges responsible for the first two categories than the latter two.

Holding colleges liable for failing to take adequate steps to protect students is complicated by the "special relationship" theory. Despite the fact that since the 1961 court decision in *Dixon v. Alabama* universities are no longer expected to act in the place of parents ("In Loco Parentis"), there are still important obligations that institutions must assume. According to Burling (1991, p. 2), "a college or university is expected to have an institutional commitment to the welfare and safety of its students. Given this public expectation, most institutions acknowledge their obligation and subsequently exercise care to protect their students by providing appropriate levels of security."

EXAMPLES OF CAMPUS CRIME
VICTIMIZATION LEGISLATION

Many states and the United States Congress have passed laws dealing with various aspects of campus crime and victimization (Bromley, 1993; Fisher and Sloan, 1995; Griffaton, 1995; Seng, 1995; Tuttle, 1991). Several state laws including those of New York, Washington, and Wisconsin, require services to be available for victims of campus crime. The New York statute, which primarily focuses on sex-related offenses, requires a campus committee to annually review security-related policies and procedures including counseling for victims. In Washington the description of programs regarding counseling, including a directory of services, is required to be part of an overall security report to be given to every student and new employee. Wisconsin law requires that every new student receive information regarding the statutory rights of crime victims and the services available at the institution or in the community to assist students who are the victims of sexual assault or sexual harassment. The California law is very comprehensive in its language regarding victim services and mandates that institutional policies state:

> Services available to victims and personnel responsible for providing those services, such as the person assigned to transport the victim to the hospital, to refer to the counseling center, and to notify the police, with the victims concurrence (Cal. Educ. Code. Ann. 1994, p. 122).

Also required in the California law is "a description of campus resources available to victims as well as appropriate off-campus services" (Cal. Educ. Code. Ann. 1994, p. 122).

FEDERAL CAMPUS CRIME LEGISLATION

The most wide-ranging and comprehensive law regarding policies and procedures for the victims of campus crime is the *Federal Crime Awareness and Campus Security Act* passed in 1990 and subsequently amended in 1992. The preamble to the law notes the increase in campus crime in general and in crimes of violence in particular. It also states that campus crime data must be shared publicly as well as noting that post-secondary institutions should develop crime prevention measures to enhance campus safety.

The Act has been criticized by some authorities (Burd, 1992a and 1992b; Seng, 1995; Seng and Koehler, 1993). In particular Seng (1995) suggests that the Act creates a misleading picture of crime on campus by not providing complete information. However, as Sloan and Fisher (1995, p. 4), note the Act has "partially improved the availability of some campus crime statistics in the United States." Griffaton (1995) suggests that the Act has been successful in increasing the general awareness about campus crime. With the passage of the

Act the "wall of silence" around campus crime does seem to be breaking down (Sloan and Fisher, 1995, p. 4).

The Act was significantly amended in 1992. The amendment mandates that institutions establish policies regarding the prevention of sex offenses and the policies must state how such offenses are to be dealt with once reported. Clearly, the intent is to require the establishment of a victim-oriented model for dealing with sex offenses on campus.

Arguably the most important area of federal legislation related to sexual violence and victimization is Title IX, which protects any person from sex-based discrimination, harassment, or violence. Title IX required that every campus has a coordinator to handle any type of complaint regarding sexual violence. The Title IX Coordinator must take immediate action to assist the victim in continuing their education without subsequent harassment or violence. This can be done through no-contact directives as well as changes to housing, work, activities, etc. Title IX also protects victims from any form of retaliation for reporting an incident and ensures that victims are safeguarded during the reporting process (KnowYourIX, 2015).

In addition to Title IX protections, the *Jeanne Clery Disclosure of Campus Security Policy and Crime Statistics Act* (known as the Clery Act) requires colleges to issue warnings to students when there are known safety risks on campus and also report any and all crimes that occur on campus in an Annual Security Report on the university website. This Act was passed in 1990 and expanded in 2013 through the *Campus Sexual Violence Elimination Act* (SaVE Act) to include all types of sexual violence, including sexual assault, domestic violence, dating violence, and stalking (KnowYourIX, 2015).

The Public Health Approach

In the past decade, the American College Health Association (ACHA) has become an active participant in attempting to address and prevent acts of violence on campus. The ACHA has specifically focused its efforts on ways to reduce serious acts of campus violence such as homicide, intimate partner violence, and rape (Carr, 2005). The ACHA's Campus Violence Committee has made a series of recommendations to support their goals. Pertinent recommendations of that committee include a focus on each university's responsibility to (Carr, 2005: p. 8):

- Address the entire continuum of violence.
- Incorporate collaboration by all campus constituents, not just student health services or police.

- Enforce codes of conduct.
- Implement tougher sanctions, including expulsion/suspension for serious misconduct.
- Create zero tolerance policies for campus violence.

The following section describes several campus victimization programs that incorporate many concepts similar to the ACHA's recommendations.

Varying Approaches of Campus Victimization Programs

Just as campuses may vary in size and complexity so too will their approaches to developing and implementing campus victimization programs (Randall, 2014). Often these programs are developed to deal with specific needs and problems of their respective campus communities. A sample of 27 universities was included in the Association of American Universities (AAU) Campus Climate Survey in 2015. This study aimed to look at how extensive sexual violence is, who the victims are, the reporting procedures of these victims, and the campus climate regarding sexual assault (Cantor et al., 2015). The results of this study highlight that there is wide variation in sexual assault and campus climate among the 27 campuses. Additionally, only one-quarter of students believed they were knowledgeable about the sexual assault victim resources available at their university. The following section provides a short overview of the different victimization programs present at each of the universities included in this survey based on their respective websites.

University Police Departments

Although the overreaching goals of sexual violence victim assistance programs are similar among the 27 universities, there are different approaches to how the programs are offered and where they are housed. Utilizing one approach, Texas A&M University offers victim assistance through its university police department. Their program also aims to assist and advocate for students who are victimized in crimes both on and off campus, and their office handles appointments and walk-ins and has a designated victim advocate and their contact information posted on their website. Their website also provides a link to the local Sexual Assault Resource Center (SARC) for anyone who would like specialized sexual victimization services (https://upd.tamu.edu/Pages/VictimsAdvocate.aspx).

Similar to Texas A&M University, the University of Florida has an Office of Victim Services that is housed in the university police department. In this capacity, a victim advocate is available 24 hours a day, seven days a week to give free and confidential support for victims of sexual violence. This advocate will support the victim throughout the different stages of the criminal justice process. Additionally, the University of Florida Police Department (UFPD) gives local and national resources for legal counsel, reporting, counseling, medical care, and education through the Sexual Trauma/Interpersonal Violence Education (STRIVE) program (http://www.police.ufl.edu/victim -services/).

In similar fashion, Washington University in St. Louis offers information for crime victims through the police. This site gives students an idea of their rights and provides contact information for counseling, medical assistance, and advocacy programs in the city of St. Louis. Additionally, the website contains a section detailing sexual assault and relationship abuse which gives important steps for individuals to follow if they are victimized. These steps provide specific contact information for the university police department and the community Sexual Assault Response Team (SART) https://police.wustl .edu/policeservices/Pages/Information-for-Victims-of-Crime.aspx).

Health and Medical Services

Other universities offer victim services through the health and medical resources available on campus. In one such case, Cornell University's Gannett Health Services offers victim assistance and advocacy for those who have experienced sexual assault and other types of violent victimization. They offer victims the ability to schedule appointments with an advocate to discuss their experience, provide information, and connect with other resources in the community for counseling or advising (http://www.gannett.cornell.edu /services/counseling/victim/advocate.cfm).

Similarly, under the University Health Services section of The University of Wisconsin, Madison website, there is a specific section, End Violence on Campus (EVOC) for sexual assault, dating violence, and stalking violence. This site contains a variety of hotlines and advice for victims/potential victims. Their program also provides advocacy and survivor services, including assistance in changing academic, living, transportation, and working situations (http://www.uhs.wisc.edu/assault/).

At Brown University, the Office of Health Education website also provides details on sexual assault and resources on campus. This program details prevention, advice, myths, and other forms of assistance for those who experience sexual assault or dating violence. Under Counseling and Psychological Services, Brown also offers therapy resources, trauma resources and immediate assistance for victims of sexual assault (http://www.brown.edu/campus-life/support/counseling-and-psychological-services/sexual-assault-and-interpersonal-violence).

Utilizing a similar medical and health resource approach, the University of Pennsylvania offers many resources for sexual assault victims through the Student Health Service office. These include medical services, counseling and psychological services, forensic assistance, and advocacy from the Penn Women's Center. Additionally, the University of Pennsylvania offers information regarding the Philadelphia Sexual Assault Response Center (PSARC), which allows for forensic examinations that are necessary for legal action (http://www.vpul.upenn.edu/shs/sexualassault.php).

Counseling Centers

In a different approach, some universities offer services through their counseling resources. For example, California Technical University's Counseling Center provides detailed information for students defining "sexual violence" and "consent." Additionally, their center provides assistance for those in need of medical attention who have been victimized, as well as a thorough description of rights related to confidentiality. In addition to the medical resources provided, the Caltech Counseling Center provides emotional support for victims and advocates on their behalf in issues related to reporting, living arrangements, and academic accommodations. A list of external assistance resources in the area and contact information is provided for students in need (https://counseling.caltech.edu/SexualAssault).

In addition to offering general counseling services, Purdue University offers an Advocacy and Support Center for those who are victims of sexual violence. This center provides assistance for students related to academic adjustments, work accommodations, housing reassignments, as well as general advocacy. Additionally, there are resources offered by the Lafayette Crisis Center which avails victims to round-the-clock assistance from a trained sexual violence advocate (http://www.edst.purdue.edu/counseling_psychology/PCGC.html).

Specialized Programs and Resources

Many universities offer services through specific programs or initiatives. For example, at the University of Texas, a program entitled "Voices against

Violence" is run by the UT Counseling and Mental Health Center to discuss issues with sexual assault and dating violence. This program contains information on what constitutes sexual violence and dating/relationship violence. Additionally, this site offers insight on prevention, risk reduction, and treatment. Their site offers a number of services to survivors of sexual violence, such as a crisis line, counseling (individual and group), advocacy, and medical attention. Additionally, their program has multiple campaigns designed to educate students about consent and sexual violence at the university (https:// socialwork.utexas.edu/cswr/institutes/idvsa/).

Similarly, the University of Pittsburgh offers the Sexual Harassment and Assault Response and Education (SHARE) program to provide counseling, medical care, and support for victims of sexual violence. This program offers confidential reporting resources and coordinates prevention and education programs for the campus as well. As with many other sites, their program offers definitions of sexual assault, relationship violence, stalking, and consent (http://www.police.pitt.edu/node/250).

Similar to the University of Pittsburgh, Cornell and Yale University offers a Sexual Harassment and Assault Response and Education (SHARE) program which lists a number of important resources for victims of sexual violence. Yale's SHARE program provides resources on the response to sexual misconduct and the university and grant counseling services for student victims. Additionally, they offer an anonymous hotline for information, advocacy, and support (http://smr.yale.edu/).

The Oasis Program was created by the Counseling and Psychological Services and Women's Resource Center at the University of Arizona. This program aims to prevent and respond to all types of interpersonal violence for students, staff, and faculty at the university. This program offers advocacy, confidential reporting, consultations, counseling, and support groups for victims. In addition, they coordinate outreach and educational efforts to prevent sexual and interpersonal violence from occurring (https://www.health .arizona.edu/hpps_oasis_program.htm)

Columbia University's Sexual Violence Response (SVR) program provides support for victims through counseling and advocacy and works toward prevention through education and outreach. This program offers on- and off-campus contact resources for victims of sexual assault, interpersonal violence, and stalking. Additionally, different other programs and offices are listed that can assist in reporting and legal assistance for victims. Beyond their advocacy focus, Columbia's SVR program allows for students to request workshops related to consent, violence, survivor support, and bystander interventions (https://health.columbia.edu/sexual-violence-response).

Michigan State University has launched a Sexual Assault Program (SAP) to assist those impacted by sexual violence and prevent these types of acts from occurring. The SAP provides crisis intervention, advocacy, therapy, support groups, and community education programs related to sexual assault. They also offer a wide variety of relevant readings for those in need of help or those who are interested in learning more about the victimization experience (http://endrape.msu.edu/).

The Aurora Center at the University of Minnesota provides services for victims of sexual assault, relationship violence, and stalking. Their website gives detailed definitions of each of these violent actions and specific resources for victims of each. This center also details all the options that are available for reporting sexual violence at the university. Additionally, there is a 24-hour helpline that is offered for assistance, advocacy, and support of those who experience sexual assault or violence (http://www1.umn.edu /aurora/).

The University of Southern California's Sexual Assault Resource Center (SARC) offers a 24-hour crisis hotline and assists victims with filing for court ordered protection or avoidance of contact letters. This allows for victim advocacy and assistance through external public safety and health resources. The SARC also provides detail on reporting options and right, as well as additional information for those who have been assaulted and those who know someone who has been assaulted (https://sarc.usc.edu/resources/).

Finally, the University of Michigan offers a Sexual Assault Prevention and Awareness Center (SAPAC) which aims to provide confidential crisis intervention, advocacy, and support for survivors of sexual assault and violence. Their site offers contact information and details on a vast multitude of resource centers in the Michigan area that may assist victims of sexual violence. The SARC's comprehensive website covers a wide variety of different programs/options and a wealth of information for sexual violence survivors (https://sapac .umich.edu/).

University Departments

The Office of Sexual Assault Prevention and Response at Harvard University is utilized to provide assistance for those who experience sexual assault, harassment, relationship violence, or stalking. They provide a 24-hour hotline and advocate for proper treatment of victims of sexual violence. The site gives detailed information on the rights and options for assault victims and provides contact information for campus, local, and national resources for the victims (http://osapr.harvard.edu/).

At the University of Missouri, the Relationship and Sexual Violence Prevention Center works to decrease the prevalence of sexual violence and assist those who are victimized. This includes providing crisis intervention and advocacy, as well as important facts and campus resources. Additionally, the university police department offers victim assistance and resources online. This site provides links to a variety of sites that can further assist the victim of a sexually violent offense (http://rsvp.missouri.edu/get-help/rsvp-center -resources/).

Ohio State University's Office of Student Conduct provides a variety of sites related to sexual violence victimization. This site gives numerous definitions of violence and consent, as well as policies related to violence and victimization. This office also provides information on the rights of the victim and the accused, the effects of false complaints, and details the use of protective or no contact orders. Additionally, OSU has launched the Sexual Civility and Empowerment Program which gives resources for support and advocacy as well as help and resources for victims on campus and in the local community (http://studentconduct.osu.edu/page.asp?id=45).

Through the Department of Public Safety, The University of North Carolina at Chapel Hill provides victims of crime external contact information for crisis centers, police departments, recovery centers, and other social services. Additionally, they offer specific resources for students who have experienced sexual violence via contact information for health services, counseling, and legal services (http://dps.unc.edu/safety/victim-assistance/).

Other universities utilize student-run groups and initiatives to handle sexual violence incidents. For example, Case Western Reserve University promotes a student group to address sexual assault and domestic violence that is co-sponsored by a local women's center, known as Sexual Assault & Violence Educators (SAVE). This group offers resources related to security, empowerment, counseling, and health services both on campus and in the local community. Their site offers specific definitions of different types of violence and details a variety of empirical statistics to demonstrate the prevalence and impact of sexual violence (http://www.case.edu/diversity/sexualconduct/assault /help.html).

Web Resource Pages

Lastly, some universities utilize a webpage with important resources through their campus website. In one such case, Iowa State University has a website specifically devoted to sexual misconduct and assault. On this site, students have access to a variety of confidential, campus, and community

212 12 · DEALING WITH COLLEGE CRIME VICTIMIZATION

resources, including medical services, law enforcement, advising, victim assistance, counseling, and shelter and support, many of which are open 24 hours a day and seven days a week. Their program offers information for supporting someone who has been sexually victimized as well as detailed information and policies related to how this type of violence is handled by the university. Furthermore, this site answers many frequently asked questions that may pertain to victims of sexual violence and their rights and options following an attack (http://www.sexualmisconduct.dso.iastate.edu/).

The University of Oregon also offers a large selection of helpful resources for victims of sexual violence, domestic violence, and stalking. Their site provides a vast assortment of agency contacts dealing with crisis assistance, on-campus services (such as counseling, crisis intervention, and sexual assault support services (SASS), evidence collection, medical care, and criminal processes). In addition, they offer an extensive staff of confidential employees who are either trained to deal with interpersonal violence at the University Counseling Center or trained to deal with medical issues at the University Health Center. Their site also gives common definitions and answers many frequently asked questions (https://safe.uoregon.edu/).

In addition, the University of Virginia provides a website detailing Sexual Violence Education and Resources which allows for support and information for victims of an assault. They provide definitions of sexual assault, intimate partner violence, and stalking, while also giving victims the ability to contact someone to get assistance immediately. Furthermore, their site offers a variety of counseling and student health resources on campus and in the local community (http://www.virginia.edu/sexualviolence/).

Finally, Dartmouth College provides a webpage specifically devoted to "Sexual Respect." This page provides definitions and on-campus and off-campus contact resources for students. It also allows students to directly report an incident if necessary. The website also gives detailed information on Title IX and the Clery Act (http://www.dartmouth.edu/sexualrespect/).

The University of South Florida: Victim Advocacy and Bystander Intervention

Offered by the Center for Victim Advocacy and Violence Prevention, USF's Advocacy Program assists USF students or employees who are victims of actual or threatened violence including assault, battery, sexual battery and attempted sexual battery. Services are available 24 hours a day, seven days a week (USF Advocacy Program, 2015). Victim services include assistance in contacting professors or supervisors about absences, assistance with referrals and follow-up medical treatment, and counseling services on and off campus; assistance with immediate changes in residence hall arrangements if needed for victims living on campus; assistance with immediate safe housing, transportation and assistance in disciplinary proceedings and/or the criminal justice system. Follow-up counseling services or other trauma assistance will be arranged for the victim as needed.

The Advocacy Program staff maintains an on-going referral network, both on and off campus. Members of USF community to whom victims may be referred, for instance, include the University Police, Counseling Center for Human Development, Employee Assistance Program, Equal Opportunity Affairs, Student Judicial Affairs, Student Health and Wellness Center, The Spring of Tampa Bay, Inc. (for domestic violence services), and individual therapists for assistance and support.

The Advocacy Program maintains a compendium of up-to-date social service resources and makes this information available to members of the USF community as needed. To accomplish this, a guide specialized for victims of sexual assault, harassment, domestic/relationship/dating violence, and stalking is provided online by USF's Advocacy Program to offer information and the contact information of a variety of confidential and non-confidential resources, including counseling, health, sexual assault services, and law enforcement agencies (USF Advocacy Program, 2015). The Advocacy Program is a member of the Hillsborough County Community Link Partnership, which links over 2000 providers of social service in Hillsborough County.

In addition to USF's Advocacy Program, as mandated by the recent amendments to the *Violence Against Women Act* (VAWA), training is administered concerning active bystander intervention. This training workshop teaches university employees to be able to intervene in the event of a potential sexual assault (American Council on Education, 2015). This program trains individuals to (1) notice a situation, (2) interpret the situation if there is a potential for danger, (3) assume responsibility to help, (4) know how to help, and (5) intervene safely. These interventions can include distracting an aggressor's attention, delegating to others, and directly approaching the situation. Through these trainings, university employees are intended to be better equipped to prevent the possibility for harm in a safe and positive way. Similar programs have been found to be effective in improving participant knowledge, their attitude towards intervening, and their efficacy of bystanders (Moynihan, Banyard, Arnold, Eckstein & Stapleton, 2011).

THE ADMINISTRATIVE APPROACH

Perhaps the most critical step to be taken in dealing with crime and specifically with sex offenses and other serious acts of violence is recognition by campus administrations that these events really do occur (Belknap and Erez, 1995; Benson, Charlton and Coodhart, 1992; Roark, 1987). To some extent such acknowledgment has been evolving over the last few decades at both the national and state levels. For example, administrative organizations such as the Association of Independent Colleges and Universities in the state of Massachusetts (AICUM), the American Council on Education (ACE), the National Association of State and University Land Grant Colleges (NASULGC), the National Association of Student Personnel Administrators (NASPA), the National Association of College and University Business Officers (NACUBO), and the International Association of Campus Law Enforcement Administrators (IACLEA) have each established guidelines for campuses to follow regarding campus crime and victimization (Bromley, 1995).

The IACLEA guidelines dictate that crime prevention is not a problem solely for police or administration, but instead, a shared problem among all members of the college campus community. In order to address this problem, the IACLEA has set nineteen positions on the management of campus law enforcement. These position statements include (among many others): ensuring that campus law enforcement has the expertise and resources to investigate crimes, ensuring that the administration has oversight over the campus police agency, the maintenance of detailed crime statistics, and community support and services to reduce criminal victimization in the campus community (IACLEA, 2008). These statements provide just a sample of the goals of the IACLEA and how they aim to best handle campus victimization.

The need for victim services programs on campuses has been supported by a variety of sources in campus crime literature. For example, Smith (1989) notes that in developing programs to deal with the crime of rape and its victims, responsibility should be shared campus-wide and not assumed only by campus police. Tomz and McGillis (1997) state that colleges have become increasingly involved in providing services to student crime victims and note that this has sometimes been accomplished in conjunction with local community victim assistance programs. The victims of certain crimes such as sexual assault, domestic violence, and hate crimes may have special needs that can best be addressed by victim assistance resources (Belknap and Erez, 1995; Powell, et al., 1994; Smith, 1989). Cerio (1989, p. 62) notes that victim service providers should also take into consideration the special needs of nontraditional campus community members such as "gays, lesbians, religious minorities, and the handicapped." In fact, in many of the victim assistance programs listed in the earlier sections of this chapter, specialized initiatives are offered to provide victimization resources for the LGBT community.

There is some evidence that post-secondary institutions have made advances acknowledging the needs of victims of crime and establishing ways to provide services to them. The United States Department of Justice published a monograph highlighting universities cited as examples of "promising practices" in providing total campus security services. Victim assistance programs were among the important services noted at the University of Pennsylvania, Penn State University, University of North Carolina, and the University of Delaware. These programs were mentioned as positive examples not found within the campus setting (Kirkland and Siegel, 1994).

In each of these programs, the services were found to be efficiently organized in order to provide easy access to victims (Kirkland and Siegel, 1994). This is obviously a critical component in the potential recovery of the victim as it assists them in dealing with the administrative processes required by the criminal Justice system.

Two nation-wide surveys of institutions of higher education also report the efforts by campuses to assist crime victims. A report by the National Center for Education Statistics found that 72% of the colleges and universities surveyed "instituted or improved in the last five years victim assistance programs" (NCES, 1997; p. 34). In his survey of campus police agencies, Reaves (2015) reported that over half of the campus law enforcement agencies surveyed (serving populations of 2,500 students or more) met with victim assistance or advocacy groups. Additionally, nearly 70% of these agencies met with sexual violence prevention groups and 60% met with domestic violence prevention groups.

Finally, in addition to developing programs to assist persons who have been crime victims, campus administrators must also play an active role in preventing victimizations. Several steps are recommended to administrators to help make their institutions safer communities.

First, campuses should require that campus police systematically review criminal activity reports from on-campus as well as those in locations near the campus for at least the prior two years. If a pattern has developed indicating that violent crimes such as rape, assault, robbery, or lewd and lascivious conduct are occurring on or near campus, police should take immediate corrective actions. Even if no pattern is evident, campus community members should be kept informed about the time and location of serious crimes and of procedures teaching how not to become a victim.

Second, campus victimization surveys should be periodically conducted in order to determine the number and location of crimes that have not been officially reported, as well as to measure the perception of safety on the part of campus community members.

Third, it is important that workshops provide students with information as to how to establish healthy non-violent relationships. Discussing sexual behavior, outlining legal consequences for assaultive behavior, and identifying resources for victims should be topics included in these workshops. As a result of the Title IX and Violence against Women Act (VAWA) amended requirements in 2013, training workshops on violence prevention, stalking, threats, assaults, domestic violence, and protective court orders are mandated for university employees (KnowYourIX, 2015). The assurance that these programs are effectually delivered and completed may improve the overall knowledge of those in the university community and hopefully can make the campus a safer place.

Fourth, the development and utilization of self-defense courses for women has been found to be a valuable adjunct to other crime control programs on many campuses. Such courses should be comprehensive in nature and would include awareness, prevention, risk reduction and avoidance, and a hands-on component for all participants.

Fifth, as noted earlier, victim assistance programs should be developed on campuses. Available services should include crisis intervention, referrals to various community services, help with criminal and student disciplinary proceedings, assistance with professors and other academic issues, help in locating safe housing, and assistance concerning parents and friends of the victim.

Finally, a comprehensive plan for responding to serious crimes should be developed by the institution. Key elements of such a plan should include identifying the specific responsibilities for campus police, student affairs officials, counseling, personnel, and student health officials. The plan should also include a mechanism for communicating with the campus community when a serious crime does occur in order to insure the accuracy and consistency of information being circulated.

Implementing Clery/Title IX

In early 2015, a meeting was held at the Georgia Institute of Technology which was hosted by the National Center for Campus Public Safety (NCCPS), the IACP University and College Police Section, and the International Association of Campus Law Enforcement Administrators to discuss and clarify the details of implementing numerous Clery Act and Title IX requirements. One of the main goals of this summit was to provide a list of best practices as it pertains to a number of different areas of compliance with these topic areas. These subjects were compiled and posted in a white paper report that was featured by the National Center for Campus Public Safety (2015). The following sections will briefly detail some of the promising practices discussed for the challenges that face universities. For more comprehensive strategies and information, see National Center for Campus Public Safety (2015).

Reporting of Sexual Violence

One of the main areas of emphasis for Clery/Title IX efforts focuses on increased reporting of criminal behavior to law enforcement. Among others, the discussants suggested that campus police agencies should focus on developing community relationships, especially with more marginalized and diverse populations. They advocated this be done through social media and outreach programs to help survivors feel more comfortable reporting their victimization to the police. Additionally, this can be accomplished through better familiarizing victims with the police and humanizing the contact made between law enforcement and the victim (National Center for Campus Public Safety, 2015). Another best practice recommendation related to impacting the reporting of sexual violence is to allow a trained advocate to be present during law enforcement's interview with the victim (National Center for Campus Public Safety, 2015).

Timely Warnings

In addition to improved relations to impact the reporting of sexual violence to police, recommendations were also made to better warn others in a timely fashion about a violent victimization. Specifically, the summit discussants suggest that the timely warning be approved by the victim prior to its release. For example, they should look for any offensive or victim-blaming language that may further victimize the survivor (National Center for Campus Public Safety, 2015). Additionally, universities should have a standard template prepared to ensure that information is released in an efficient manner. A second suggested practice is to send a follow-up message to those at the university with the results of the investigation (National Center for Campus Public Safety, 2015).

Training

Another aspect of Clery/Title IX implementation is the training of university employees in sexual violence victimization and certain requirements as a member of the campus community. One main suggestion is to develop advisory boards to establish training standards and certification processes (National Center for Campus Public Safety, 2015). Additionally, the summit recommended that table-top exercises are conducted using realistic incidents as examples (National Center for Campus Public Safety, 2015). Finally, training should be guided by facts and data collected by campus surveys (such as Climate Surveys) (National Center for Campus Public Safety, 2015).

Victim/Survivor Services

The summit also recommended a number of services to be offered for those who are victims of sexual violence. One such recommendation was for universities to form a Title IX committee to assist the university's Title IX Coordinator in their campus duties and also to partner with other nearby schools to share resources (National Center for Campus Public Safety, 2015). Additionally, campus administrators are recommended to review the procedures and practices set at the university with a victims' rights attorney (National Center for Campus Public Safety, 2015).

Investigations, Prosecutors, and On-Campus Hearings

The final section of promising practices relate to how investigations and campus hearings are held in accordance with Clery/Title IX. One specific best practice in this portion of the requirements is to not ask the victim if they would like to prosecute or offer the option of not prosecuting. As such, all sexual assault cases should be provided to a prosecutor (National Center for Campus Public Safety, 2015). Another recommendation is to share all information between local law enforcement agencies and campus police agencies regarding sexual offenders who have been arrested in the area (National Center for Campus Public Safety, 2015). Through these and many other recommendations, practitioners hope to improve the implementation of Clery/Title IX and better equip university administrators and police to deal with sexual violence victimization.

CONCLUSION

Anticipating and responding to campus crime victimization will continue to be a challenge for higher education decision-makers in the 21st century. The changing demographics of student populations, the growth in physical size of institutions and the number of students, are all factors to be considered when addressing campus victimization issues. National-level research such as that conducted by Fisher, et al. (2000), Hart (2003), Baum and Klaus (2005), and Sinozich and Langton (2014) certainly provides some insights for those responsible for reducing campus victimization and providing essential services to crime victims. However, while national-level initiatives are important, it is also important that executives at colleges and universities conduct similar research with respect to the nature and extent of campus crime at their own campuses. This will allow the various legal, public health, administrative, and programmatic efforts to be "tailored" to the unique needs of their campus community. Although many positive changes have been made since the passing of the Clery Act in the 1990s, campus victimization remains a major issue. With the recent progress of the new Title IX requirements, college campuses must continue to remain vigilant and proactive to address the safety of the students who attend the university. Campus policy-makers must continue to provide leadership and, with the assistance of other key campus constituents, develop comprehensive approaches to effectively and compassionately deal with the various aspects of campus crime victimization.

Final Note

The authors would like to give a special thank you to Dr. Ráchael Powers (Department of Criminology) and Joni Bernbaum (Center for Victim Advocacy) at the University of South Florida for their assistance in reviewing and giving feedback on this chapter.

References

American Council on Education. (2014). "New Requirements Imposed by the Violence Against Women Reauthorization Act." Retrieved from http://www.acenet.edu/news-room/Documents/VAWA-Summary.pdf on December 3, 2015.

American College Health Association. (2015). National College Health Assessment: Spring 2015 Reference Group Executive Summary. Retrieved on December 3, 2015 from http://www.acha-ncha.org/docs/NCHA-II_WEB_SPRING_2015_REFERENCE_GROUP_EXECUTIVE_SUMMARY.pdf.

Bachman, R. (1994). *Violence Against Women*. Washington, DC: U.S. Department of Justice.

Baier, S. Rosenweig, M., and Whipple, E. (1991). "Patterns of Sexual Behavior, Coercion and Victimization of University Students." *Journal of College Student Development*, (32): 310–322.

Barrick, K., Krebs, C. P., and Lindquist, C. H. (2013). "Intimate partner violence victimization among undergraduate women at historically black colleges and universities (HBCUs)." *Violence Against Women*, 19(8): 1014–1033.

Baum, K., and Klaus, P. (2005). "Violent Victimization of College Students, 1995–2002." Washington, D.C.: U.S. Department of Justice, Bureau of Justice Statistics.

Bausell, C., Bausell, B., and Siegel, D. (1991). *The Links Among Drugs, Alcohol, and Campus Crime: Research Results From the Campus Violence Prevention Center's Second Victimization Survey*. Towson, Maryland: Towson State University, Center for the Study and Prevention of Campus Crime.

Belknap, J., and Erez, E. (1995). "The Victimization of Women on College Campuses: Courtship Violence, Date Rape and Sexual Harassment." In B. Fisher and J. Sloan (eds.), *Campus Crime: Legal, Social and Policy Perspectives*. (pp. 156–178) Springfield, IL: Charles C. Thomas.

Benson, D., Charlton, C., and Coodhart, F. (1992). "Acquaintance Rape on Campus." *Journal of American College Health*. 40: 157–165.

Berkowitz, A. (1992). "College Men as Perpetrators of Acquaintance Rape and Sexual Assault: A Review of Cunent Research." *Journal of American College Health*, 40(4): 175–180.

Bogal-Allbritten, R., and Allbritten, W. (1991). "Courtship Violence and Campus: A National Survey of Student Affairs Professionals." *NASPA Journal*, 28(4): 312–318.

Brantingham P., Brantingham P., and Scagrave, J. (1995). "Crime and Fear of Crime at a Canadian University." In B.S. Fisher and J.S. Sloan (eds.), *Campus Crime Legal, Social and Policy Perspectives*. Springfield, IL: Charles C. Thomas.

Bromley, M. (2007). "The Evolution of Campus Policing: Different Models for Different Eras." In B.S. Fisher and J.S. Sloan (eds.), *Campus Crime Legal, Social and Policy Perspectives, 2nd ed.* Springfield, IL: Charles C. Thomas.

Bromley, M. (1995). "Securing the Campus: Political and Economic Forces Affecting Decision Makers." In B.S. Fisher and J.S. Sloan (eds.), *Campus Crime Legal, Social and Policy Perspectives*. Springfield, IL: Charles C. Thomas.

Bromley, M. (1993). "The Impact of Recently Enacted Statutes in Civil Law Suits on Security Policies at Post-Secondary Institutions." *The Journal of Police and Criminal Psychology.* 9(2): 46–52.

Bromley, M.L., and Territo, L. (1990). *College Crime Prevention and Personal Safety Awareness.* Springfield, IL: Charles C. Thomas.

Burd, S. (1992a). "Colleges Issue Federally Required Reports on Campus Crime Rates." *The Chronicle of Higher Education,* September 2, p. A-25.

Burd, S. (1992b). "Colleges Issue Federally Required Reports on Campus-Crime Rates, Arrests, Policies." *The Chronicle of Higher Education,* September 2, p. A-25.

Burling, P. (1991). *Crime on Campus: Analyzing and Managing the Increasing Risk of Institutional Liability.* Washington, D.C.: National Association of College and University Attorneys.

Burling, P. (1993). *Acquaintance Rape on Campus: A Model for Institutional Response.* Washington, D.C.: National Association of College and University Attorneys.

Cantor, D., Fisher, W., Chibnaill, S., Townsend, R., Lee, H., Bruce, C., and Thomas, G. (2015). Report on the AAU campus climate survey on sexual assault and sexual misconduct. Retrieved on December 3, 2015 from http://sexualassaulttaskforce.harvard.edu/files/taskforce/files/final _report_harvard_9.21.15.

Carr, J. (2005) *American College Health Association Campus Violence White Paper.* Baltimore, MD: American College Health Association.

Castelli, J. (1990). "Campus Crime 101." *The New York Times Education Life,* November 4, 1.

Cerio, N. (1989). "Counseling Victims and Perpetrators of Campus Violence." In J.N. Sherrill and D.G. Siegel (eds.) *Responding to Violence on Campus. New Directions for Student Services.* San Francisco: Jossey-Bass.

Cokey, M., Sherrill, J., Cave, R., and Chapman, G.R. (1988). "Awareness of Campus Violence by Students and Administrators," *Response.* 11(1): 3–6.

Coronel, S., Coll, S., and Kravitz, D. (2015). " 'A rape on campus': What went wrong?" *RollingStone.com.* Retrieved from http://www.rollingstone.com /culture/features/a-rape-on-campus-what-went-wrong-20150405 on December 3, 2015.

Erdely, S. (2014). "A rape on campus: a brutal assault and struggle for justice at UVA." *RollingStone.com.* Archived from the original on December 19, 2014. Retrieved on December 3, 2015.

Esposito, D., and Stormer, D. (1989) "The Multiple Roles of Campus Law Enforcement." *Campus Law Enforcement Journal*, 19(3): 26–30.

Field, K. (2015). "How Much Can Campus-Crime Reports Tell Us About Sexual Assault?" *The Chronicle of Higher Education*, November 25, 2015.

Fisher, B., Cullen, F., and Turner, M. (2000). "The Sexual Victimization of College Women." Washington, D.C.: U.S. Department of Justice, National Institute of Justice.

Fisher, B., and Sloan, J. (1995). *Campus Crime: Legal, Social, and Policy Perspectives.* Springfield, IL: Charles C. Thomas.

Forke, C. M., Myers, R. K., Catallozzi, M., and Schwarz, D. F. (2008). "Relationship violence among female and male college undergraduate students." *Archives of Pediatrics and Adolescent Medicine*, 162(7): 634–641.

Gordon, N.T., and Riger, S. (1989). *The Female Fear.* New York: Free Press.

Griffaton, M.C. (1995). "State-Level Initiatives and Campus Crime." In B. Fisher and J. Sloan (eds.), Campus Crime: Legal, Social and Policy Perspectives. Springfield IL: Charles C. Thomas.

Hart, T. (2003). "Violent Victimization of College Students, 1995–2000." Washington, D.C.: U. S. Department of Justice, Bureau of Justice Statistics.

International Association of Campus Law Enforcement Administrators (IACLEA). (1997). *Campus Crime Report, 1994–1995.* Hartford, CT: International Association of Campus Law Enforcement Administrators.

International Association of Campus Law Enforcement Administrators (IACLEA). (2008). *Position Statements.* Retrieved from http://www.iaclea.org/visitors/about/positonstatements.cfm on December 10, 2015.

Kalette, D. (1990). "Colleges Confront Liability." *U.S.A. Today,* September 14, 6A.

Kaplan, W. A. (1990). *The Law of Higher Education,* 2nd Ed. San Francisco, CA: Jossey-Bass Publishers.

Kaukinen, C., Gover, A. R., and Hartman, J. L. (2012). "College women's experiences of dating violence in casual and exclusive relationships." *American Journal of Criminal Justice*, 37(2): 146–162.

Kilpatrick, D. G., Resnick, H. S., Ruggiero, K. J., Conoscenti, L. M., and McCauley, J. (2007). *Drug-facilitated, incapacitated, and forcible rape: A national study.* Charleston, SC: Medical University of South Carolina, National Crime Victims Research and Treatment Center.

Kirkland, C., and Siegel, D. (1994). *Campus Security: A First Look at Promising Practices.* Washington, DC: U.S. Department of Education.

KnowYourIX. (2015). "Know Your IX: Empowering students to stop sexual violence." Retrieved from http://knowyourix.org on December 3, 2015.

Koss, M.P, Gidycz, C.A., and Wisniewski, N. (1987). "The Scope of Rape: Incidence and Prevalence of Sexual Aggression and Victimization in a National Sample of Higher Education Students." *Journal of Consulting and Clinical Psychology*, 55(2): 162–170.

Langford, T. (2004). *Preventing Violence and Promoting Safety in Higher Education Settings*. Washington, D.C.: U.S. Department of Education.

Lederman, D. (1993). "Colleges Report 7,500 Violent Crimes on Their Campuses in First Annual Statements Required Under Federal Law." *The Chronicle of Higher Education*, January 20, A32–A43.

Lederman, D. (1994a). "Crime on the Campus." *The Chronicle of Higher Education*, February 3, A33.

Lederman, D. (1994b). "Weapons on Campus." *The Chronicle of Higher Education*, March 9, A33.

Lively, K. (1996). "Drug Arrests Rise Again." *The Chronicle of Higher Education*, April 26, A37.

Lively, K. (1997). "Campus Drug Arrests Increased 18 Percent in 1995: Reports of Other Crimes Fell." *The Chronicle of Higher Education*, March 21, A44.

Makepeace, J.M. (1981). "Courtship Violence among College Students." *Family Relations*, 30(1): 97–102.

Maloy, C.E. (1991). Paper presented at the Fifth National Conference on Violence, Towson State University, Towson, Maryland.

Mangan, K. (2015). "What 'Yes Means Yes' Means for Colleges' Sex-Assault Investigations." *The Chronicle of Higher Education*, September 3, 2015.

Mathews, A. (1993). "The Campus Crime War." *The New York Times Magazine*, March 7, 38–47.

McIntire, M.E. (2015). "Conversation About Sexual Violence Is Often a New One for College Freshmen." *The Chronicle of Higher Education*, August 26, 2015.

Moynihan, M. M., Banyard, V. L., Arnold, J. S., Eckstein, R. P., and Stapleton, J. G. (2011). "Sisterhood may be powerful for reducing sexual and intimate partner violence: an evaluation of the Bringing in the Bystander in-person program with sorority members." *Violence Against Women*, 17(6): 703–719.

National Center for Campus Public Safety. (2015). "Practitioners' Discussion of Implementing Clery/Title IX: Report on the Summit II." Retrieved from

http://nccpsafety.org/assets/files/library/NCCPS_Summit_II_Paper
_FINAL051815.pdf on December 21, 2015.

National Center for Educational Statistics. (1997). *Campus Crime and Security at Post Secondary Institutions.* Washington, DC: U.S. Department of Education.

Nichols, D. (1986). *The Administration of Public Safety in Higher Education.* Springfield, IL: Charles C. Thomas.

Ordovensky, P. (1990). "Students Easy 'Prey' on Campus." *U.S.A. Today,* December 3, 1A.

Powell, J. (1981) "The History and Proper Role of Campus Security." *Security World,* 8(1): 18–25.

Powell, J.W., Pander, M.S., and Nielsen, R.C. (1994). *Campus Security and Law Enforcement,* 2nd edition. Boston, MA: Butterworth-Heinemann.

Randall, A. (2014). "Additional Campus Prevention Program Examples, Gathered by the Department of Justice." In *Preventing Sexual Violence on College Campuses: Lessons from Research and Practice.* Retrieved from notalone.gov/assets/evidence-based-strategies-for-the-prevention-of-sv-perpetration.pdf on December 3, 2015.

Reaves, B. (2015). "*Campus Law Enforcement 2011–2012.*" Washington, D.C.: United States Department of Justice.

Roark, M. (1987). "Preventing Violence on Campus." *Journal of Counseling and Development,* March (65): 367–371.

Sellers, C. S., and Bromley, M.L. (1996). "Violent Behavior in College Student Dating Relationships: Implications for Campus Service Providers." *Journal of Contemporary Criminal Justice,* 12(1): 1–27.

Seng, M.J., and Koehler, N.S. (1993). "The Crime Awareness and Campus Security Act: A Critical Analysis." *Journal of Crime and Justice* 16(1): 97–110.

Seng, M. (1995). "The Crime Awareness and Campus Security Act: Some Observations, Critical Comments, and Suggestions." In B.S. Fisher and J.J. Sloan, *Campus Crime: Legal, Social and Policy Perspectives.* Springfield, IL: Charles C. Thomas.

Siegel, D., and Raymond, C. (1992). "An Ecological Approach to Violent Crime on Campus." *Journal of Security Administration,* 15(2): 19–29.

Sigler, R., and Koehler, N.S. (1993). "Victimization and Crime on Campus." *International Review of Victimology,* 2(1): 331–343.

Sinozich, S., and Langton, L (2014). "Rape and Sexual Assault Victimization Among College-Age Females, 1995–2013." Washington, D.C.: U. S. Department of Justice, Bureau of Justice Statistics.

Sloan, J. (1992a) "The Modern Campus Police: An Analysis of Their Evolution, Structure, and Function." *American Journal of Police*, 11(1): 85–104.

Sloan, J. (1992b). "Campus Crime and Campus Communities: An Analysis of Campus Police and Security." *Journal of Security Administration*, 15(2): 31–45.

Sloan, J.J. (1994). "The Correlates of Campus Crime: An Analysis of Reported Crimes on University Campuses." *Journal of Criminal Justice*, 22(1): 51–62.

Sloan, J., and Fisher, B. (1995). "Campus Crime: Legal, Social, and Policy Contexts." In B.S. Fisher and J. Sloan (eds.) *Campus Crime: Legal, Social, and Policy Perspectives.* Springfield, IL: Charles C. Thomas.

Smith, M. (1989) *Campus Crime and Campus Police: A Handbook for Police Officers and Administrators.* Asheville, NC: College Administration Publications, Inc.

Smith, M.C. (1995). "Vexations of Victims of Campus Crime." In B. Fisher and J. Sloan (eds.), *Campus Crime: Legal, Social and Policy Perspectives.* Springfield IL: Charles C. Thomas.

Territo, L., Halsted, J., and Bromley, M. (2004). *Crime and Justice in America: A Human Perspective.* Newton, MA: Butterworth-Heinemann.

Thomason, A. (2015). "15% of Female Freshmen are Raped While Incapacitated, Study Suggests." *The Chronicle of Higher Education*, November 18, 2015.

Tomz, J., and McGillis, D. (1997). *Serving Crime Victims and Witnesses.* Washington, DC: U.S. Department of Justice.

Torrey, S., and Lee, R. (1987). Curbing Dating Violence: Campus-Wide Strategies. *Journal of National Association for Women Deans, Administrators, and Counselors*, 51(1): 3–8.

Tuttle, D.F. (1991). "Campus Crime Disclosure Legislation." *Campus Law Enforcement Journal*, 21(1): 19–21.

USF Advocacy Program (2015). "Guide for Victims of Sexual Assault & Harassment, Domestic, Relationship & Dating Violence, and Stalking." Retrieved from http://sa.usf.edu/advocacy/docs/VAVP_Victim_Guide_FINAL_web.pdf on December 10, 2015.

United States Department of Justice, F.B.I. (1997). *Crime in the United States 1996. Uniform Crime Report.* Washington, DC: U.S. Government Printing Office.

Ward, S.K., Chapman, S., White, S., and Williams, K. (1991). "Acquaintance Rape and the College Social Scene." *Family Relations*, 40(1): 65–71.

Wechsler, H., Davenport, A., Dowdall, G., Moeykens, B., and Lastillo, S. (1994). "Health and Behavioral Consequences of Binge Drinking in College." *The Journal of the American Medical Association*, 272(21): 1672–1677.

Ziering, A. (Producer), and Dick, K. (Director). (2015). *The Hunting Ground* [Motion picture]. United States: The Weinstein Company.

CASES

Dixon v. The Alabama Board of Education, 294F.2d.150 (1961).

STATUTES

Cal. Educ. Code Ann., §§67380, 67390 to 67393, 94380 (1994).

Student Right-to-Know and Campus Security Act, Public Law No. 101–542 (1990); amended by Public Law No. 102–26, Sec. 10(c) (1991); 20 U.S.C. 1092(f).

CHAPTER 13

An Overview of College Sexual Assault: Federal Legislation and Campus Responses

Beverly Dolinsky and Courtney Gurska
Endicott College

One in five women and one in 16 men are sexually assaulted while attending college (National Sexual Violence Resource Center, 2015). The prevalence of college sexual assault was first documented in 1987 by Koss, Gidycz, and Wisniewski and studies since then have found little has changed in the past 30 years (Cantor, Fisher, Chibnall, Townsend, Lee, Bruce & Thomas, 2015; Fisher, Cullen & Turner, 2000; Krebs, Lindquist, Warner, Fisher & Martin, 2007). Surveying over 150,000 students from 27 universities in the spring of 2015, the American Association of Universities reported the 11.7% rate of nonconsensual sexual contact was as high as or slightly higher than what had been previously reported (Cantor et al., 2015). First year students were the most likely to report having experienced a sexual assault and only 28% of assaults were reported to an organization or agency. In piloting a standardized Campus Climate Survey to nine universities in 2015, the reported rates of female sexual assault ranged from 4–20% with an average rate of 10% for the nine institutions (Krebs, Lindquist, Berzofsky, Shook-Sa & Peterson, 2016). In short, the rate of sexual victimization on a college campus is alarmingly commonplace. Schools are required by Federal law to put into place policies and procedures to protect students from assault. However, until recently few colleges were doing this in a comprehensive and intentional manner.

Legislative Responses to Addressing Campus Sexual Assault

In 1972, the foundation for colleges and universities to be held liable for sexual assault on college campuses was laid with the implementation of Title IX of the Education Act (United States Department of Justice, 1972; United States Department of Justice, Civil Rights Division, 2001). An overview of how this law has evolved over the next 40 years is summarized in Figure 1.

Figure 1: An Overview of Sexual Assault Legislation Directed Towards Educationally Based Institutions

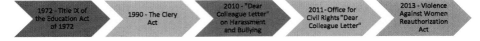

The Department of Education's Office for Civil Rights (OCR) oversees adherence to the Title IX regulations by schools. The role of the Office of Civil Rights in overseeing Title IX complaints includes helping to resolve complaints, to initiate reviews of cases that are particularly severe, and to offer assistance to institutions who are voluntarily seeking to enhance compliance. Paralleling Title IX, The Clery Act was being established and implemented across college campuses (Clery Center for Security on Campus, 2012). This law, instituted in 1990, requires all colleges and universities who receive federal financial aid to share information about the crimes on their campus as well as the safety policies and procedures that are designed to keep students safe on the campus.

The Federal government in 2010 emphasized a school's responsibility in addressing sexual assault in a "Dear Colleague Letter" [DCL] on Harassment and Bullying issued by the Office for Civil Rights (United States Department of Education, Office for Civil Rights, 2010). Addressed to schools, colleges and universities, the letter highlighted how educational institutions are obligated to protect students from harassment and bullying based on race, sex and disability. It was not until the publication of the 2011 Office of Civil Rights "Dear Colleague Letter" that sexual assault on college campuses was directly addressed (Department of Education, Office for Civil Rights, 2011). The letter emphasized the institutions' obligations to respond to sexual harassment and sexual violence. It re-emphasized that sexual harassment consists of unwelcome sexual contact that results in a hostile environment interfering or limiting a student's ability to participate in the school's programs. In addition, it highlighted that sexual assault occurs when there is a lack of consent and/or the student is unable to give consent due to the victim's use of alcohol or drugs, or an intellectual or physical disability.

Although as a result of the "Dear Colleague Letter" colleges were now taking their role more seriously, it was becoming clear that more still needed to be done. Reports of sexual assault in the Clery Annual Safety Reports were remaining near zero while self-reports via victimization surveys indicated sexual assault was continuing to be experienced at a high level. In March 2013, President Obama signed the Reauthorization of the Violence against Women Act (Violence Against Women Reauthorization Act of 2013) that *"amended the Clery Act to require institutions to compile statistics not only for reported sexual assaults but for complaints of dating violence, domestic violence, and stalking as well as to include certain policies, procedures, and programs pertaining to these incidents in their annual security reports"* (Federal Register, 2014, para 1). The amendment required colleges to provide training to new students and employees as well as provide sexual victimization and harassment primary prevention and awareness programs. The changes to the VAWA act also required colleges to adjust their policies and procedures in numerous ways including publishing the steps, timelines and decision making processes for sexual assault disciplinary proceedings and providing a list of sanctions that can be imposed for students found responsible for a sexual assault as well as a description of protective measures used to support the victim. The regulations became effective on July 1, 2015.

Responses to Sexual Assault

Numerous actions have occurred in the advent of the legislation holding educational institutions responsible for preventing and responding to sexual assault complaints. These responses are summarized in Figure 2.

Campus Climate Surveys

The White House Task Force to Protect Students from Sexual Assault has recommended the voluntary use of campus climate surveys and has provided a model for such a survey as well as the methodology to implement the surveys (DeGue, 2016; Krebs et al., 2016; NotAlone.gov, 2015; NotAlone.gov, 2016). The report of the Task Force emphasized the importance for Colleges to listen to their students' experiences to gauge the severity of the issue on their campus, assess students' attitudes towards sexual assault and knowledge of pre-

Figure 2: Responses to Sexual Assault Legislation

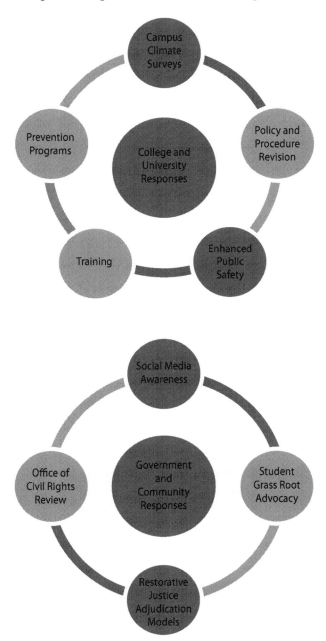

vention methods. The buy-in for Campus Climate Surveys has been mixed. The University of New Hampshire has one of the longest records in completing such a survey and has been capturing student campus sexual assault experiences for 25 years. Other institutions have been required to implement climate surveys as a result of accommodations made to settle OCR complaints. An example is the University of Montana-Missoula, a case that received wide media attention and is the focus of the book entitled *Missoula* (Krakauer, 2015). In this narrative, Krakauer details the sexual assault complaints by several female University of Montana students against members of the football team. A yearlong review by the Office of Civil Rights found the University lacking in a number of policies and procedures and the case became a model for subsequent investigations. Still, other institutions are holding off conducting the surveys due to concern with negative publicity, questioning the accuracy of self-report, voluntary surveys and questioning the value and usefulness of the knowledge obtained (Harvey, 2014). It is too early to report how effective these surveys have been in improving training and prevention programs, but the focus to ensure that institutions do use this data proactively is being called for at the Federal level.

Policy and Procedure Revision

The DCL and VAWA have required all colleges and universities to carefully examine their sexual assault policies and procedures to ensure they meet all of the guidelines within these laws. To support institutions, the Department of Justice has created an online clearinghouse for colleges and universities and includes information on policy, responding and preventing sexual assault (Center for Changing our Campus Culture, 2015).

The definition of consent has been especially focused on in policy revision. Those responsible for policy struggle on how to write clear expectations of how students can gain affirmative consent from partners. Student conduct officers also struggle on making a decision in a student conduct case for the same reasons. Does the absence of a "no" imply consent? Does the absence of a "yes" imply the lack of consent? One policy being considered is being termed the "Yes means Yes" policy. In 2014, the state of California was the first state to set uniform definitions of consent for private and public colleges with New York soon to follow. Grinnell College has been cited as a case study for implementing a "yes means yes" policy (Wilson, 2014c). The goal of these new laws and policies are to have the focus of a sexual assault complaint be on whether the offender had gained consent rather than the more common demand of the victim to prove that they had said "no" or were unable to do so based on being impaired physically or mentally. There has been considerable debate on the viability of such a policy in practice as well as the legal limits of the policy given the policy reverses the assumption of innocence and requires the target of the complaint to prove that the partner had explicitly given consent. Schools now have to decide if the "yes means yes" policy is one that should not only be a standard for proper conduct and training but central to the student conduct litigation process.

A second major point of contention in rewriting the policies has focused on the concept of due process. Although it is clear colleges must use the "more likely than not" standard in investigating a sexual assault complaint, the accused and their families have become more vocal in questioning this lesser standard. As policies and procedures have been revised to support the victim, more of the individuals accused of these crimes, their families and legal representatives have been filing institutional and legal complaints. These students believe they have not received a fair and impartial review of the case, are presumed guilty and are receiving unduly harsh punishments. Ironically, the perpetrators are arguing that Title IX is biased against them. Men found responsible for rape on their college campuses have sued their institutions and filed OCR Title IX complaints (Wilson, 2014a, 2014b). Desired settlement requests have included a reversal of the decision based on an appeal as well as a request to expunge their conduct record so that these charges do not negatively impact the futures of students found responsible.

Public Safety Enhancements

The Department of Education's Office for Civil Rights requires colleges to investigate reports of college sexual assault immediately and fairly as well as to ensure the safety of the individual who has filed the complaint even while the investigation is still pending. In response, public safety departments have been encouraged to enhance their officer training. The *Center for Changing our Campus Culture (2015)* has provided resources to: 1) improve the investigation of a complaint; and 2) develop emergency response policy and forensic trauma interviews. Similar training is being offered by many other nonprofit and for-profit organizations.

In addition to implementing sexual violence and bystander intervention education programs, campus safety departments are increasing safety mechanisms available to students. The popular but rarely useful "Blue Light" notification system (free-standing towers installed across a campus with an integrated security phone system) continues to be an advertising presence on college campuses. Safety escorts are popular. In a nod to the extensive availability of smart phones, the newest strategy has been the adoption of special cell phone "apps" designed to provide notification in case of an emergency as well as bystander support. Popular "apps" include *CampusSafe, Circle of 6,* and *EmergenSee* (Button, 2014). The value of these apps in reducing college sexual assault has yet to be empirically established but the advertising found on the app sites and in campus safety public relations material strongly implies their value. Whether these statements are true remains to be determined.

Training: Professionalizing First Responder and Investigation Responses

The Department of Justice Center for *Changing Our Campus (2015)* online clearinghouse provides numerous recommendations for training on a college campus. The most emphasized trainings focus around first responders and investigators. Colleges are now required to train all new employees on their responsibilities to report sexual harassment and violence. The college also needs to arrange for training of the Title IX officer as well as individuals who are being identified in policy documents as individuals where a sexual harassment complaint can be placed. The training needs to highlight the trauma experienced by sexual assault victims. The professionals need to know the resources available to victims and be able to guide the victim through the process.

Prevention Programs

The *Division of Violence Prevention within the Center for Disease Control* systematically reviewed 140 studies in order to develop a document summarizing the best practices in reducing and preventing sexual violence within a community (DeGue, 2014). Programs identified as ineffective included brief, one session educational programs typical in summer orientations and residence hall programs. It was concluded that although these brief inoculation type programs may raise awareness, they rarely predict changes in proactive behavior resulting in increased safety precautions, bystander intervention or the filing of complaints (Daigle, Fisher & Stewart, 2009). Instead comprehensive programs across years and the college campus are recommended. Some promising prevention programs that are in need of further empirical research included *Coaching Boys into Men* (Futures without Violence, 2016), *One in Four Program (One in Four, 2016),* the *Red Watch Band program (Stonybrook University, 2016), Green Dot (Green Dot, Etc., 2010)* and the *Bringing in the Bystander* developed by Banyard, Moynihan and Plante (2007) at the University of New Hampshire. Via education, the primary objective of these programs is to promote healthy relationships and reduce interpersonal violence by learning strategies for prevention and intervention. Recent research has found support for bystander education programs to reduce rape myth acceptance and increased bystander efficacy within college students (Reed, Hines, Armstrong & Cameron, 2015).

Social Media Awareness

To emphasize that it is everyone's responsibility to prevent college sexual violence, President Obama and Vice President Biden started the *"It's On Us"* social media campaign asking celebrities, companies, colleges, and individual citizens to pledge to

1) *intervene instead of being a bystander.*
2) *Recognize that any time consent is not — or cannot — be given, it is sexual assault and it is a crime*
3) *do everything you can to create an environment where sexual assault is unacceptable, and all survivors are supported (White House, Office of the Vice President, 2015, para. 6).*

Simultaneously the White House unveiled the *NotAlone.gov* website that gives students and college officials guidance on how to prevent and respond to college sexual assault. In addition, the *"No More"* campaign was ushered out in 2015 using celebrities, especially male celebrities and athletes voicing the primary message that it is time to halt domestic violence and sexual assault. Additional popular social media campaigns used at colleges include *Know Your Power, The Red Flag Campaign, The White Ribbon Campaign,* and *Walk A Mile In Her Shoes Campaign* (DeGue, 2014). Each of these programs provides education on what sexual assault is and who is victimized as well as emphasizes the important role students play in reducing sexual assaults via bystander intervention. Although some of these campaigns have been supported empirically, more research is needed to assess their effectiveness.

Student Grassroots Advocacy Campaigns

Several grassroots student advocacy groups have gained national attention addressing the pervasiveness of college sexual assault. Using social media, a number of students across the country became aware of students who had similar sexual assault experiences as well as similar unsatisfactory experiences with how the colleges addressed the complaint. As a result, a group of these students from Amherst College and the University of South Carolina launched a website entitled "Know Your Title IX." The website provides legal and public relations advice. In addition, tactics to continue a victim's college education are shared as well as strategies to develop sexual assault prevention campaigns on a campus (Bombardieri, 2014). How these grassroots movements began, their actions and their impact were documented in the film *The Hunting Ground* released in 2015. This type of informal networking using social media has continued to increase in size and has amplified the attention colleges have faced in their often inadequate response to addressing college sexual assault.

Restorative Justice Adjudication Models

Apart from training, the types of investigative and adjudicative systems that work best are being examined. Best practices regarding who should gather the evidence, hear the case, make the decision, and hear the appeal are all being discussed. Some schools are continuing to use the traditional administrative/conduct hearing board model. This model tends to contradict the spirit of Title IX as they can be hostile towards the victim and fail to protect either the complainant or the larger community (Kirven, 2014). Others are adopting a "single investigator" model where a trained investigator hears the complaint from both the victim and the offender perspective and makes a decision. The "restorative justice" model is a third model gaining momentum. Protecting the victim from further victimization via the investigation and adjudication process is central to the restorative justice process. The process believes that a crime has a community wide impact including the victim, the victim's family, the offender's family, as well as the greater community within which the crime occurred. Forms of restorative justice include victim-offender dialogues, victim impact panels, community reparation panels, and circles of support. Rather than focusing on fault or responsibility, the restorative justice process empowers the victim to make decisions regarding the process. Within an informal, voluntary mediation method, the victim voices the impact of the offense, the offender acknowledges this impact and a reparation plan is created mutually agreed upon by both victim and offender. The plan should support the victim's healing process, reinforce the community's expectations for appropriate behavior, and expects the offender to behave in a socially responsible manner in the future. Evidence for the effectiveness of the restorative justice model is still being examined especially as it pertains to sexual assault on adults (Koss, 2014; Koss, Wilgus & Williamsen, 2014). Several college campuses are exploring the use of restorative justice models to address Title IX complaints via the *CAMPUS PRISM* (2016) project.

Office of Civil Rights Response

When reviewing a Title IX complaint, the Office of Civil Rights can withdraw federal financial aid to institutions that are not in compliance with Title IX as well as refer cases to the Department of Justice for litigation. However, neither of these two actions is common. The Office of Civil Rights is much more likely to negotiate resolutions with institutions to allow them to become compliant. Such actions include revising policies and procedures, improving community preventative education methods, and providing enhanced victim support services.

At the time of writing, there were a total of 273 cases being investigated by the OCR. The average length of time to resolve a case is one year and three months with 18% of the cases resolved. The statuses of all cases are available via *The Chronicle of Higher Education's Campus Sexual Assault under Investigation* website (2016). The majority of the OCR cases have been based on the mishandling of sexual assault reports on college campus, which in turn resulted in an alleged hostile learning environment for the victims. The three most common resolutions agreed upon between the OCR and a school has included: 1) updating Title IX Policies and Grievance Procedures; 2) providing trainings to all members of the school community; and 3) conducting climate surveys to assess the effectiveness of the resolution steps.

Concluding Remarks

Sexual assault is pervasive on a college campus and statistics of sexual assault victimization have not changed over the past thirty years. Despite significant enhancement and enforcement in Federal laws to prevent and respond to sexual assault, there is still much more that needs to be done:

- For the majority of institutions of higher education, changes to policies and procedures to respond and prevent sexual assault are occurring as a result of the recent changes to Federal laws. Colleges have not acted in a selfless manner to prevent victimization but have acted in a selfish manner to avoid liability, negative publicity, and loss of potential revenue.

The Office of Civil Rights will need to enforce these guidelines in a way that is meaningful to ensure effective campus change.

- Rape myth acceptance remains pervasive. Victims, offenders, college officials, responsible for addressing complaints continue to blame the victim, diminish the seriousness of rape as well as the impact of rape on the victim. Although new training requires education on this, changing attitudes and more importantly behavior is extremely difficult. Strategies to decrease rape myth acceptance attitudes must continue to be developed and implemented. The victim will not be supported until rape myth acceptance attitudes are eliminated.
- Training and education does not guarantee changes in historically biased attitudes towards victims. College officials need to set up case review processes that assess for biased, negative practices against victims.
- There needs to be a united and consistent philosophy on a college campus that the victim's needs and safety are of foremost importance. Best practices in comprehensive approaches in supporting the sexual assault victim need to be identified and implemented on the campus and in collaboration with community victim advocacy agencies.
- Consent or the lack there of can be very difficult to determine when alcohol, differing perceptions, and a lack of witnesses are available. Individuals trained in sexual assault and their complexities should be the ones reviewing the cases given this.
- Each sexual assault case is unique. Decisions regarding responsibility as well as sanctions must therefore be approached in a unique way. Yet, colleges should strive to use similar and equitable decision criteria, sanctions and resolutions. It is an exceedingly difficult tightrope to balance and again calls for trained professionals to handle these cases.
- Students and their families need to be better educated on the differences between the college adjudication process and the legal process. The "more likely than not" standard is significantly different than due process. Victims, offenders and their families can confuse the processes resulting in frustration, anger and appeals regarding decisions made.
- Clery statistics are not accurate reflections of college sexual assault. Colleges should complete campus climate surveys and these should be published to support the safety of the students.
- Comprehensive and frequent training for all students on campus sexual assault, prevention methods and bystander interview needs to be improved.
- Restorative justice models are showing promise for their focus on empowering the victim, supporting their healing, involving the com-

munity in the process and attempting to redress the offending behavior to avoid recidivism. The effectiveness of these models in supporting both the victim and the community need to be empirically examined.

REFERENCES

Banyard, V. L, Moynihan, M. M. & Plante, E. G. (2007). Sexual violence prevention through bystander intervention: An experimental evaluation. *Journal of Community Psychology, 35(4)*, 463–481.

Bombardieri, M. (2014, May 3). Students' efforts put campus sex assaults into spotlight. *Boston Globe*. Retrieved from https://www.bostonglobe.com /metro/2014/05/02/student-activism-white-house-pressure-elevated-sexual -assault-college-campuses-national-concern/JiMUJDdai4ub1mTuEREPaL /story.html

Button, K. (2014). 10 mobile apps making campuses safer. *EducationDive*. Retrieved From http://www.educationdive.com/news/10-mobile-apps-making -campuses-safer/241575/.

CAMPUS PRISM. (2016). Promoting restorative initiatives for sexual misconduct on college campuses. Retrieved from http://www.skidmore.edu /campusrj/prism.php.

Cantor, D., Fisher, B., Chibnall, S., Townsend, R., Lee, H., Bruce, C. & Thomas, G. (2015). Report on the AAU campus climate survey on sexual assault and sexual misconduct. Westat. Retrieved from https://www.aau.edu /uploadedFiles/AAU_Publications/AAU_Reports/Sexual_Assault _Campus_Survey/AAU_Campus_Climate_Survey_12_14_15.pdf.

Center for Changing our Campus Culture (2015). Retrieved from http://www .changingourcampus.org/.

Chronicle of Higher Education Campus sexual assault under investigation Website (2016). Retrieved from http://projects.chronicle.com/titleix/.

Clery Center for Security on Campus (2012). Jeanne Clery Act. Retrieved from http://clerycenter.org/jeanne-clery-act.

Daigle, L. E., Fisher, B. S. & Stewart, M. (2009). The effectiveness of sexual victimization prevention among college students: A summary of "what works". *Victims and Offenders, 4*, 398–404.

DeGue, S. (2014). Preventing sexual violence on college campuses: Lessons from research and practice. *The White House Task Force to Protect Students from Sexual Assault*. Retrieved from https://www.notalone.gov/assets /evidence-based-strategies-for-the-prevention-of-sv-perpetration.pdf.

Federal Register. (2014, Oct 20). Violence against women act. Retrieved from https://www.federalregister.gov/articles/2014/10/20/2014-24284/violence -against-women-act.

Fisher, B.S., Cullen, F. T. & Turner, M.G. (2000). *The sexual victimization of college women*. Washington, D.C., United States Department of Justice, Office of Justice Programs. Retrieved from https://www.ncjrs.gov/pdffiles1 /nij/182369.pdf.

Futures without Violence. (2016). Coaching boys into men. Retrieved from *http://www.futureswithoutviolence.org/engaging-men/coaching-boys-into -men/*.

Green Dot, Etc. (2010). Ending violence one green dot at a time. Retrieved from https://www.livethegreendot.com/.

Harvey, T. (2014, May 12). To curb sexual assault on campuses, surveys become a priority. *Chronicle of Higher Education*. Retrieved from http://chronicle .com/article/To-Curb-Sexual-Assault-on/146475.

Kirven, S. (2014). Isolation to empowerment: A review of the campus rape adjudication process. *Journal of International Criminal Justice Research, 2,* 1–15.

Koss, M. P. (2014). The RESTORE of restorative justice for sex crimes: Vision, process and outcomes. *Journal of Interpersonal Violence, 29(9),* 1623–1660.

Koss, M. P. , Gidycz, C. A. & Wisniewski, N., (1987). The scope of rape: Incidence and prevalence of sexual aggression and victimization in a national sample of higher education students. *Journal of Clinical and Consulting Psychology, 55(2), 162–170.*

Koss, M. P., Wilgus, J. K. & Williamsen, K. M., 2014. Campus sexual misconduct: Restorative justice approaches to enhance compliance with Title IX guidance. *Trauma, Violence & Abuse, 15,* 242–257.

Krakauer, J. (2015). Missoula: Rape and the justice system in a college town. New York, NY: Anchor Books.

Krebs, C., Lindquist, C., Berzofsky, M., Shook-Sa, B. & Petersen, K. (2016). Campus climate survey validation study final technical report. *Bureau of Justice Statistics*. Retrieved from http://www.bjs.gov/content/pub/pdf /ccsvsftr.pdf.

Krebs, C. P., Lindquist, C. H., Warner, T. D., Fisher, B. S. & Martin, S. L. (2007). The campus sexual assault (CSA) study. *The United States Department of Justice.* Retrieved from https://www.ncjrs.gov/pdffiles1/nij/grants/221153 .pdf.

National Sexual Violence Resource Center. (2015). Statistics about sexual violence. Retrieved from http://www.nsvrc.org/sites/default/files/publications _nsvrc_factsheet_media-packet_statistics-about-sexual-violence_0.pdf.

NotAlone.gov (2015). Resource guide to prevent and improve the response to sexual violence at colleges and universities. Retrieved from https://www .notalone.gov/assets/task-force-resource-guide-sep-15.pdf.

NotAlone.gov (2016). Climate surveys: Useful tools to help colleges and universities in their efforts to reduce and prevent sexual assault. Retrieved from https://www.notalone.gov/assets/ovw-climate-survey.pdf.

One in Four Program. (2016). One in four: An overview. Retrieved from http:// www.oneinfourusa.org/overview.php.

Reed, K. M., Hines, D. A., Armstrong, J. L. & Cameron, A. Y. (2015). Experimental evaluation of a bystander prevention program for sexual assault and dating violence. *Psychology of Violence, 5(1)*, 95–102.

Stonybrook University. (2016). Red watch band. Retrieved from http://www .stonybrook.edu/commcms/rwb/.

United States Department of Justice. (1972). Overview of title IX of the education amendments of 1972. Retrieved from http://www.justice.gov/crt /overview-title-ix-education-amendments-1972-20-usc-1681-et-seq.

United States Department of Justice, Civil Rights Division. (2001, January 11). *Title IX Legal manual.* Washington, D.C.: *United States Department of Justice, Civil Rights Division.* Retried from http://www.justice.gov/sites/default /files/crt/legacy/2010/12/14/ixlegal.pdf

United States Department of Education, Office for Civil Rights. (2010). Dear colleague letter harassment and bullying (October 26, 2010) Background, Summary, and Fast Facts. Retrieved from http://www2.ed.gov/about /offices/list/ocr/docs/dcl-factsheet-201010.pdf

United States Department of Education, Office for Civil Rights. (2011). Dear Colleague Letter: Office of the Assistant Secretary. Retrieved from http:// www2.ed.gov/about/offices/list/ocr/letters/colleague-201104.html.

U.S. Department of Education: Office of Post Secondary Education. (2011). The handbook for Campus Safety and Security Reporting. Retrieved from http://www2.ed.gov/admins/lead/safety/handbook.pdf.

Violence Against Women Reauthorization Act. (2013). S. 47, 113th Cong. Retrieved from https://www.gpo.gov/fdsys/pkg/BILLS-113s47enr/pdf/BILLS-113s47enr.pdf.

White House, Office of the Vice President. (2015, Nov 9). Vice President Joe Biden Op:Ed: It's on us to stop campus sexual assault. Retrieved from https://www.whitehouse.gov/the-press-office/2015/11/09/vice-president-joe-biden-op-ed-its-us-stop-campus-sexual-assault.

Wilson, R. (2014a, Sept 1). More college men are fighting back against sexual assault cases. Chronicle of Higher Education. Retrieved from http://chronicle.com/article/Presumed-Guilty/148529/.

Wilson, R. (2014b, Sep. 5). Presumed guilty: College men accused of rape say the scales are tipped against them. *Chronicle of Higher Education*, A38-A42.

Wilson, R. (2014c, October 10). How "yes means yes" already works on one campus. *Chronicle of Higher Education*, A4, A6.

CHAPTER 14

Isolation to Empowerment: A Review of the Campus Rape Adjudication Process[*]

Stephane Jasmin Kirven
SACRED HEART UNIVERSITY

INTRODUCTION

In the fall of 2012 at Columbia University, an Ivy League college in New York City, Emma a sophomore and Paul her friend since freshmen year had sex. Across college campuses in America co-eds having sex is not an uncommon occurrence. However, in this case something went terribly wrong. Emma is alleging that Paul, with whom she had consensual sex twice the previous school year, forced himself upon her and sexually assaulted[1] her. Unfortunately, the incidents of sexual assault is becoming a more common occurrence on college[2] campuses across America today.

Two years after the alleged assaults, Emma initiated a grievance with the Columbia University disciplinary Board. As she relayed the graphic details of the harrowing experience of her sexual assault, she encountered disbelief and skepticism. Ms. Sulkowicz[3] was asked to explain how anal sex without

---

[*] This book chapter was previously published in the *Journal of International Criminal Justice Research*, Volume 2, September 2014.

1. Although the term "sexual assault" includes a wide range of behavior, this article focuses on the severest form of assault and as completed or attempted rape. The term sexual assault is used throughout this article to reference such conduct.

2. The article uses the terms colleges, universities and schools interchangeably to reference post-secondary institutions.

3. Though victims of sexual violence are afforded anonymity the three victims Emma Sulkowicz, Anna Clark and Angie Epifano referenced in this article have

lubrication is possible. The panel displayed insensitivity and disturbing ignorance for individuals who had supposedly been trained for this role. The university investigators had taken inaccurate and incomplete notes and the offender had been granted months of postponements while she was warned, repeatedly, that she could not discuss the case with anyone. At the hearing, she heard the offender testify that she had imagined that he coerced her. A week later, she got an email informing her that the panel had held the man "not responsible." "I didn't even cry at first," she said softly, recalling that moment. "I don't know. Has anything ever happened to you that was just so bad that you felt like you became a shell of a human being?" The university's adjudication process, she said, left her feeling even more traumatized and unsafe (Perez-Pena & Taylor, 2014, p. A1).

Rape is a serious and prevalent problem at colleges and universities across the United States. One in five college women are victims of acquaintance rape during their academic career and less than 5% come forward to report they have been assaulted (Fisher, Cullen & Turner, 2000). This is the reality on university and college campuses today. Although most schools are well intentioned and claim to support the victim, the typical grievance process is often quite hostile and irresponsive to the victim's needs as the immediate focus of the school is to protect their public reputation to ensure continued community and financial support (Cantalupo, 2011). At many schools, the grievance process and results often lack a fair and equitable resolution as many victims feel retaliated against or are made to feel that they are responsible for their own victimization. For many student victims, the campus grievance process is the only means available for redress and justice which makes it imperative for college and universities to design and implement an effective process.

This article will first review the present state of sexual assaults on campus and then review the Title IX standards and the campus adjudication system of such cases. Next, this article will analyze how the current system of adjudication fails to meet the victims' needs and fails to protect or include the community in redressing the harm. After highlighting the inadequacies in the present campus adjudication system, the article introduces restorative justice as a victim oriented approach to reforming the present adjudicatory process in sexual assault cases. Finally, this article concludes with a proposed model of restorative justice as a response to sexual assault cases on campus. Although the author recognizes that the restorative justice approach may not be appro-

---

revealed their identity and gone public with their stories in the hope of bringing attention to campus sexual assaults.

priate in every case, the author argues that restorative justice offers solutions that includes the community and helps both victims and offenders while balancing the need for punitive and remedial measures.

I. The State of Sexual Assault on Campus, Title IX Standards and the Grievance Process

Rape is a human rights violation creating long-term, physical and mental health problems for the victim. According to research findings, college women are at a higher risk for rape than women of a comparable age group in the general population highlighting the high rate of sexual violence on college campuses. (Fisher, Cullen & Turner, 2000). Furthermore, the naiveté and lack of maturity of freshman or sophomore women in college puts them at even greater risk of sexual assault than older students. (Sampson, 2002).

Studies have discovered multiple risk factors that put women in college in danger of sexual assault. First, young women come into contact with young men in a variety of places on college campuses in different situations without adult supervision thus creating opportunity for these assaults to happen. Moreover, these situations often involve alcohol or other substances that can lead to incapacitation. Finally, there are a disproportionate number of rapes reported when the perpetrators are athletes and a disproportionate number of gang rapes reported when the perpetrators are fraternity members (Fisher et. al. 2000).

At universities and colleges, acquaintance rape accounts for 90% of victimizations (Sampson, 2002). Acquaintance rape, in which the victim knows the attacker, differs from stranger rape, in which the victim does not know the attacker (Fisher et. al. 2000; Sampson, 2002). Society, as well as colleges and universities, treats acquaintance rape less seriously than stranger rape, in part because of the misconception that acquaintance rape is somehow not "real rape" since the parties are known to each other (Erhlich, 1998).

In response to the increasing number of female sexual assaults on campuses, Congress passed on March 7, 2013 the Violence Against Women Reauthorization Act that included the Campus Sexual Violence Act ("SaVE Act") to address the rising tide of violence against women. These provisions broadened the reporting and response requirements of colleges and universities under Title IX which was originally signed into law in 1972.

Title IX prohibits discrimination on the basis of sex in education programs or activities in schools that receive federal funding. When students are sexually assaulted or harassed, they are deprived of equal and free access to an education. As a matter of law, sexual harassment of students which includes acts of sexual violence is a form of sex discrimination prohibited by Title IX. In 2011, the U.S. Department of Education Office of Civil Rights ("OCR)" issued a "Dear Colleague" letter to college and university administrators about the implementation of Title IX of the Education Amendments of 1972 in regards to campus sexual assault cases. The Dear Colleague letter suggests procedural requirements for responding to a report of sexual assault, as well as proactive, educational measures schools are to undertake.

Under the Dear Colleague Letter, schools are required to develop and distribute policies regarding sexual harassment, designate a Title IX coordinator to oversee the school's duties, train staff and students in sexual harassment and violence issues, and establish an investigation procedure and an adjudication process. The letter however failed to articulate specific procedural safeguards, rules for the examination of evidence, or guidelines for the conduct of adjudication or hearing processes for cases of campus sexual violence (OCR, 2011). Consequently, colleges and universities have developed and implemented their own procedures, which vary greatly from campus to campus. Some schools have implemented procedures though initially well intended, may ultimately be judged as arbitrary and capricious and open the gate for lawsuits from alleged victims who feel that their claim was mishandled.

Without much guidance from the OCR, most colleges and universities have created judicial boards comprised of students, faculty and/or staff (Reardon, 2005). Often these individuals have limited training in sexual violence and act as investigators as opposed to fact finders. There is a board chair who plays a similar role to a judge in a jury trial. The judicial board renders findings of guilt on the basis of evidence presented at a hearing (Reardon, 2005). All outsiders are banned from the hearing including lawyers, friends and family. Some schools will allow an advisor to be present but they must participate in a non-advocacy role.

While some see judicial boards as the most effective means of resolving sexual misconduct claims, judicial boards[4] are a quasi-judicial process and by their nature are adversarial. The victim is often relegated to a position of witness as opposed to complainant. By definition, a quasi-judicial hearing is not designed to make a victim whole again however it should not be expected to be hostile and retaliatory against the victim. Research on victims' experiences

---

4. Colleges and Universities use a wide variety of names to refer to the disciplinary boards i.e. hearing panel, hearing board or judicial board, but the core function of such boards is the same.

with the adversarial quasi-judicial system has shown that it is not the best practice for sexual misconduct resolution (Cantalupo, 2009). Victims report feelings of re-traumatization, disempowerment and isolation. Under surmounting pressure from the U.S. Department of Education's Office of Civil Rights and the rising voices of survivors of sexual assault on campus, college and universities are forced to confront and address the inadequacies of the present quasi-judicial process and look for ways to enhance justice outcomes for victims of sexual assault.

II. Inadequacies of the Campus Grievance Process

Rape is often defined as a disempowering act of violence (Du Toit, 2009). Rape survivors will often describe rape as denying them their status of personhood (Henderson, 1988). "The needs of the rape victims are at times diametrically opposed to the judicial process. Victims need social acknowledgment and support while the system requires them to endure a public challenge to their credibility." Victims need an opportunity to tell their stories in their own way . . . the hearing requires them to respond to a set of questions that does not reflect a coherent and meaningful narrative (Herman, 2005, p. 574). Rape survivors often need "to have input into how to resolve the violation, receive answers to questions, observe offender remorse and experience a justice process that counteracts isolation in the aftermath of the crime" (Koss, 2006, PP 208–209; Lacey, 2008).

A. The Campus Grievance Process Fails to Serve Victims' Needs

Research finds that the adversarial process of adjudication for campus sexual assault is grounded in patriarchal ideology and cultural norms that blame women for their victimization (Herman, 2005; Koss, 2006). Rape survivors are often forced to testify about graphic details of the rape while their credibility and the experience of their trauma is being scrutinized and questioned (Ullman, 2010). The adversarial model often leaves the victim feeling as if they are the one on trial (Koss, 2006). The potential for re-traumatization of the victim, starts with the police interrogation requiring victims to discuss graphic and personal details of their trauma experience often with little sensitivity to the emotional state of the victim (Koss, 2006). The re-traumatization continues with the grievance process where the victim is made to relive the rape while the cross-examination of the victim is geared towards the University's agenda of protecting their reputation or safeguarding their star athlete (Cantalupo, 2011), as was the case at Hobart and Williams Smith College.

The case of Anna Clark a freshman at Hobart and William Smith College in upstate New York illustrates the failings of the campus grievance hearing process. Similar, to Emma's story in the introduction of this article, the grievance process reveals a blatant dismissal and disregard for the female campus rape victim. The New York Times headline read "Reporting Rape and Wishing She Hadn't, How One College Handled a Sexual Assault Complaint" (Bogdanich, 2014). The headline speaks to the feelings of campus rape victims across the United States.

According to the New York Times, Anna was raped by three football players on the night of a fraternity party. There was a witness to the rape, medical records revealed a blunt force trauma consistent with the rape and there was a record of text messages from a desperate Anna to a friend trying to get help. As a member of the football team the witness declined to testify.

At the hearing, Anna had no advocate to speak up on her behalf. She was interrupted several times by panelists as she tried to answer and at times they misrepresented evidence and asked her about a police report that she had not seen. Further review of the hearing records reveal that the administrator who convened the hearing panel chose not to disclose the medical records from Anna's rape kit to the two other panelists. One panel member did not appear to know what a rape exam entails and why it was unpleasant. Instead, according to the New York Times, the panel asked Anna what Anna had drunk and who she may have kissed and how she had danced. One administrator asked Anna "whether the football player's penis had been 'inside of you' or had he been 'having sex with you.'" (Bogdanich, 2014, p. A1)

Similarly, in Emma's case one administrator asked Emma who had been anally raped "how is it possible to have anal sex without lubrication" (Perez-Pena, 2014, p.A1). A serious look at the records of these hearings reveals a pattern of blaming the victim, administrative incompetence and reflects an ignorance of sexual assault that can be deeply traumatizing for rape victims through this process. In a U.S Senate study of 400 schools, it was found that one third failed to properly train officials adjudicating sexual assault claims (U.S. Senate Subcommittee on Financial & Contracting Oversight, 2014). Unfortunately, the conduct of the administrators at these hearings reveal the norm as opposed to the exception.

In both cases, the University failed to expel the boys involved. When Anna was informed that she could appeal the decision she was directed to look at page thirteen. Page thirteen said nothing about appeals. Instead it contained a section titled "false allegations." This revealed that the university continued to deny Anna her rape experience.

Perhaps one of the worst examples of disbelief and hostility towards a campus rape victim is the story of Angie Epifano, a student at Amherst College. Angie was institutionalized in a psychiatric hospital after talking to counselors at the school about her experience of sexual assault. She was later forced to go on leave, denied the opportunity to study abroad and eventually ended up withdrawing from the school (Epifano, 2012). While Angie's experience was particularly harrowing, the systematic failure of the grievance process to demonstrate sensitivity to the needs of the rape victims again is the norm as opposed to the exception in the adjudication process of campus sexual assault cases.

From investigation to adjudication, decision and appeal, campus rape victims are shamed and blamed for their own victimization. Research reveals that when the grievance process fails to acknowledge the harm that was committed to the victim it leaves them isolated and disempowered (Koss, 2006). Furthermore, victims experience a secondary victimization and traumatization when they are blamed or not believed (Ulman, 2010). Their credibility is examined more closely than that of other crime victims (Koss, 2000).

If administrators listen closely to the protest voices of victims of sexual assault across the country, it reflects a dissatisfaction with a grievance process that denies them a voice and fails to acknowledge and recognize the harm caused. It is calling for much-needed reform (Koss, 2006).

B. The Campus Grievance Process Fails to Protect the Community

The grievance process often fails to acknowledge that a crime was committed and the perpetrator faces no meaningful punishment. The perpetrators are left to believe that there was nothing wrong in their behavior leading them to feel empowered and emboldened to continue the same pattern of behavior posing a threat to members of the community. According to a recent investigation into the outcomes of disciplinary proceedings at 26 higher education institutions, the study found that many schools, upon report of a sexual assault, failed to initiate an investigation or dismissed the complaint before reaching the grievance process (Lombardi, 2010). Of the cases that did proceed those found responsible for sexual assault often faced little or no punishment, even when the assailant was adjudicated "responsible." This rarely led to expulsion even in cases where the assailant was a repeat offender (Lombardi, 2010).

When underlying actions and beliefs of the perpetrator goes unchallenged they see no reason for behavior modification nor do they see a need for remorse (Bibas & Bierschbach, 2004). Furthermore, with no consequence to their actions offenders face no deterrence in repeat offending, thus continuing to pose a threat to the community.

C. The Campus Grievance Process Fails to Involve the Community to Address the Harm

One of the significant problems in the grievance process in cases of sexual assault on many university campuses around the country is the secrecy around the complaint and the disciplinary process. Many schools have gag orders and confidentiality requirements barring victims and perpetrators from discussing the matter outside the grievance hearing. While administrators claim student privacy rights as a reason not to release the information, (Lombardi, 2010) this is false (OCR, 2011). To the contrary, federal law allows the release of such information when students are found responsible for violent acts against other students (OCR, 2011).

This shroud of secrecy fails to recognize and address the way in which the action harmed the community and fails to allow community participation. In failing to allow community participation, the school fails to validate the harm caused to the entire community (Herman, 2005); Koss and Harvey (1991) argue that rape is an issue that the entire community must address because the offender's behavior is often developed from community socialization and a value system that encourages the offender's action. Accordingly, the community must be allowed to collectively address the harm and determine the appropriate remedies (Braithwaite, 1989). Koss and Harvey reference the power of the community to impact the victim and state that as the community acts on behalf of the victim, the victim will build her personal and social power and her sense of self (Koss & Harvey, 1991; Cantalupo, 2011). Studies show that one of the most desired outcomes reported by survivors of sexual assault is community acknowledgement (Herman, 2005).

Under the mandate of the new law, schools are not only required to respond promptly, investigate allegations and provide grievance procedure but they must also affirmatively take steps to educate and transform the campus culture to prevent rape. Since many rape survivors are prevented by confidentiality policies from speaking about their experience outside of the school disciplinary proceeding, the grievance process disallows community participation in the process to acknowledge and redress the harm. Consequently, it denies the campus an opportunity for a communal dialogue about sexual assaults and the culture of rape and thus undermines the school's ability to uses these incidences as "teaching moments" to serve rape prevention goals under the new federal guidelines. (Violence Against Women's Act, 2013) Research supports that individuals who are educated about sexual assaults are more likely to be empathetic towards rape victims, less likely to rape and are more likely to intervene to stop a sexual assault (Schewe, 2002). Lastly, without a community oriented response to the sexual assault, the grievance process is less likely to have a deterrent effect in preventing future rapes.

III. Restorative Justice

The empirical data tells us that women are sexually assaulted at a high rate on college campuses and are failing to report the incidences. When women do report they express feelings of traumatization and disempowerment with the grievance process and feelings of dissatisfaction with the outcomes. The disciplinary process at most schools follows the adversarial format modeled after the criminal justice system which tends to protect the accused students at the expense of the victim (Cantalupo, 2011). The failings of the current system makes it incumbent upon society and institutions of higher education to reform the process to support rape victims and include the community in redressing the harm. This article argues that restorative justice offers a response that meets the justice needs of the victim and complies with the goals and requirements of Title IX. Restorative justice offers the social acknowledgement, the validation and redress of harm that victims of sexual assault seek (Koss, 2006).

Restorative justice is defined in many ways, but generally refers to a nontraditional approach to crime and justice intended to repair harm to victims, hold offenders accountable, and restore safety to victims, relationships and communities (Umbreit & Armour, 2010). Schools may be reluctant to use restorative justice programs to resolve allegations of sexual assaults confusing it with mediation, which is strictly prohibited by the OCR. To the contrary, mediation and restorative justice are fundamentally different. Mediation is designed to resolve a dispute whereas restorative justice is designed to address the harm caused by an offense, hold the offender accountable, repair the harm and heal and empower the victim (Braithwaite, 2002). Although restorative justice is used on college campuses today to address issues of plagiarism, vandalism and bullying, restorative justice has never been used on a college campus to address sexual assault or rape. Nonetheless, restorative justice offers an opportunity to reform the grievance process in such a way as to address the harm, empower the victim and include the community while balancing the needs for punitive and remedial measures.

There is an experiential and a holistic quality to restorative justice that makes this approach well suited to address acquaintance rape on college campuses (Karp, 2004). It allows for healing after the harm and the building of community. Restorative justice takes an invitational approach involving victim, offender and community to participate in the justice process (Braithwaite, 1995). Under this approach the offender is accountable to both the individual harmed and to the community. Victims feel a measure of vindication and validation when the offender admits responsibility and the community acknowledges the harm (Koss, 2008). Victims want offenders to "visibly and publicly" acknowledge the consequences of their actions as well as wishing to give the offenders "the emotional baggage they have been carrying" (Miller, 2011, pp. 178–179). Braithwaite argues that all "social processes of expressing disapproval that have the intention or effect of involving remorse in an offender are a more effective deterrent to crime than formal punishment." (Braithwaite, 1995, p. 191) Moreover, restorative justice provides an opportunity to educate members at large on gender violence and rape prevention because it includes the community (Karp, 2004).

In standing contrast to the current grievance process, restorative justice allows the victim's voice to be heard (Koss & Achilles, 2008). It transforms the role of the victim from a passive bystander to an active participant. Whereas the grievance process seeks to stifle the victim with gag orders and nondisclosure agreements, the restorative justice process allows the victim to have a voice in the process, a voice in redressing the harm and more importantly allows the victim a voice to tell her story. As Kay Pranis (2002, p. 30) states "Listening respectfully to a victim's story is a way of giving them power . . . a positive kind of power." Miller suggests "that the face to face dialogue gives victims back their power: the asymmetry of power that was present during the crime and the case processing was reconfigured." (Miller, 2011 p. 178)

There are many practices that reflect the restorative justice focus but victim studies show that the empowerment model is the best model for responding to sexual assaults (Koss, 2006). This practice holds that "justice and fair treatment" are equally the right of both the victim and offender (Barton, 2003

p. 46). The restorative justice approach invites all stakeholders to participate, to feel validated, to acknowledge the harm and make amends. The empowerment practice takes the form of a facilitated conference and brings offender and victim and ideally family and friends to address the violence and ensure that the environment remains safe and productive (Barton, 2003). By consensus, a contract is drawn up by the group to restore to the victim what has been lost (e.g., dignity, property, etc.). In contrast to the adversarial quasi-judicial process, the conferencing meeting involves the offender taking responsibility and the victim voicing the impact of the crime (Braithwaite, 2002). The offender acknowledges and responds to what he has heard and the meeting concludes with discussions formalizing the offender's plan of amends to repair the harm to the victim.

In many cases of acquaintance rape, sanctions imposed on the offender do not bring resolution for the victim of the crime committed (Koss, 2006). Victim studies reveal that it is often the expression of accountability and remorse from the offender that takes the victim to a place of healing and restoration (Braithwaite, 2002; Koss, 2006). The offender's apology for the offense committed offers symbolic reparation for the harm caused. To the extent that restorative justice models offer such healing there is much to benefit from this approach. There is some evidence that suggest that conferences also reduce repeat offending (Braithwaite, 2002). Offenders also express satisfaction with the fairness of the conference process and all those involved come away with high levels of satisfaction (Braithwaite, 2002).

Although restorative justice is presently not used on college campuses to address crimes of sexual assault, it is being used in Arizona in an innovative program called RESTORE (Responsibility and Equity for Sexual Transgressions Offering a Restorative Experience). Restore was developed in Arizona under the leadership of Mary Koss who brought together the needs of sexual assault victims and the principles of restorative justice. Restore was the first project to explicitly use feminist and restorative justice principles to address victims' justice needs of telling one's story, validation and participation. The mission is to facilitate a survivor-centered, community driven resolution of selected individual sex crimes that creates and carries out a plan for accountability, healing and public safety (Koss, 2006).

IV. The Proposal

Given the need for reform of the present grievance process in campus sexual assault cases, colleges and universities should look to adopt the RESTORE empowerment model to add restorative justice elements to the current adjudication process. Its main objective would be to meet victims' justice needs and foster a credible deterrence of sexual violence on campuses. The program would focus on support for victims, offender accountability and responsibility, community participation and community education. All of which are consistent with the spirit of Title IX. The program would be premised on the victim's voluntary participation and the offender's accepting responsibility for the harm. The program would be restricted to first time offenders. The stakeholders would receive the assistance and counseling of trained facilitators. Victims and family members would have access to counseling and the criminal justice system for additional remedies, such as restraining orders if needed. In practice, restorative justice may operate either within or outside the traditional justice system (Zehr, 2002).

Unlike the present grievance process on college campuses, the restorative justice approach would allow all participants to share their perspectives and through a collaborative process, the parties would discuss and determine how to repair the harm. Victims and offenders would have four to six persons that are closest to them accompany them in the conference. The participation of the broader community holds the parties accountable ensuring a safe and productive environment. Together the parties explore the harm in question and the acts that precipitated it, collaborating to create an agreement on what should be done to repair the harm (Pranis, 2002). In contrast to the quasijudicial adjudication approach, the victim plays an active role in crafting the remedy to meet their needs of resolution and healing (Daly, 2002). The proscribed remedy can vary from individual apologies to civil restitution.

Restorative justice does not purport to be a panacea to sexual assault violence (Daly, 2002) however the restorative justice approach to campus rape cases offers a novel approach to victims' needs where the traditional adversarial system has failed. "The restorative justice program for campus rape could work in tandem with existing remedies as an alternative to traditional grievance procedures or parallel to traditional methods of adjudication" (Brenner, 2013). Some feminists argue that restorative justice offers a more meaningful response for the victim then the traditional criminal justice system (Braithwaite, 2002; Koss, 2006). This is especially true with acquaintance rape on campus where more often than not victims may not be interested in formal prosecution.

Conclusion

Pursuant to Title IX, when sexual violence occurs on campus and universities students are denied fair and equal access to an education. For the institution, it represents a failure in its obligations to its students and a breakdown in its institutional mission (Cantalupo, 2011). The current grievance quasi-judicial system used to respond to acquaintance rape at college and universities today fails to meet victims' needs for justice (Lacey, 2008; Cantalupo, 2009), as was illustrated in the narratives of the Emma Sulkowicz, Anna Clark, Angie Epifano and the countless other victims of campus sexual assault. The marginalization and lack of justice for campus rape victims is a reoccurring theme at college and universities across the United States today.

As argued above, the current quasi-judicial grievance system used by most schools to respond to sexual violence on campus fails to be survivor-oriented, fails to hold offenders accountable (Cantalupo, 2009; Lombardi, 2010) and fails to have a community-oriented response. Sexual assault on campus is further complicated by the fact that these assaults occur between individuals who are known to each other as friends or acquaintances and by the fact that these assaults occur in familiar and comfortable surroundings (Fisher et. al., 2001). As such, the traditional adversarial quasi-judicial model has proven to be ineffective in addressing this type of violence (Braithwaite, 2002).

In order to effectively respond to this epidemic of sexual violence against women on college campuses, society needs to re-conceptualize its response to rape and sexual assault on campus. To the extent that the present system routinely fails victim of sexual assault (Koss, 2006), the author argues that the restorative justice process is one approach available to respond to sexual assault on campus. Restorative justice offers the elements of retribution, rehabilitation, reintegration, individual and public protection while addressing the survivor's needs to be heard and meeting their desires for justice (Koss, 2006). Restorative justice can bring the victim from a place of isolation to a place of empowerment.

References

Barton, C. (2003). *Restorative justice: The empowerment model.* Annandale, Australia: Hawkins Press.

Bibas, S. & Bierschbach, R (2004). Integrating remorse and apology into criminal procedure. *Yale Law Journal,* 114.

Bogdanich, W. (2014, July 12). Reporting rape, and wishing she hadn't. *The New York Times,* p. A1.

Bohmer, C. & Parrot, A. (1993). *Sexual assault on campus: the problem and the solution.* New York, NY: Lexington Books.

Braithwaite, J. (1999). *Crime, shame, and reintegration.* New York, NY: Cambridge University Press.

Braithwaite, J. (2002). *Restorative justice & responsive regulation.* New York, NY: Oxford University Press.

Brenner, A. (2013). Transforming campus culture to prevent rape: the possibility and promise of restorative justice as a response to campus sexual violence. *Harvard Journal of Law & Gender, 10.*

Cantalupo, N.C. (2009) Campus violence: Understanding the extraordinary through the ordinary *Journal of College and University Law, 35,* pp. 613–690, Georgetown Public Law and Legal Theory Research Paper No. 1457343.

Cantalupo, N.C. (2010). How should colleges and universities respond to peer sexual violence on campus? What the current legal environment tells us. *NASPA Journal About Women in Higher Education, 3,* pp. 49–84, Georgetown Public Law and Legal Research Paper No. 10-54, doi: 10.2202/1940-7882.1044

Cantalupo, N.C. (2011) Burying our heads in the sand: lack of knowledge, Knowledge avoidance and the persistent problem of campus peer sexual violence. *Loyola University Chicago Law Journal, 43,* pp. 205, 2011, Georgetown Public Law Research Paper No. 11-41.

Curtis-Fawley, S. & Daly, K. (2005). Gendered violence and restorative justice: the views of victim advocates. *Violence Against Women, 11,* 603–638. doi: 10.1177/1077801205274488

Daly, K. (2005). Restorative justice and sexual assault: An archival study of court and conference cases. *British Journal of Criminology,* 334–356, doi: 10.1093/bjc/azi071

Daly, K. (2002). Restorative justice: the real story. *Punishment & Society, 4,* 55–79, doi: 10.1177/14624740222228464

Du Toit, L. (2009). *A philosophical investigation of rape: The making and unmaking of the feminine self.* New York: Routledge.

Epifano, A. (2012, October 17) An account of sexual assault at Amherst College, *The Amherst Student. 142-6.* Retrieved from http://amherststudent.amherst.edu

Estrich, S. (1987). *Real rape.* Cambridge, MA: Harvard University Press.

Fisher, B., Cullen, F. & Turner, M. (2000). *The sexual victimization of college women*. Washington, DC: U.S. Dept. of Justice, Office of Justice Programs, National Institute of Justice. Retrieved from https://www.ncjrs.gov/pdffiles1/nij/182369.pdf

Herman, J. (1997). *Trauma and recovery, The aftermath of violence-from domestic abuse to political terror*. (Rev. ed.). New York, NY: BasicBooks.

Hopkins, C. (2005). Incorporating feminist theory and insights into a restorative justice response to sex offenses. *Violence Against Women, 693–723*.

Karp, D. (2004). Restorative justice on the college campus promoting student growth and responsibility, and reawakening the spirit of campus community (pp. 48–60). Springfield, Ill.: C.C. Thomas Publisher.

Koss, M. (2000). Blame, shame, and community: justice responses to violence against women. *American Psychologist, 55*, 1332–1343.

Koss, M. (1985). The hidden rape victim: personality, attitudinal and situational characteristics. *Psychology of Women Quarterly, 9*, 193–212. doi: 10.1111/j.1471-6402

Koss, M. (2006). Restoring rape survivors: Justice, advocacy, and a call to action. *Annals New York Academy of Sciences*, 206–234.

Koss, M. & Achilles, M. (2008). Restorative justice responses to sexual assault. *National online resource center on violence against women*, Retrieved http://www.vawnet.org/assoc_files_vawnet/ar_restorativejustice.pdf

Koss, M. & Harvey, M. (1991). *The rape victim: clinical and community interventions* (2nd ed.). Newbury Park, C.A.: Sage Publications.

Lacey, N. (1997). *Unspeakable subjects, impossible rights: Sexuality, integrity and criminal law, Women a Cultural Review*. New York, NY: Oxford University Press.

Lombardi, K. (2009). Sexual assault on campus shrouded in secrecy, High rates of rape, closed hearings, and confusing laws. *The Center for Public Integrity*. Retrieved http://www.publicintegrity.org/2009/12/01/9047/sexual-assault-campus-shrouded-secrecy

Lombardi, K. (2010). A lack of consequences for sexual assaults, Students found "responsible" face modest penalties, while victims are traumatized. *The Center for Public Integrity*, Retrieved http://www.publicintegrity.org/2010/02/24/4360/lack-consequences-sexual-assault

Miller, S. (2010). *After the crime: The power of restorative justice dialogues between victims and violent offenders*. New York, NY: New York University Press.

Pérez-Peña, R. & Lovett, I. (2013, April 18). 2 More Colleges Accused of Mishandling Assaults. *The New York Times*, p. A14. Retrieved http://www.nytimes.com/2013/04/19/education/swarthmore-and-occidental-colleges-are-accused-of-mishandling-sexual-assault-cases.html

Pérez-Peña, R. & Taylor, K. (2014, May 3). Fight against sexual assaults holds colleges to account. *The New York Times*, p. A1. Retrieved http://www.nytimes.com/2014/05/04/us/fight-against-sex-crimes-holds-colleges-to-account.html

Reardon, K. (2005) Acquaintance Rape at Private Colleges and Universities: Providing for Victims' Educational and Civil Rights, *38, Suffolk University Law Review*, 38, 395, 407–12. Sampson, R. (2002). Acquaintance rape of college students. Washington, DC: U.S. Department of Justice Office of Community Oriented Policing Services. (#99-CK- WX-K004)

Schewe, P. (2002). *Preventing violence in relationships: Interventions across the life span.* Washington, D.C.: American Psychological Association, 107–36.

U.S. Department of Education, Office of Civil Rights (2011), *Dear Colleague Letter: Sexual Violence*, Washington, D.C., Retrieved from http://www2.ed.gov/about/offices/list/ocr/letters/colleague-201104.pdf.

U.S. Department of Education, Office of Civil Rights (2011), Revised sexual harassment guidance: Harassment of students by school employees, other students, or third parties. Washington, D.C., Retrieved http://www2.ed.gov/about/offices/list/ocr/docs/shguide.pdf

U.S. Senate Subcommittee on Financial & Contracting Oversight (2014), Sexual violence on campus: How too many Institutions of higher education are failing to protect students. Washington, D.C., Retrieved http://www.mccaskill.senate.gov/SurveyReportwithAppendix.pdf

Title IX of the Education Amendments of 1972, 20 U.S.C. §1681 et seq.

Ullman, S. (2010). *Talking about sexual assault: Society's response to survivors.* Washington, DC: American Psychological Association.

Umbreit, M. & Armour, M. (2010). *Restorative justice dialogue: An essential guide for research and practice.* New York, NY: Springer Publishing Company.

Violence Against Women Reauthorization Act of 2013, 42 USC 13701

Zehr, H. (2003). *The little book of restorative justice.* Intercourse, PA: Good Books.

CHAPTER 15

Youth Internet Victimization

Christine Bryce
Virginia Commonwealth University

*The internet is a city and, like any great city, it has monumental librar-
ies and theatres and museums and places in which you can learn and
pick up information, and there are facilities for you that are astounding—
specialised museums, not just general ones.*

*But there are also slums, and there are red light districts, and there
are really sleazy areas where you wouldn't want your children wander-
ing alone.* (Fry, 2009)

The Internet provides a tremendous wealth of information and communi-
cations media. Comprised of public, private, commercial, non-profit, educational, and personal websites as well as blogs, the World Wide Web gives
anyone with a connection the ability to instantly reach an audience of billions.
Coupled with email, social media, and instant messaging the Internet allows
instant feedback and multi-modal communication. The Internet provides
methods of sending and receiving various types of data, including images,
text, video and audio clips, and other files.

In 1995, approximately 35 million people worldwide used the Internet;
today close to 3 billion people use the Internet (Meeker, 2015). Additionally,
in 1995, 80 million people had mobile phones; today almost 5 and a half billion people have cell phones and forty percent of these use smartphones (2015).
During the past decade, major technological changes have shaped how today's
youth interacts. The Internet became faster; high-speed and WIFI were intro-
duced. The biggest change was smartphones. The Internet has morphed from

an occasional pastime to an instant, fast daily companion to adolescents. A staggering "92% of teens report going online daily—including 24% who say they go online 'almost constantly,'" according to a new study from Pew Research Center (Lenhart, 2015).

According to research by Mary Meeker (2015), for eighty-seven percent of Millennials, their smartphone "never leaves their side (night or day.)" Another 80% of Millennials report that the "first thing I do is reach for my smartphone." Seventy-eight percent spend more than two hours every day using their smartphones, and of these, most use their smartphone's built-in cameras and post the pictures/videos they capture to social media (Meeker, 2015). According to the Pew Research Center, approximately 95% of juveniles aged 10–17 use the Internet on a regular basis (Lenhart, 2015). Essentially, almost all American youngsters have at least some presence on the Internet, and for the majority of them, it's a daily presence. Marc Prensky (2001) posited that today's youth are digital natives. Today's kids were born into an already digital world, spend vast amounts of their time in digital spaces, and use digital technologies on a daily basis (2001). They go online using computers, smartphones, laptops, tablets, cell phones, MP3 players, gaming devices, e-readers, and more.

The areas most frequented by teenagers are social media sites such as Facebook, Snapchat, Instagram, Tumblr, Twitter, WhatsApp, and Google+. Approximately 81% of them use social media (Lenhart, 2015). Youth are also texting, sexting, taking pictures, sharing pictures, and playing games on their cell phones or smartphones. Kids are using Google, Wikipedia, and other tools to assist with their homework. They frequent gaming websites and play in large multi-user virtual worlds like Minecraft and Farmville. They download MP3s or use iTunes, they upload and watch videos on YouTube, and they download and play the latest apps. While email may be used to communicate with adults, teachers, and other authorities, Facebook, Snapchat, WhatsApp, Instagram, and other such sites have become the primary communication tool for teens. Most teens use social networking sites to interact with their known friends and acquaintances. Teens, by and large, do not surf to strangers' profiles on social media.

Social media sites (also referred to as social networking sites) like Facebook (the most popular social network site) are domains where individual users join and create individual profiles. Registered users can then "add friends" within the system through an invitation that can either be accepted or declined. User profile pages serve as an individual's digital representation of their opinions, tastes, fashion, identity, and their many "selfies" (self-made digital pictures). Individuals can upload photos, link to group pages such as schools attended and employment, declare their unique interests, list favorite musicians, and describe themselves textually and through associated "liked" media. These sites also allow friends to comment on or "like" each other's profile page, uploaded images, shared items, and status update posts.

Social media sites also provide numerous communication tools. Most have instant messaging, an in-app email system, open group and closed group pages where people can post messages that all "friends" or group members can read, and a blog (short for web log: a regularly updated narrative like a journal or diary displayed in reverse chronology) where users can post entries for either friends or the public at large. Some social media sites, like Twitter (a microblog), allow for brief "tweets" — the user's under 144-word "thoughts" on any given topic. These "tweets" are completely public, and anyone can "follow" particular Twitter accounts. Friend or Buddy lists allow users to connect their sites to the sites of other users and to detect whether their "friend" is currently on-line.

Snapchat has an estimated 200 million registered accounts, Instagram has 400 million user accounts, Twitter has 320 million users, and Facebook has approximately 1.55 Billion active accounts. While Facebook has more users of all ages worldwide, in the United States among youth, Instagram has become the favorite.

Other than social media sites, multiplayer gaming websites remain popular as do the in-app gaming features within social media sites. Gaming sites or real-time gaming apps allow members to interact and play games with (or against) other users. These sites and apps are essentially expanded versions of popular computer games where multiple people play in the same virtual environment. Online games include traditional card games, chess, and board games, but the majority of online games involve combat of some kind, "Dungeons and Dragons" style fantasy role-playing, and military simulation. Team play is an important aspect of these games and most sites include group chat and instant messaging to support in-game cooperation. Many gaming sites also include out-of-game chat-rooms for discussing game related issues.

Chat rooms, while once tremendously popular, have all but disappeared with the rise of social media sites. As discussed above, social media sites allow for the creation of public and private groups where users engage in group discussions by broadcasting typed messages to other group members. Public groups are open to anyone; closed groups are by invitation only. Further, chat rooms have been replaced by texting and messaging apps. An estimated 91% of teens use their mobile carrier texting service or a messaging app on their phone (such as Whatsapp or Kik.) Teens report texting anywhere from 30 to 100 texts per day (Lenhart, 2015).

Parents of today's key sources of concern with their children's Internet use include sexting, cyberbullying, "Internet addiction," and privacy concerns. Parents typically worry most about the activities of their younger children and utilize defense technologies and set strict limits. With older youth (14+) most parents rely on open communication with their children, and will limit cell phone/smartphone/tablet/etc. use as a punishment for various infractions.

Educators of youth have done an excellent job of incorporating online safety education in schools. Because of this effort, most youth are familiar with many of the hidden dangers of the Internet. According to published statistics and media reports, many youth will be victimized online. Parents, educators and law enforcement officials have been contending with Internet victimization for the past decade and have developed several excellent prevention programs. The greatest challenge facing parents, educators, and law enforcement is remaining aware, current, and vigilant.

Internet victimization can include a variety of crimes. However, the most prevalent and frequently debated regarding youth are sexual solicitation, unwanted exposure to sexual material, and harassment or bullying. As defined by the Crimes against Children Research Center (Wolak, Mitchell, and Finkelhor, 2006):

> **Sexual Solicitations and Approaches:** Requests to engage in sexual activities or sexual talk or give personal sexual information that were unwanted or, whether wanted or not, made by an adult.
>
> **Aggressive Sexual Solicitation:** Sexual solicitations involving offline contact with the perpetrator through regular mail, by telephone, or in person or attempts or requests for offline contact.
>
> **Unwanted Exposure to Sexual Materials:** Without seeking or expecting sexual material, being exposed to pictures of naked people or people having sex when doing online searches, surfing the web, opening email or instant messages, or opening links in email or instant messages.
>
> **Harassment:** Threats or other offensive behavior (not sexual solicitation), sent online to the youth or posted online about the youth for others to see.

Since the explosion of the popularity of the Internet, the news media regularly presents Americans with snippets and factoids of Internet crimes against children which paint a grisly picture of the sinister side of the Internet. These headlines leap from the television screen (or smartphone/tablet screen) to shock the reader:

USA Today:
80% of children under 5 use Internet weekly.

Huffington Post:
9% to 35% of young people are victims of some form of electronic violence.

New York Times:
Screen Addiction is taking a toll on children.

Inside Edition:
Stranger Danger! Man Lures Teenage Girls Through the Internet, Shows How Easy it Is

Independent (U.K.):
Internet is lawless jungle too dangerous for children to use former government adviser warns

The news media highly publicizes a comparatively small number of cases with gripping headlines such as, "Man Charged with Raping Girl he Met on Internet," "Missing Child Met Internet Lover," "Girl Flew Overseas to Meet Internet Boyfriend." These and similar media reports and political statements frequently refer to the dangers of the social-networking websites. The statistics presented by the media and politicians have increased a parenting nightmare about sexual predators lurking online. For parents (and politicians) struggling to understand a scene navigated by technology frequently far out their reach, they are often left wondering: what is happening to youth on the Internet?

A TV spot created in 2005 but still widely circulated by Merkley & Partners (pro bono) for the Ad Council was aimed at getting the attention of teenage girls. This ad switches between shots of a teenage girl and a man, whose talking mouth is initially the only part of his body that is shown. Each takes turns speaking. In the back and forth "dialogue," the man says, "Meeting a teen girl online is easy" and "meeting them is the goal, that's when things get really interesting." In between the man's comments, the girl says, "Attention from older guys is flattering, they get me more than guys my age," and asks, "if you trust someone, what's wrong with meeting?" At the end of the ad, the voiceover, read by another teenage girl, says, "Online predators know what they're doing. Do you?" (Ad Council, 2005).

Another TV spot depicts a bedroom being searched in crime-show style against a background of dramatic crime-showesque music. A teenaged girl voices over the scene and music with, "Before you start an online relationship with a guy . . ." Then after an evidence technician puts a computer keyboard into a plastic bag (shown above), she continues, ". . . think about how it could end." The Ad ends with the text: "One in five kids online is sexually solicited" (Ad Council, 2005).

A popular educator and parent website by the National Center for Missing and Exploited Children, NetSmartz, has similar effective video campaigns geared towards youth. These videos made for youth and their parents include: "Julie's Journey," a story about a girl named Julie who runs away to be with her Internet lover; "Two Kinds of Stupid," a story about a boy who posted a picture on Facebook of himself (with some friends) drinking at a party — the picture went "viral" and the boys were suspended and kicked off their sports team, ending any chances of a college scholarship; "The Cyberbully Virus" depicts a young girl suffering from cyberbullying; and "Photo Fate," a powerful story showing a girl "sexting" a topless picture of herself to her boyfriend and how quickly her photo spread (Netsmartz, 2015).

Parents, politicians, and educators alike are voicing concerns about how much information teens reveal about themselves through their online profiles. Parents and educators find images of teens drinking or posing provocatively or sexually, discussions of illicit drug use, or signs of bullying and other abusive behavior on social networking sites. Many teens do upload inappropriate self-made images of themselves and others. It would appear that many of today's teens have different notions of privacy than their parents and other adults: teens feel more comfortable sharing aspects of their lives (for example, their sexual identities) that previous generations would have kept private. Teens who have not been better educated about posting personal information on the Internet (and sometimes those who have) do not fully understand the risks of making certain information public. Some underage teens have found themselves charged with the creation, possession, and transmittal of child pornography from "sexting" nude images of themselves to boyfriends and girlfriends. Schools are uncertain what level of responsibility they should have over what their students do online — some are worried about what students do on school-issued computers and others attempts to extend their administration into what teens are doing during after school hours and off school grounds.

The available research on youth Internet use and safety has increased tremendously since the early 2000s. The Internet Crimes Against Children Research Center based at the University of New Hampshire has conducted numerous studies of youth internet practices.

According to the Third Youth Internet Safety Survey (YISS-3), 9% of Internet users ages 10 to 17 were exposed to unwanted sexual solicitations. This figure, in fact, illustrates a decline in unwanted exposure from 13% in 2005 and 19% in 2000. Researchers indicated that this decrease might be attributed to changes in online behaviors. For instance, the disappearance of chat rooms — youth have shifted from using chat rooms to using social media sites. The researchers also suggest that youth use more caution and discernment now on the Internet due to Internet safety education. They also indicate that the numerous successful prosecutions of adults has led to a reduction of offenders and offenses (Jones, Mitchell, and Finklehor, 2011).

About three percent of the youth surveyed reported that solicitors tried to make contact in person by telephone or tried to set up a meeting. A small percent of the youth formed close friendships with people they met online who were five or more years older. Of these, one percent had a face-to-face meeting with an older person they met online. The online relationships with adults five or more years older that became sexual included: adult requesting a sexually explicit photo, adult sending a sexually explicit photo, adult requesting or instructing self-touching sexual contact, and other related behavior that showed sexual interest (Mitchell, Jones, Finklehor, and Wolak, 2014), see examples below:

> "A person wanted pictures and stuff and she got mad when I didn't send them and I blocked her, it was someone I didn't know before our internet interaction."   —Boy, 13

> "I was on ChatRoulette with my friends because we thought it would be funny, and someone asked us to take our shirts off, and so we just hit next."   —Girl, 17

> "Well he showed up at my job, and he was a nice enough guy, and he asked for my number, and we were texting throughout the 2+weeks, and he would ask me if I wanted to hang out in the middle of the night and if I would be willing to meet him someplace."   —Girl, 17

> "I was on Facebook, a guy asked me if I was a virgin, and if I wanted to have sex. Also, this guy asked me to send a picture of my breast, and this really bothered me."   —Girl, 14

From the survey of 10–17-year-olds, sexual solicitations were more common among older youth (16–17). No ten-year-olds and only a few 11–12 year-olds reported sexual solicitations. Seventy-five percent of the Internet predator victims were female, and almost all of the internet predator offenders were male. The predators tend to meet their victims in social networking sites (Mitchell, et al., 2014). Predators befriend and romance victims over a longer period of time — sometimes several months — and foster the relationship to the point of sending pictures, exchanging phone calls, and sending gifts and money (Wolak, et al., 2006).

The 2010 (YISS-3) study also indicated a substantial decrease in youth exposure to unwanted pornography from 34% in 2005 to 23% in 2010 (Jones, et al, 2011). However, there is still an abundance of pornographic material available for those youth that seek it, with an estimated 13–23 percent intentionally viewing X-rated materials (Jones, et al., 2011). The researchers theorize the decrease of unwanted exposure is attributed to the use of spamware, filters, and related defense technologies.

An estimated 11 percent of youth responding to the survey reported online harassment (threats or offensive language emailed, instant messaged, or posted online) — often referred to as cyberbullying. This shows a gradual increase. Researches believe this correlates to the recent increase of bullying in schools and believe that the Internet is another area where bullies lurk (Jones, et al., 2011). From an earlier study in 2005 (YISS-2), twenty-eight percent of youth surveyed also reported that they made "rude or nasty comments to someone on the Internet," and nine percent admitted they "used the Internet to harass or embarrass someone they were mad at." Researcher Janis Wolak indicated that the harshness of school life is exacerbated by the Internet. "Kids are receiving and dishing more of it out," according to Wolak (Wolak, et al., 2006).

An emerging concern amongst parents, educators, and politicians is the seeming rise of youth suicide. They worry that online harassment (cyberbullying) victimization leads to suicide. Many have raised the question: is the Internet promoting suicide? Statistically, the number of teens committing suicide decreased until 2009 (down 38% from 1990–2007) (Child Trends, 2010). However, according to data from the CDC, the rates have increased slightly from 2010–2015, where the rate was 3.15% in 2000 to 3.63% in 2015. This increase made suicide the second leading cause of death for youth 15–24 and the third leading cause of death for 10–14-year-olds. According to researchers at Oxford University (Daine, Hawton, Singaravelu, Stewart, Simkin and Montgomery, 2013):

> Youth who self-harm or are suicidal often make use of the internet. It is most commonly used for constructive reasons such as seeking support and coping strategies, but may exert a negative influence, normalising self-harm and potentially discouraging disclosure or professional help-seeking. The internet has created channels of communication that can be misused to 'cyber-bully' peers; both cyber-

bullying and general internet use have been found to correlate with increased risk of self-harm, suicidal ideation, and depression. Correlations have also been found between internet exposure and violent methods of self-harm.

Further, the aforementioned research also discovered almost 60% of teens reported that they had researched the topic of suicide online. A staggering 80% of teens that survived attempted suicide reported that they had first researched how to commit their self-harm act online. Of the young people who cut themselves, 74% said that they had done Internet research first (Daine, et al. 2013). The research team concluded that, "Internet use may exert both positive and negative effects on young people at risk of self-harm or suicide." (Daine, et al., 2013)

Regarding fears of cyberbullying, Dr. Justin Patchin, co-director of the Cyberbullying Research Center said:

> The internet is no more a 'lawless jungle' than the schoolyard, the shopping mall, or the living room. There is no evidence that I am aware of that the risk of physical (or even emotional or psychological) harm is higher among children who regularly use the Internet compared to those who don't. In the US, it is clear from numerous data sources that young people are more likely to be victimized at school than online. And that is really saying something because the school is one of the safest places for kids to be. Every study that I have looked at that has explored both bullying at school and bullying online shows that the former occurs with greater frequency than the latter (Balkam, 2014).

The original "one in five" figure from the 2000 Youth Internet Safety Survey has been used heavily by the media and political machinations. However, the statistic is both outdated and is only from a very small sampling (1500) of millions of youth Internet users. Further, the language of the "one in five children are sexually solicited online," does not differentiate the type of sexual solicitation or approach which could include requests to "engage in sexual activities or sexual talk or to give personal sexual information online." Few have looked carefully at the study results to find that almost half of online sexual solicitations to teens were from other teens — 42%. Additionally, very few of incidents of sexual solicitation were reported to law enforcement, ISPs, or other authorities (Mitchell, et al., 2014).

A common myth is the assumption that online predators are pedophiles targeting children ages 5–10. A majority of parents and politicians believe that quite young children (5 to 10 years old) are at the most risk on the Internet. The information presented by the media and political messages can cause parents to believe that online predators are pedophiles who lie to young children about their identities, age, and motives, trick young children into giving their names and addresses, and abduct young children and commit violent offenses. In fact, the majority of online predators seek teen-aged youth from 12–17. As a result of the myth, many parents, while stringent in protecting 5–10-year-olds, relax their rules for teens, allowing them unlimited, unmonitored Internet access and allow teens to have personal computers, laptops, or game systems in their rooms; smartphones; and tablets with which they can spend hours surfing the Internet.

Additionally, the results of the studies indicate the errors of the myth. One, the majority of offenders were not deceptive about their ages (only 5% of offenders claimed to be age 17 or younger to their victims). Two, when deceptions occurred, they typically regarded the offender's physical appearance. Finally, and perhaps most important, the vast majority of victims of Internet sex crimes were teens aged 13 to 15 (Wolak, et al., 2004).

As stated by law enforcement and researchers alike, the Internet has made the predator's job easy. With the millions of youth using the Internet coupled with the anonymity the Internet provides, predators have an almost unlimited supply of potential victims. However, as parents, educators, and children themselves have become more aware about the potential "stranger danger" online, the number of successful predation has dropped significantly. Additionally, a 2003 National Crime Victimization Survey reported a significant decrease of reported child sexual abuse from 1992 to 2003 with 150,000 cases (1992) to 90,000 (2003). Also, a January 2010 4th National Incidence Study Report to Congress confirms a similar decline with 217,700 incidents reported in 1993 to 135,300 incidents reported in 2005 — a 38% decrease.

Further, many of the unwanted solicitations reported came from fellow youth. This includes unwanted date requests and sexual teasing from fellow teens. Of the adult solicitations, the majority was from people 18–25, and both wanted and unwanted solicitations are included. In other words, if an 18-year-old asks out a 17-year-old online (in other words, a high school senior asks out a high school junior) and both consent, this would still be seen as an online sexual solicitation. Only a small number of the online solicitations included a request for a physical encounter; most sexual solicitations were for cybersex. While the study shows that youth are faced with uncomfortable or offensive experiences online, there is no concurrent research of how many are faced with uncomfortable or offensive experiences at school, public places, or other teen locations (Jenkins, 2006).

A pertinent question that arises when presented with these statistics is why were these young teen victims falling for much older men? To begin, many females in the 13 to 15 age range are already sexually active. According to a 2005 CDC study of nearly every high school student in the USA, 46% of teens are sexually active. The numbers increase with age, 25% of sexually active teens become active before they turn 16 while 58% of females and 51% of males become sexually active by the time they are 18 (CDC, 2006). When teens are already having sexual encounters with their peers, how can they be convinced that a sexual relationship with an older adult is wrong? Many teen girls are especially vulnerable to the fantasy the online predators offer them — how can they resist the sex-appeal of the "older," "more mature," "he loves me," "he buys me presents," "he's so sophisticated" male? The Internet can promote intimacy (real or imagined) and allow relationships to develop based on fantasy and projection.

American society's tendency to glorify and sell sex certainly doesn't help matters. Today's youth are desensitized to sex and pornographic or suggestive images. They are constantly bombarded by images of sexually-charged or sexually-seductive scenes in television and movies. Current teen celebrities and idols are sexually posed, scantily-clad young women singing, dancing, and "twerking." Even the checkout line at the supermarket is laden with images of scantily-clad celebrities.

Parents and educators do have a few options available to them. A variety of "defense" technologies are available to parents and educators. Spyware and Adware blocking software as well as spam-blocking and pop-up blocking software can eradicate a great amount of the exposure to unwanted sexual images youth receive through pop-ups and "cookie"-based advertising (Cookies are a small record of websites visited by a computer, stored on the computer, and used by websites to generate individual advertising. For instance, if a person visits a mortgage website, then the ads this person will see on various web pages they then visit which use cookie-based advertising will pertain to mortgages.). Installing a working firewall can protect personal files stored on the computer from being "hacked" into. Installing and regularly updating anti-virus software can prevent computer viruses, including some newer viruses that download pornographic images to a computer. Finally, a variety of content-control software (such as Net Nanny) exists for parents (and schools) to control the content allowed (or more specifically, not allowed) for viewing on the Internet.

Windows 10, the newest Windows platform at the time of this writing, allows parents to create and manage user accounts on all Windows products for their children. Tablets like Amazon's Kindle or Leappad's Platinum offer content-limited Internet access and reviewed/approved content for children. Many of these products and some smartphones also allow a screen limit. Again, many parents remain vigilant for their younger children, but cease to provide these limitations to their teens. If a parent chooses to remove restrictions on Internet use, they should maintain open and frequent communication with their teens regarding their Internet use.

In addition to defense technologies available to parents and educators, more law enforcement agencies are devoting resources to monitor social networking, chat room, and gaming sites. The primary goal is to catch the predator before he strikes (FBI, 2006).

Rather than knee-jerk reactions to possibly sensationalized statistics and media reports, politicians, too, must remain current and well-educated regarding the technologies and youth hotspots on the Internet. While regulation in schools certainly seems to have its place, the Internet has become what the mall and playgrounds were to older generations.

Proponents of social-networking sites emphasize that with such a small number of sexual solicitation/predator cases reported nationwide, and more than 80 million youth using these sites, these cyber places are in fact safer than most teens' local malls, parks, or even homes. According to Alex Koroknay-Palicz, executive director of the National Youth Rights Organization, "We're trying to get the public to understand that these websites . . . [are really] positive sites that a few isolated criminals are misusing" (NYRA, 2006).

Many of the social networking sites have implemented features worthy of merit. A Facebook ad campaign geared towards encouraging its voting aged users to participate in upcoming elections. Facebook, Twitter, Instagram, and Snapchat all have public pages for politicians, special causes, and other worthy interests.

A scare campaign isn't needed, but parents do need to be educated about the possible dangers and in turn set ground rules for their children's Internet use and educate their children about the possible dangers online. In addition to the defense technologies listed above, parents need to take responsibility for the computers, tablets, smartphones, and other connected devices in their home and how they are used. Ideally, all devices connected to the Internet in a family household should be in a central, "public" location of the home where parents or other responsible adults can regularly visually and through checking internet history and cookies monitor their children's Internet activities.

Ultimately, the responsibility for protecting children is up to parents. Parents need not be afraid to set limits and rules. Perry Aftab of WiredSafety.com puts the problem some parents face very succinctly:

They're afraid of their kids. They somehow think because technology is involved, they're no longer the parent. Get real. You're the parent. If you don't like it, unplug the computer. If they don't follow your rules, no Internet at all. If you're not the parent and if you're not going to step in, no Website on earth is going to be able to help your child be safe (Stafford, 2006).

Parents also need to educate themselves about the technologies that their Internet-using children utilize. Parents should know what their children are doing on their various devices. If a son or daughter has a Facebook or Instagram account, then the parent should both have their own Facebook or Instagram account and regularly monitor their child's account. Parents should know any aliases that their child may be using online (Schrobsdorff, 2006). They need to look at their child's web page(s) and review any information and pictures that might be on it (Stafford, 2006). In addition to their child's posts, parents should monitor what their "child's friends [and enemies] are posting regarding your child's identity" (NetSmartz.org, 2006).

Parents (and educators) need to continuously stress that the Internet is not private. Words and images can quite possibly remain on the Internet forever. They need to sit down with their child, no matter what their age, and have a frank conversation about what is appropriate and not appropriate information to put on the internet and the reasons why. Youth need to choose wisely what words, images, and information they post on the Internet.

REFERENCES

Ad Council (2005). Online sexual exploitation. Retrieved July 20, 2006 from http://www.adcouncil.org/default.aspx?id=56

Anderson, M. (2016, January 7). Parents, Teens and Digital Monitoring. Retrieved January 8, 2016, from http://www.pewinternet.org/2016/01/07/parents-teens-and-digital-monitoring/

Associated Press (2006, April 11). MySpace.com makes new online safety push. Retrieved June 20, 2006, from MSNBC.com Web site: http://www.msnbc.msn.com/id/12256764/print/1/displaymode/1098.

Balkam, S. (2014, August 13). Is the Internet Really a "Lawless Jungle?" Retrieved December 13, 2015, from http://www.theguardian.com/technology/2014/aug/15/online-safety-internet-sexting-cyberbullying-children

CDC-Centers for Disease Control (2006). Youth risk behavior surveillance — United States, 2005. Morbidity and Mortality Weekly Report Surveillance Summaries, July 9, 2006, vol. 55, No. SS-5.

Child Trends. (2010). Suicidal Teens. Retrieved January 5, 2016, from http://www.childtrends.org/?indicators=suicidal-teens

Daine, K., Hawton, K., Singaravelu, V., Stewart, A., Simkin. S. & Montgomery P. (2013) The Power of the Web: A Systematic Review of Studies of the Influence of the Internet on Self-Harm and Suicide in Young People. PLoS ONE 8(10): e77555. doi:10.1371/journal.pone.0077555

FBI-Federal Bureau of Investigation (2006). Keeping kids safe online: Advice from an fbi cyber agent. Retrieved June 9, 2006, from Federal Bureau of Investigation — Press Room Web site: http://fbi.gov/page2/april06/ccctf_interview042806.htm

Finkelhor, D., Mitchell, K.J. & Wolak, J. (2000). Online victimization: A report on the nation's youth. Alexandria, VA: National Center for Missing and Exploited Children. (CV38)

Finkelhor, D. (2011). The Internet, Youth Safety and the Problem of "Juvenoia." *Crimes Against Children Research Center*, 1–32.

Fry, S. (2009). Stephen Fry: The Internet and me. Retrieved from http://news.bbc.co.uk/2/hi/7926509.stm

Jenkins, H. (2006). MySpace and deleting online predators act. Retrieved July 20, 2006, from http://www.digitaldivide.net/articles/view.php?ArticleID=592

Jones, L., Mitchell, K. & Finkelhor, D. (2011). Trends in Youth Internet Victimization: Findings From Three Youth Internet Safety Surveys 2000–2010. *Journal of Adolescent Health*, 179–186.

Lenhart, A. (2015, April 8). Teens, Social Media & Technology Overview 2015. Retrieved December 8, 2015, from http://www.pewinternet.org/2015/04/09/teens-social-media-technology-2015/

Mitchell, K., Jones, L., Finkelhor, D. & Wolak, J. (2014). Trends in Child Victimization: Final Report. *Crimes Against Children Research Center*.

Mitchell, K., Jones, L., Turner, H., Shattuck, A. & Wolak, J. (2015). The Role of Technology in Peer Harassment: Does It Amplify Harm for Youth? *Psychology of Violence*, 1–12.

Meeker, M. (2015, May 27). INTERNET TRENDS 2015 — CODE CONFERENCE. Retrieved January 5, 2016, from http://kpcbweb2.s3.amazonaws.com/files/90/Internet_Trends_2015.pdf?1432738078

National Sex Offender Public Website. (2015). Facts and Statistics. Retrieved January 4, 2016, from https://www.nsopw.gov/en/Education/FactsStatistics#reference

NetSmartz.org (2006). Blog beware. NetSmartz Workshop, Retrieved June 9, 2006, from http://www.netsmartz.org/news/blogbeware.htm.

Netsmartz (2015). Netsmartz Real-Life Stories. Retrieved November 11, 2015, from http://www.netsmartz.org/RealLifeStories

Netsmartz Workshop (2016). Retrieved January 8, 2016, from http://www.netsmartz.org/

Norris, M. (2006, April 11). MySpace adds a security monitor. NPR, Retrieved 2006, June 18, from http://www.npr.org/templates/story/story.php?storyId=5336688.

NYRA-National Youth Rights Association (2006). MySpace Restrictions. Retrieved July 20, 2006, from http://www.youthrights.org/nyranews2006.shtml

Prensky, M. (2001). Digital Natives, Digital Immigrants. *On the Horizon, 9* (No. 5), 1–6.

Schrobsdorff, S. (2006). Predator's Playground. Retrieved June 18, 2006, from Q&A: How to keep teens safe on mySpace.com — Newsweek National News — MSNBC Web site: http://www.msnbc.msn.com/id/11065951/site/newsweek/print/1displaymode/1098.

WISQARS (2015, December 8). Retrieved January 4, 2016, from http://www.cdc.gov/injury/wisqars/

Wolak, J., Mitchell, K., and Finkelhor, D. (2006). Online victimization of youth: Five years later. National Center for Missing and Exploited Children Bulletin — #07-06-025. Alexandria, VA. (CV138)

Wolak, J., Finkelhor, D. and Mitchell, K.J. (2004). Internet-initiated sex crimes against minors: Implications for prevention based on findings from a national study. Journal of Adolescent Health, 35(5), 424–433. (CV71)

Contributors'
Biographical Information

Christopher M. Bellas is an associate professor in the Department of Criminal Justice & Forensic Sciences at Youngstown State University. He earned a BA in political science from Edinboro University of Pennsylvania, an MS in criminal justice from Youngstown State University and an MA and PhD in political science from Kent State University with a concentration in justice studies. His research areas focus on juries in death penalty cases, courts and constitutional law, criminology, and victimology.

Tammy Bracewell is an assistant professor at Texas A&M University-Central Texas. She earned her PhD in criminal justice at Texas State University. She currently holds a Master Peace Officer License in the State of Texas and has previously worked as a municipal police detective investigating crimes against children and sex crimes. Additionally, she has served as a program director and forensic interviewer at a Children's Advocacy Center. Her areas of expertise include child maltreatment, child advocacy centers, and sexual assaults. Her current research focuses on the utility of multidisciplinary teams regarding child sexual abuse.

Max L. Bromley is an associate professor emeritus in the Department of Criminology and director of the Master's in Criminal Justice Administration Program at the University of South Florida. Prior to becoming a full-time faculty member in 1996 he served as the associate director of public safety at the University of South Florida and worked in the criminal justice field for almost 25 years. He has written dozens of scholarly articles and technical documents on a variety of campus crime and campus policing issues and has co-authored three books.

Christine Bryce is a part-time professor in the Criminal Justice program at Virginia Commonwealth University. Professor Bryce came to VCU in 2004 while working as a computer forensic investigator for the Virginia State Police. Previously, she was a Virginia State Police Academy Instructor. She has also worked as a social worker in the City of Richmond Public Schools. She has contributed chapters to several textbooks as well as presented guest lectures to community groups in her areas of interest. She regularly teaches classes in: Computer crimes, computer forensics, corrections, economic and organized crime, gender and crime, and mental health issues in the criminal justice system. Her research interests are digital crime, mental health issues in the criminal justice system, community corrections, aging prison populations and long-term care needs, theory and dynamics of gender and crime, parenting the Internet, and writing and rhetoric in government and public affairs. Bryce holds a B.S.W. from Virginia Commonwealth University and a M.A. from the University of Richmond.

Beverly Dolinsky holds a PhD in social psychology and works at Endicott College in Beverly, Massachusetts. During her 25-year tenure at Endicott, she has acted as vice president of student affairs, the college's Title IX officer, dean of the School of Arts and Sciences, and is currently a professor of psychology. Beverly has played a leading role in many initiatives including the creation of new Baccalaureate degrees, a revision of the core curriculum, a strategically planned co-curricular residence life programing model and the implementation of comprehensive health and wellness programs. As vice president of student affairs, she oversaw the student conduct process promoting the use of a restorative justice process. Her scholarship is focused within the areas of higher education curricular design and pedagogy as well as student development policies and programming.

Kathleen Dunn is a professor of criminal justice in the School of Justice Studies at Roger Williams University, where she teaches courses in constitutional law, criminal law and procedure, and human rights law. She holds a PhD in sociology from Brown University, and a JD from Boston University. Her research interests include comparative criminal justice, international human rights law, and the role of the International Criminal Court in enforcing human rights law.

Michelle Foster is an assistant professor at Kent State University. She earned her Bachelor of Arts degree from Pennsylvania State University and two Master of Arts degrees from Kent State University, one in political science and one in justice studies. Mrs. Foster's other publications include a book anthology for use in criminology courses titled *Enduring Issues in Law and Society*, two journal articles published in the OCCJE online journal and various essays in criminology encyclopedias. She also devotes her time to her local community by being a 5th- and 6th-grade Catechism teacher and a Co-Leader for the Northeast Ohio Girl Scouts.

Randy Gainey is a professor in the Department of Sociology and Criminal Justice at Old Dominion University. His research focuses on elder abuse, disparities in sentencing decisions, alternatives to incarceration, and neighborhood characteristics and crime. He is co-author of four books: *Family Violence and Criminal Justice: A Life-Course Approach*, now in its third edition, *Drugs and Policing, Deviance and Social Control: A Sociological Perspective* and *Perspectives on Deviance and Social Control*. His articles have recently appeared in *Criminology, Justice Quarterly, Theoretical Criminology, The Prison Journal, The Journal of Criminal Justice*, and *The Journal of Crime and Justice*.

Jill A. Gordon is a professor of criminal justice and associate dean for faculty and academic affairs in the L. Douglas Wilder School of Government and Public Affairs at Virginia Commonwealth University. Her research interests center on correctional employees' attitudes toward work, clients and the organization and assessment of correctional policy and programs. She is currently working on a multi-site project examining perceptions of culture and climate among correctional officers and inmates. Her work has appeared in numerous outlets including *Justice Quarterly, International Journal of Offender Therapy and Comparative Criminology,* and *Journal of Crime and Justice*.

Courtney Gurska received her Bachelor's Degree in psychology in the spring of 2016 and is pursuing her Master's in Social Work at Boston University. As an undergraduate, she worked at Massachusetts General Hospital within the Center for Addiction Medicine where she assisted several research projects focusing on marijuana addiction. In addition, she is a medical advocate intern at the Boston Area Rape Crisis Center where she assists sexual assault survivors in the hospital by providing them with medical options and victim support resources.

Robert A. Jerin is professor of criminal justice and victimology at Endicott College. He received the PhD in Criminal Justice in 1987 from Sam Houston State University. Dr. Jerin has taught a variety of criminal justice and victimology courses over the past 25+years, including the development of courses on victimology, domestic violence, and the victimization of children. While teaching he has also volunteered as an advocate for victims of domestic and sexual violence with numerous private domestic violence organization since 1993. Dr. Jerin was previously on the steering committee and educational curriculum committee for the Massachusetts' Victims' Assistance Academy.

Jerin is a life member of the National Organization for Victim Assistance and the American Society of Victimology, where he also served as a board member. He is also a life member of Academy of Criminal Justice Sciences (ACJS) and the chairperson of its Academic Program Review Committee. He previously established the victimology section as part of the Academy of Criminal Justice Sciences and is the past chairperson of the section. He is also a member of the American Society of Criminology (ASC) and along with Dr. Bonnie Fisher started the Division of Victimology (DOV) within ASC, which he currently acts as co-chair. Dr. Jerin is a member of the World Society of Victimology and a member of its UN Liaison Committee. In 2005, Dr. Jerin was the recipient of the John P. J. Dussich award from the American Society of Victimology for his many and significant contributions to the field of Victimology. In 2011, he was presented with the Gerhard Mueller Innovator Award by the Northeastern Association of Criminal Justice Sciences in recognition of significant contributions within the criminal justice system as a scholar-practitioner. He co-edited a special edition of the *Journal of Criminal Justice* with Dr. Bonnie Fisher entitled "The Evolution of Victimology" in December of 2014. His most recent book, *The Victims of Crime,* co-authored with Dr. Laura Moriarty, was published in January 2010 by Pearson Publishing. This was his third book with Dr. Moriarty focusing on crime victims and victimology. He has published numerous book chapters and scholarly articles, some of which can be found in the *American Journal of Police, Criminal Justice Policy Review, Journal of Criminal Justice and Popular Culture* and *Tokiwa International Victimology Institute Journal.* He has also contributed to the Encyclopedia of Victimology, the Encyclopedia of Corrections and other reference materials within the criminal justice and victimological disciplines.

Stephane Jasmin Kirven is a graduate of Tufts University and Georgetown University Law Center. Stephane is an assistant professor of criminal justice and an attorney who specializes in education law. She has published in the areas of gender bias in the legal profession, restorative justice and Title IX.

Karel Kurst-Swanger is a professor at the State University of New York at Oswego in the Department of Public Justice. She received her PhD in political science/public policy and administration from Binghamton University, and a MSEd in counselor education and BS in criminal justice from the State University of New York at Brockport. She is the author of two books: *Worship and Sin: An Exploration of Religion-related Crime in the U.S.* (Peter Lang) and *Violence in the Home: Multidisciplinary Perspectives* (Oxford University Press) and numerous other publications. Her research interests center on a wide range of topics in criminal justice/human services and she serves as a consultant for many non-profit and public organizations facilitating strategic planning and multidisciplinary collaborations, and the resolution of management/

organizational issues. She is currently serving as the coordinator of the Broome County Child Fatality Review Team. She has also served as the executive director of the Crime Victims Assistance Center, Inc., Binghamton, New York, and the coordinator of the Victim Assistance Unit of the Rochester City Police Department in Rochester, New York.

Monica Leisey is a graduate of Virginia Commonwealth University and an assistant professor in the Salem State University School of Social Work. Her areas of scholarship include the pedagogy of social work and social work leadership. Dr. Leisey has successfully submitted grants to both NIH and the DOJ. She is currently serving as the coordinator of the Master of Social Work Program, and is responsible for managing the MSW program for approximately 350 students. Dr. Leisey also chairs the Salem State University Collaboration Committee and serves on the President's Advisory Committee on Diversity, Affirmative Action, Equity and Social Justice and the Graduate Education Council. Recently, Dr. Leisey was sponsored to attend the HERS Bryn Mawr Summer Institute by the Council on Social Work Education and Salem State University.

Stephanie Manzi is the dean of the School of Justice Studies at Roger Williams University, where she teaches courses in criminology, victimology, policing, and research methods. She holds a PhD in criminology from the University of Maryland, College Park. She is currently working on a grant to reduce violent crime in the city of Providence, Rhode Island, and serves as a core team member in the learning collaborative between the National Governors Association and the National Parole Resource Center to update state executives about evidence-based practices for paroling authorities.

Marie Mele is a graduate of Rutgers University, where she obtained a PhD in criminal justice. Her research interests include repeat victimization and intimate partner violence. Dr. Mele has several publications on the correlates of repeat victimization, domestic violence protection orders, and victim advocacy. Before joining academia, Dr. Mele worked as an advocate for domestic violence victims. She is currently a faculty member with the Department of Criminal Justice at Monmouth University, offering courses in criminology, research methodology, and victimology.

Matthew E. McDermott is completing the Master of the Arts in Public Policy at Monmouth University. He received the Bachelor of Arts in history from James Madison University in 2013. McDermott's areas of research interest are in social and cultural policy areas such as immigration.

Robyn Diehl McDougle is an associate professor in the criminal justice program, faculty director of the Office of Public Policy Outreach, and interim director for the Commonwealth Education Policy Institute at Virginia Commonwealth University. Dr. McDougle received the PhD in developmental psychology from Virginia Commonwealth University. Her primary area of research is program evaluation, project impact and the impact of violent crime on youth and community development. Her research involves working with service-based organizations and law enforcement agencies to evaluate the efficacy of programs offered to residents in communities that suffer many of the negative consequences resulting from high levels of crime, specifically violent crime.

Laura J. Moriarty is the provost and vice president for academic affairs at Monmouth University, where she is a tenured professor in the Department of Criminal Justice. She holds the PhD in criminal justice from Sam Houston State University. Moriarty is a past president of the Academy of Criminal Justice Sciences and the Southern Criminal Justice Association, and has served as editor of *ACJS Today*. She is a recipient of the ACJS Founders Award for outstanding service to ACJS and the profession. Moriarty's publications appear in a wide variety of criminal justice outlets.

Nicholas M. Perez is an assistant professor in the School of Criminology, Criminal Justice, and Emergency Management in the College of Health and Human Services at California State University, Long Beach. He received the PhD in criminology from the University of South Florida in 2016. His dissertation examined the role of childhood trauma in the development of violent behavior in Department of Juvenile Justice youth. Prior to completing his doctoral degree, Nicholas earned his MS in criminal justice (2012) and a BA in sociology (2010) from the University of Central Florida. His main research interests include the development of delinquent behavior, policing, childhood trauma, and bullying/hazing violence. He has recently had articles accepted for publication in *Child Abuse and Neglect, Journal of Criminal Justice Education, Security Journal,* and *Policing: An International Journal of Police Strategies & Management*

Brian K. Payne is the vice provost for academic affairs at Old Dominion University, where he is tenured in the Department of Sociology and Criminal Justice. He is a former editor of the *American Journal of Criminal Justice* and past president of the Southern Criminal Justice Association and the Academy of Criminal Justice Sciences. He recently guest-edited an issue of *Criminal Jus-*

tice Studies focusing on "Cybersecurity and Criminal Justice." As vice provost, he led the development of the Center for Cybersecurity Education and Research at Old Dominion University. The center brings together faculty from several different academic departments to address cybersecurity as an interdisciplinary problem. Payne is the author or co-author of more than 160 journal articles and seven books, including *White-Collar Crime: The Essentials* (Sage), *Family Violence and Criminal Justice* (Elsevier, with Randy Gainey), and *Crime and Elder Abuse: An Integrated Perspective* (Charles C Thomas). He is currently co-authoring (with Will Oliver and Nancy Marion) *Introduction to Criminal Justice: A Balanced Approach* (Sage).

Sara Plummer is currently the assistant director of the BASW program at Rutgers University. She has over ten years of teaching experience and has taught on the Bachelor, Master, and PhD level. Most recently, she was the assessment coordinator and core faculty member at Walden University. Her practice experience includes being both a social worker and an assistant director at Barrier Free Living, Inc., an agency that provided services to individuals with disabilities who were survivors of abuse in NYC, and a psychiatric social worker at Southside Regional Medical Center in Virginia. Her research and scholarly focus is on intimate partner violence and the abuse of people with disabilities.

Christina Policastro is an assistant professor of criminal justice in the Department of Social, Cultural, and Justice Studies at the University of Tennessee at Chattanooga. She received her PhD in criminal justice and criminology from Georgia State University in 2013. Policastro's dissertation examined the applicability of lifestyles/routine activities theory to victimization of the elderly. Her primary research interests are in the area of victimization with a specific focus on elder abuse and intimate partner violence. She has published articles on diverse topics including perceptions of intimate partner violence victims, pre-professionals' knowledge of elder abuse, trajectories of recurring victimization among persons with serious mental illness, and durable medical equipment fraud. Her work has been published in journals such as the *Journal of Quantitative Criminology, Journal of Interpersonal Violence,* and *Journal of Elder Abuse & Neglect.*

Elizabeth Quinn is an assistant professor at Middle Tennessee State University in Murfreesboro, TN. She received her PhD from Sam Houston State University in Huntsville, Texas, in 2004 and has focused her teaching, research and service activities in the areas of victim services and problem-oriented policing. Her field experience includes work as a corrections liaison with juveniles in Wisconsin and work with sexual assault victims in Wisconsin and North Carolina. She was privileged to serve on the board of directors of a rape crisis center for four years, including appointments as board treasurer and board secretary for three of those years, and assisted with grant writing, training and fundraising. She has been published in *Women & Criminal Justice, Applied Psychology in Criminal Justice, Contemporary Justice Review, ACJS Assessment Forum,* and *Crime Prevention and Community Safety.* She has written four book chapters exploring different victimological and victims' rights issues and a technical report on the victimization experience presented to the Texas State Legislature. Most recently, Dr. Quinn, along with Dr. Sara Brightman (Fayetteville State University), published a new textbook on crime victimization, offering students a broader look at burgeoning issues and working with victims overall.

Breea Willingham is an assistant professor of criminal justice at Plattsburgh State University of New York. Her research areas include Black women's prison writing, higher education in prisons, Black women and police violence, the impact of incarceration on Black fathers and their children, and race and crime. Dr. Willingham worked as a newspaper reporter covering crime and education for 10 years before entering academia. She is currently writing a book on Black women and police violence, due to be released in 2017.

Mary Wilson is an associate professor in the Department of Sociology, teaching in the Criminology and Justice Studies Program at the Kent State Trumbull Campus. She completed her doctorate in political science with a specific concentration in justice studies at Kent State University. She teaches undergraduate courses in criminology and criminal justice. Her research interests cover a range of topics including Megan's law; justice system policies; elder abuse; DNA technology and privacy issues in criminal justice; crime victim services and compensation, including the rights of crime victims; and victimology.

Carolyn J. Zeppa holds a BFA in dance from Fordham University and The Alvin Ailey School as well as an MA in criminology and criminal justice from Eastern Michigan University, and is pursuing her PhD in public policy and administration with specialization in criminal justice at Virginia Commonwealth University's L. Douglas Wilder School of Government and Public Affairs. Her research focus includes policing studies, particularly policing technologies and occupational culture, and crime and media studies.

INDEX